BEGINNING WRITERS IN THE ZONE OF PROXIMAL DEVELOPMENT

BEGINNING WRITERS IN THE ZONE OF PROXIMAL DEVELOPMENT

Elizabeth Petrick Steward
State University of New York at Plattsburgh

LEA

LAWRENCE ERLBAUM ASSOCIATES, PUBLISHERS
1995   Hillsdale, New Jersey   Hove, UK

Lawrence Erlbaum Associates, Inc., Publishers
365 Broadway
Hillsdale, New Jersey 07642

Cover design by Debbie Karrel

Library of Congress Cataloging-in-Publication Data

Petrick Steward, Elizabeth.
     Beginning writers in the zone of proximal development / Elizabeth
Petrick Steward.
          p.   cm.
     Includes bibliographical references and index.
     ISBN 0-8058-1302-0.   ISBN 0-8058-1866-9 (pbk.)
     1. Children—Writing.   2. Literacy.   3. Children—Language
acquisition.   I. Title.
LB 1139.W7S84   1994
372.6'23—dc20   94-34727
                                                          CIP

Books published by Lawrence Erlbaum Associates are printed on acid-free
paper, and their bindings are chosen for strength and durability.

Printed in the United States of America
10 9 8 7 6 5 4 3 2 1

To Farnham, of course

Contents

Preface

How can this book be characterized? First, it is the empirical story of a group of young learners as they strive to master the powerful mental tool of written language—a description of how a class of children produce a set of their own "books." The children are not merely *pretending* to write; they are genuinely authors, in control of the text worlds they create, first with spoken language and pictures, and later with written words. Second, the story is told within the structure of Vygotsky's sociocultural developmental theory, with a particular focus on the *zone of proximal development,* that period of sensitivity in which learning advances. The mechanism of change is *verbal mediation—* talk among peers and teacher as they discuss work-in-progress—which moves the children through the zone of proximal development. Finally, this book is a resource. I focus mostly on one child, Jeremy, because he provided a pivotal event that moved the whole class forward. But to present just Jeremy's books is to tell only part of a wonderfully complex and fascinating story. To complete the picture, the books of all the children in the class, along with the accompanying conference dialogue, are presented in an Appendix. Each of the 11 children has a unique experience on the class's collective road to literacy, and many aspects of this corpus have yet to be explored. I sincerely hope that those who study children's writing can make use of this collection, to investigate, interpret, and enjoy the early writing of Jeremy, Brenton, Celeste, Damon, Jeff, John, Jodi, Gene, Michelle, Tyler, and Todd.

As this book progressed, I came to understand more clearly that it is not only beginning writers who work collaboratively. Far from being a solitary effort, this book is as much the work of others as it is my own. Neill Wenger, the teacher of the class described in this book, is a very special person. He is an intuitively gifted teacher, and fortunately for early literacy research, he is a compulsive collector and record keeper. It is his meticulous documentation that provides the foundation for this volume, and without his foresight we would never have heard the voices that are recorded in this book. He is also a good friend and a generous colleague. Dr. Sylvia Farnham-Diggory, with her editing and encouragement, helped and supported me through my own personal zone of proximal development as I worked on this project. She is mentor, model, and inspiration, and I am truly grateful. Mark Grabowski's eternal patience with technological matters and the secretarial assistance of Bette Perna and Kathy Murphy were also necessary parts of this enterprise; many other friends and colleagues helped in countless important ways, and I offer my thanks to each of them. Finally, I thank my daughter Jill for her love and support.

I would also like to express my appreciation to the editors at Lawrence Erlbaum Associates, who supported the unusual format of this book with its multitude of illustrations. Data reduction in works of qualitative research is often difficult as well as problematical; presentation of the corpus in its entirety adds immeasurably to the usefulness of this volume.

—Elizabeth Petrick Steward

1

BACKGROUND

"Can you read, Courtney?"

"No! I'm only 5 years old!"

"Can you write?"

"Yes, I can. I can write."

"What can you write?"

"I can write houses, and monsters . . . and my name, I think."

Courtney knows she cannot read, but she has been "writing" long before she came to kindergarten. Yet, as Courtney's example demonstrates, she has an unconventional view of what writing is. Does this mean she is preliterate? Does real literacy commence only with school instruction? With the mastery of conventional forms?

In recent years, inspired in part by studies of children's emergent language, there has been a surge of research into what is now called *emergent literacy*. The research can be characterized most generally as a search for the developmental precursors of literacy—"bridges," as they are sometimes called, to formal literacy. Children are alleged to go through predictable developmental progressions as they spontaneously acquire knowledge of how to write down speech—knowledge that will eventually be subject to the corrections of academic training.

But the analogy between the emergence of spoken and written language cannot be carried very far. There are persuasive arguments that spoken language is biologically rooted; its emergence follows a specialized evolutionary pattern (Liebermann, 1984). Written language, though parasitic to some degree on spoken language, is a recent cultural invention. There has not been enough

time, as evolution goes, for a *writing acquisition device,* parallel to the *language acquisition device,* to have evolved in human brains. Hence, the lawful regularities of emergent literacy—if such regularities do in fact exist—must be sought in general learning theory, which can then be used as a frame for a theory specific to written language.

As is characteristic of any new field, research into emergent literacy is descriptive and taxonomic. Attempts are being made to "plug into" established theories (such as Piaget's), but the value of this is still unclear. Is it merely an exercise in metaphor? Or will it generate testable predictions? The point of making connections with a powerful theory is that it gets you somewhere you could not get without it.

It is my thesis that Vygotsky's theory provides the model needed by the field of emergent literacy. It addresses the heart of the matter: how children—in developmentally lawful ways—draw from an environment of language, print, and people to construct new ways of symbolizing ideas.

To support my thesis, I analyze a corpus of early writing—almost the very first writing of 11 young children—to see if the developmental progressions described by Vygotsky actually occur. I find that they do indeed occur, in both individual and collective forms, and that they provide strong support for the value and power of Vygotsky's theoretical framework.

In particular, I document the complexity of the relationship between young children's drawing and their developing insight into the nature of writing. For example, when children first "write" their name, they may in fact be producing a drawing. When they draw a sun and a stick figure, they may be "writing" a story about a boy in the sunshine. The insight into the difference between these two symbol systems (drawing and writing) is a crucial moment of growth. Many such moments are captured in the work reported here.

Additionally, I document the complexity of the relationship between what children say and what they put down on paper, and their developing insight into the nature of the difference between speech and writing. Again, the corpus reveals crucial moments of growth.

In this introductory chapter, I first survey descriptive research which has bearing on my own—research into the connections between (a) writing and drawing, and (b) writing and spoken language. I then summarize two widely cited attempts to systematize such descriptive data. The inadequacies of these attempts have spurred me to adopt the Vygotskyan theoretical framework set forth in chapter 2. After laying the theoretical groundwork, I recast the information provided in chapter 1 in terms of a Vygotskyan perspective.

WRITING AND DRAWING

One of the most striking aspects of early writing behavior is the close relationship between writing and drawing (Bissex, 1980; Clay, 1975; Gardner, 1980; Harste, Woodward, & Burke, 1984; Kellogg, 1970). As earlier conversation with Courtney illustrates, young children often talk about writing and drawing as if the two processes are synonymous. A 7-year-old talks about "drawing a story" (Barrs, 1988); when a 5-year-old is asked what he is going to write, he replies, "How should I know? I haven't drawed it yet" (Calkins, 1986).

The connection between writing and drawing is well known, and the manner in which children's writing grows out of pictorials parallels the historical development of written language, whose earlier instances were pictorial. The forerunners of writing are pictorial, such as the "writing" of North American Indians or Mayans (Frawley, 1987).

The relationships among different symbolic systems as they correspond to the development of writing was cogently described by Vygotsky (1978), in a characteristically rich and dense chapter. Vygotsky posited that "make-believe play, drawing and writing can be viewed as different moments in an essentially united process of development of written language" (p. 116). He found the very beginnings of this process in *gesture*, which he calls "writing in air" (p. 107).

A representation of these transformations was sketched by Emig (1981, p. 24) and is shown in Fig. 1.1.

Symbolic play provides the crucial link between a concrete object and its abstraction into a sign: at first one object substitutes for another in play (e.g., a stick

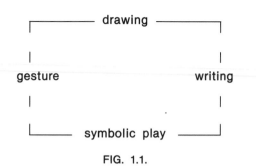

FIG. 1.1.

becomes a horse to be ridden); later, one object signifies another (a penknife used as a "doctor" in a play drama falls off the table, and the child exclaims, "The doctor has fallen!") (Vygotsky, 1978, p. 110).

Early drawing is the other bridge between gestures and writing. Gesture becomes interwoven with scribbles, and a critical moment comes when the child realizes his lines can have meaning. Vygotsky described the earliest phase of true writing as the use of idiosyncratic markers (such as pictograms or rebuses) that a child might produce to graphically represent something. Vygotsky called these *first order representations,* marks and drawings which directly stand for objects and actions. The "basic discovery" (1978, p.115), according to Vygotsky, is the realization that we can draw speech as well as things. This is *second order symbolism,* where written symbols represent words, which are in turn symbols for objects and actions.

In an essay describing the links between drawing and writing, Barrs (1988) uses the term *pictographic* for Vygotsky's idiosyncratic markers. She suggests that many children employ a "pictographic hypothesis" about writing at some point. Barrs presents observational evidence to support a gender dimension: Boys rather than girls are more inclined to go on using pictures as a means of storytelling.

A different description of the progression from scribble into writing and drawing is found in Kellogg's (1970) work. Kellogg agrees that both writing and drawing make use of the same base of representational experience, but says that the *use* of the lines differs. Whereas Vygotsky's description of the process is based on a strong theoretical view, Kellogg's work is atheoretical and empirical.

Kellogg (1970) collected and examined a corpus of thousands of children's drawings, and produced a descriptive classification that has the appearance of a developmental progression (although she did not claim it as such), from *basic scribbles*, to *diagrams* (such as crosses), to *shapes*, and finally to *combinations* of shapes, at which point the child is functioning as an artist.

Kellogg found certain formations that she believes to

be universal. Primary among them are the mandala (a circle or square divided into halves or quarters), radials, and suns. She described a developmental progression in the use of these forms: children typically produce the mandala first (the key into pictorials), followed by suns; finally children draw human figures.

Kellogg (1970) considered the motivating force behind art to be aesthetic rather than communicative. She cites differences between children's art and letter forms; both use lines from basic scribbles, but in children's art the lines are used to make self-taught formations, learned from scratch by each new generation of children—line sequences appear independently of pictorial associations. Language symbols, in contrast, are passed on from generation to generation, within cultural limits. Kellogg maintains that the place of scribbling in written language is limited to promoting eye–hand coordination that will be needed for writing (she suggests that children should be taught cursive writing from the beginning of instruction).

Kellogg (1970) believes that most letters are made as gestalts prior to formal writing instruction, in patterns or implied shapes. The task of the child in beginning writing, then, is to learn to perceive differences in *aesthetic* positions (usually centrally placed) versus the conventional *linguistic* positions of top–bottom and left–right. (Similarly, Clay, 1975, described the entering writer's task as the child's gradual awareness of those arbitrary customs used in written English.)

In an influential series of studies designed to investigate the patterns of early writing development in preschool children, Harste et al. (1984) found that young children do indeed differentiate between writing and drawing. The scribbled marks of 3-year-old children reflect a clear distinction between art and writing. The decisions children make are strongly influenced by the kinesthetics of the written form of their names. Three-year-old Nathan's "writing" is linear (reflecting the up-and-down strokes of the initial *N*), whereas his "drawing" is circular and centrally positioned. Shannon, age 3, does the opposite: She writes with a series of linearly organized circles (like the *S* in *Shannon*) and draws with centrally placed up-and-down lines.

Harste et al. (1984) demonstrated that children's writing is socially based—children make marks that reflect the written language of their culture. For example, a 4-year-old from the United States "writes" (in unconventional script) with wavy lines that go from top to bottom, and left to right. A 4-year-old from Saudi Arabia produces curlicues and dots, and an Israeli 4-year-old prints a series of rectangular and triangular shapes, left-to-right, then right-to-left, that "looks like Hebrew, but it's not" (p. 82).

Gardner (1980) investigated the significance of drawing as it relates to writing, within a larger developmental system. He found that interest in writing antedates schooling; by age 2, certain activities are already marked off as "writing." A certain class of marks are "words," and children make perceptual copies of cursive script.

Gardner (1980), like Harste, et al. (1984), found that cultural influences are important, and is cautious about declaring "universal" forms (as Kellogg, 1970, does). He cites cross-cultural studies where, for example, Balinese children fill up all spaces, and Japanese children adeptly use delicacy and balance. Gardner places drawing within a larger and more general developmental framework, and, like Vygotsky, draws parallels between children's developing art work and other systems of "symbolic play," such as bedtime prattle (Weir, 1962, cited in Gardner, 1980), in which the child plays with the sounds of language in a way analogous to her play with integrating marks on a page in her effort to gain control of the symbol systems of her culture.

Early discovery of the ability to make marks—with anything, such as cereal, or in sand—leads to the discovery of a marker's function as a tool to make marks. The child works at integrating natural motions of arm, wrist, elbow, and fingers into patterns, and finally into representations.

Early scribbles are *contrasting*: circular or wavy (made with fixed elbow and rotating forearm); dots (percussive); straight lines (stiff fingers, arms moving); or angles (wrist must be constantly adjusted). Gardner (1980) proposed the theory of maximum contrasts: It is the contrast that pleases the child—kinesthetic as well as visual. The quality of the production also contrasts, like the percussion of dots versus the smoothness of wavy lines.

Beyond the physical action of scribbling itself, children are interested in the marks that are produced. Hubbard (1989) reported a study in which children's markers were replaced with those that left no traces on the paper. Even very young children soon lost interest in the scribbling activity if their efforts did not result in visible marks on the paper. The researchers concluded that the children were interested in not only the kinetic activity, but the actual scribble marks themselves (Gibson & Yonas, 1968, in Hubbard, 1989).

Harste et al. (1984) and Gardner (1980) found that children are able to distinguish between writing and drawing at very early ages, 2 or 3 years. Ferreiro and Teberosky (1982), however, noted that there is "difficulty in finding the precise difference between writing and drawing" (p. 185) with young children. These researchers conducted a series of studies in Argentina in the Piagetian tradition, and obtained data through the use of the clinical interview. A 4-year-old responded to the question, "Do you know how to write?" with, "Yes, a little toy," and she drew a tadpole figure. Asked to write *boy*, she once again responded with a figure, but with a second request to write *boy*, she produced a "cursive-like string in which curves alternate with wavy lines" (p. 186).

Ferreiro and Teberosky (1982) found that children's difficulty in differentiating between writing and drawing activities is a "momentary, passing thing" (p. 185). In fact, children at initial reading levels (i.e., at about 6 years) can move back and forth between picture and text with ease.

Consistent with other researchers' findings, Ferreiro and Teberosky (1982) agree that children write in ways that are very different from the ways in which they draw; the question is "whether they use drawing as an escape from the difficult task of writing or whether drawing serves a certain function in relation to writing" (p. 186). They favor the second interpretation, as drawing seems to support writing in terms of insuring its meaning. Barrs (1988) reported that when children want to make their meaning clear, they include a picture; for example, a child who discovers that neither he nor his teacher can read back his "writing" includes a picture above questionable words. Grinnell and Burris (1983) reported that when children are learning to write on their own, the pictures often need to carry a large part of the story; writing and drawing are so integrated that both must be considered to decipher the message.

Children's apparent conflation between writing and drawing corresponds to the historical development of written language. Early writing systems such as the word–syllabic representations of the Egyptians are a transition between pictorials and abstract symbols, and include elements of both (Frawley, 1987).

Hubbard (1989), in her study of writing activities in a first grade classroom, demonstrated that children's drawing and writing continue to diverge, while at the same time children are learning to use the two symbol systems to complement each other. Not only did the children in Hubbard's study use words and pictures in an integrated way, but they were able to shift strategies to make their communication more effective. When action lines in a drawing did not quite express all the aspects of movement the child intended, a verb which expressed the strength of the imagery was used; for example, a drawn line describing the trajectory of a falling pumpkin was replaced with the more evocative "plopped." When relational words like *on* or *over* proved imprecise, children complemented the text with a diagram, picture, or map. A number of the children in Hubbard's study made vivid use of pop-out pictures to

show the nature of the intended motion: "I spring up," a child read, and attempted to demonstrate her picture that was supposed to " . . . like, *spring* up . . . 'cept . . . I have to fix it" (p. 115).

Summary: Writing and Drawing

Although writing and drawing spring from the same roots, children differentiate between the two symbol systems very early. When they are struggling to control the new symbol system that is written text, children must often fall back on an earlier learned system, that of drawing, in order to communicate their message. Early literary efforts are usually an integrated combination of illustration and text.

WRITING AND SPOKEN LANGUAGE

Writing is, at one level, a transcription of the sounds of language, "drawing speech," as Vygotsky says (1978, p. 107). In the previous section, we examined some of the ways in which young literacy learners come to understand that the marks they make on paper can have meaning, even before the conventional phoneme/grapheme relationships are learned and used. Building on gestures and early scribbles, young writers structure their graphic products toward an ever more mature approximation of conventional writing.

Written text is far more than a graphic representation, however, and children are working on higher level text structures at the same time they are working out the graphics. In the relationship between drawing and writing discussed previously, we see that children make use of a more familiar symbol system—drawing—when exploring the new system of writing, and they fall back on drawing when the meaning of their written communication is threatened. In the same way, higher level rhetorical structures grow out of and are supported by a symbol system that is more nearly under the child's control, that of *spoken language*.

Oral and Literate Language

Luria (1982) defines two basic forms of the speech utterance: (a) oral (which includes dialogue, or conversation; and monologue, or narrative); and (b) written speech. The argument that children must learn to switch from operating in an "oral" language society to a "literate" society (Egan, 1987; Goody, 1977: Havelock, 1986; Ong, 1982) is intuitively appealing. It is certainly true that children operate with only the spoken language symbol system for several years prior to learning to control written language. Egan (1987) made the point that, during this period, children utilize many of the oral storage strategies employed by oral societies to assist memory—rhymes, rhythm, meter, and the story form, for example.

Egan maintains that oral forms and patterns continue into adulthood (although in the shadow of literate behaviors), even in literate societies; this is clearly true. What is arguable is the oral-to-literate notion that literacy does not begin until the child begins formal schooling, at which point the learner must confront a whole new way of thinking. Schooling is singled out as the critical process that transforms children's language from utterance to text (Olson, 1977).

The distinction between oral and literate styles of communication can better be described as a continuum, instead of a dichotomy (Gee, 1985). Most authors agree that one of the most important aspects of oral language is its *context-bound* nature, whereas literate language is characterized as *decontextualized* and abstract.

Vygotskyan theory maintains that cultural knowledge (including language) is learned by the child in social interaction with adults or more knowledgeable peers in the society. The children in this study are part of a literate culture, and the discussion is therefore limited to literate societies. Given these two assumptions—that cultural knowledge is learned from society, and that the society is literate—there is ample evidence that children begin to learn literacy patterns from the time of their earliest verbal interactions with parents and other caretakers (e.g., Bruner, 1985; Snow, 1983). Children from "mainstream" homes bring to school the foundations of literate styles of speech (Gee, 1985; Heath, 1983). Young learners are immersed in print in their environment and surrounded by literate others who continually interact with written text, even in so-called "deprived" or "impoverished" sectors of a literate culture (Heath, (1983; Taylor & Dorsey-Gaines, 1988; Teale, 1986).

There are clearly activities using spoken language, like storybook reading, that serve to teach the child the "written register" (Green & Morgan, 1981). At the same time, there are speech activities that have no connection to literate behaviors. However, classifying certain modes of speech (like dialogue or monologue) as exclusively literate or exclusively oral is not possible; either may serve literacy, or may not, depending on the goal of the activity. I conclude therefore that the path to literacy is not *through* oral language, but *side by side* with it (or, more accurately, intertwined with it) from the very beginning.

Language Modes

Sulzby (1982, 1986) described a sequence of *language modes* in kindergarten children that captures the gradual transition into written language, beginning with the conversational mode and leading to handwritten stories. In her 1982 study, Sulzby examined differences between two kinds of oral production—storytelling and story dictation—by 24 kindergarten children. The children are subsequently asked to "re-read" their stories, and judgments of language mode (conversation, storytelling or narrative, dictation, or written story) are obtained.

Conversation, or information exchanged between two speakers, is the earliest mode the child acquires. The roots of conversation have been well documented in accounts of turn taking observed in mother–infant dyads (e.g., Bruner, 1985). Conversation, which is a dialogue, is followed by *narrative*, or storytelling, which is a monologue. Once the child has internalized the concept of taking turns speaking with a conversational partner, he can hold the dialogue model in mind and take both its parts, producing the monologue.

Sulzby also noted changes in prosody and other conventions that are appropriate to the mode being used. During storytelling, one speaker maintains a monologue and others listen; if the listener stops the storyteller for clarification, it is considered an interruption, and is clearly marked prosodically as outside the narration.

The demarcation between the text of the narrative and extratextual comments is clear even in the written transcripts of such verbal exchanges. Joshua, a first-grade child, told a story about a bad day. With a storytelling intonation, he began, "Once upon a time I woke up and my cat got in my mom's lunch . . . "

The examiner broke in, "I thought you said [earlier] it was breakfast?"

"Yeah, well, it was lunch. Once upon a time I woke up and my cat . . . "

Besides conversation and narrative, Sulzby (1982) found that children also are able to discriminate a third mode, *dictation*. In the dictating mode, one person is the speaker, who must maintain the oral monologue, and a second person is the scribe. One task of the speaker is to compose a message appropriate for written language, that is, for reading by an absent audience. Therefore, the dictation mode is more abstract than narration, more literate. A second task in dictation is to adapt to the needs of the scribe, who has to write; this demands clear speech, slow intonation, and segmentation of speech that is coordinated with the conventions of the writing system.

The fourth mode in Sulzby's (1982) studies is the *handwritten message*. The person conveying the message uses a graphic code; she is a writer, not a speaker. In this mode, the child must deal with the constraints of written language, such as spelling, punctuation, message structure, and composition. There is no audience, not even the scribe.

The children in Sulzby's studies were able to sound as if they were dictating when asked to dictate, and to maintain an oral monologue when they were telling a story. Sulzby found that children make another discrimination between told and dictated stories when she asked them to retell (or "re-read") their stories: Children adapted their told (narrative) stories toward the related oral mode of conversation (e.g., they ask questions or wait for the listener to take a turn); they adapted their dictated stories toward the literate mode of handwritten stories (e.g., they inserted pauses between words and waited for the scribe to finish before going on). Therefore, the children considered dictated stories to be more like written text than like oral language.

The Importance of Narratives

During the preschool years, the child's preferred mode of discourse is the *narrative*, one kind of monologue (Gundlach, 1981). Gee (1985) states that perhaps the primary way human beings make sense of experience is by casting it in a narrative form: "This is an ability that develops early and rapidly in children, without explicit training or instruction" (p. 11). Gee argues that narrativization ("This happened, then that happened . . . ") is a universal human experience, as is language itself. The narrative is not only the dominant mode of discourse in early years, it is one way children move towards literacy—through stories heard, told, and read about themselves and others (Scollon & Scollon, 1981, in Galda & Pellegrini, 1988). Children learn to write in many cases by writing personal narratives (as, e.g., the children in the classroom that is the focus of the present study).

Children's early narrative efforts are not well organized. Applebee (1978), who based his analysis of a collection of young children's stories on Vygotsky's general theory of development, calls the child's earliest efforts "heaps," or unrelated collections of statements, which are closely bound to the context. It is only by knowing the context that the reader can make sense of children's early efforts. In one of the studies conducted by Harste et al. (1984), only 4 of 48 dictated stories contain an explicit global proposition to which all the others are tied; for 12 more stories, a global proposition could be implied. Thirty stories are contextually dependent, and the reader must be familiar with the context before the story can be comprehended.

Young children have only a nascent ability to employ different narrative genres. Hicks (1990a, 1990b) investigated the command young children have of various narrative genres. When children were asked to narrate a short silent film in various narrative styles (an "on-line" narration of the film, a "news report," and an embellished story), most of her subjects produced lists. The youngest children especially had difficulty shifting their ways of telling events. However, through careful contextual analysis of the children's transcripts, Hicks found clear but subtle differentiation among the narrative forms for all her subjects, leading her to conclude that children in primary grades are able to produce distinct narrative genres.

In another study conducted by Galda and Pellegrini (1988), the researchers had dyads of children play with two sets of manipulanda, plain blocks (functionally ambiguous) and a doctor's kit (functionally explicit), while they recorded the children's speech. The researchers first determined that the children were *able* to produce decontextualized language if the situation demanded it; but they found that the children tended to produce *personalized narratives* (vs. *paradigmatic*, or decontextualized language) when confronted with an ambiguous situation (the plain blocks) or a problematic situation (peer disagreement). That is, when the situation became difficult, the children fell back upon an earlier learned, more reliable language form. The narrative form of speaking is a form of language that is usually context-bound and personal, as contrasted with the abstract paradigmatic mode, and temporally precedes decontextualized forms of speaking. Galda and Pellegrini hypothesized that the familiar, contextually anchored narrative form acts as a *scaffold* (Bruner's metaphor; Wood, Bruner, & Ross, 1976) for the developing abstract language. In an earlier section, we saw that when children's attempts to use conventional orthography fail to convey their meaning, they fall back upon drawing, which is more nearly under their control. Similarly, children begin to use the newer form of discourse (paradigmatic, or literary language), but when the goal of making meaning becomes difficult, an earlier and more completely learned form (narrative) is employed to support the developing one.

Other Genres

Young children have some degree of control over a number of verbal language forms (e.g., conversation and the narrative story) and can use them appropriately. Children also recognize different forms of written communication. The relationship to art is evident: Written messages convey meaning, not only with words, but in their visual form. It is the visual configuration, and not the written text, that carries the meaning. "Relative sizes, ways of placing and arranging words and sentences on a page . . . are habitual means of communication" (Schwartz, in Smolken, Conlan, & Yaden, 1988, p. 60).

By the time children are ready for first grade, they already have a wide repertoire of organizational structures which clearly mark genre (Harste et al., 1984; Hicks, 1990a). Lists, notes, letters, stories, and maps are some of the forms that children produce. Children explore these forms through the medium of spoken language as well. When children are presented with a written document in one of these forms, there is a structural variation in their oral response appropriate to the document they are "reading," for example, a list sounds like a list. A request for a story often elicits the beginning phrase, "Once upon a time . . . " (Gundlach, 1981). Harste et al. found that children as young as 3 attend to salient structures in various kinds of written text.

Text patterns influence spoken language even before reading begins. Cook-Gumperz and Gumperz (1981) cite an example of a conversation between two 3-year old girls as they play at "reading" to each other. Not only are intonation and prosody appropriate to "reading a story," but the girls also organize the conversation in a specific reading formula, *X was Y*:

The dog was happy.

The park was trees.

It   was lovely.

Even without having grasped the word/symbol/sound correspondence, the influence of the written word on the spoken is evident.

Decontextualized Language

How does the child acquire his knowledge of the different modes of language? Snow (1983) traced a path that parallels the child's development from the highly contextualized conversational mode to decreasing reliance on present or previous interactions: "Full-blown adult literacy is the ultimate decontextualized skill" (p. 175).

Snow (1983) maintains that in order to develop conversational competence, a child needs a familiar partner who will ask the expected questions and give the expected answers: "Memory provides the context that physical environment cannot" (p. 176). This kind of *literate interaction* (in middle-class homes at least; cf. Heath, 1983; Gee, 1985) includes the use of conversation to build shared histories between mother and child, where the mother asks the child questions about shared

events and thereby helps the child to tell stories about and to build internal representations, or abstractions, about those shared events.[1]

Snow contends that building shared, permanent histories is a characteristic of literate societies where information is storable and permanent. This contrasts with nonliterate societies with an oral approach to language, where shared representations are reconstructed as needed; whereas information is not permanent in oral societies, it endures through epigrams or proverbs, with details filled in when required.

The use of *routines* is important in Snow's reconstruction of how literate modes of language are acquired (such as the "reading" routine *X was Y*, described previously, from Cook-Gumperz and Gumperz, 1981). Routines are not rigid and unexpandable, but are highly predictable, and therefore are "ideal contexts for language learning" (Snow, 1983, p. 177).

Social Book Reading

There is "widespread agreement in the research and teaching communities that experience in being read to contributes directly to early literacy development" (Teale, 1986, p. 196). Storybook reading is not the only early literacy activity engaged in by children and caretakers (e.g., Heath, 1983, Taylor & Dorsey-Gaines, 1988, Teale, 1986); however, it is widely studied because this activity clearly reveals, first, the importance of *routines* in literacy learning and, second, *adult mediation* in the co-construction of literacy.

In a widely cited study, Ninio and Bruner (1978) demonstrated that interactional patterns between mother and child during picture-book reading are highly routinized; they are simutaneously repetitive and innovative. Snow (1983) cited the example of ABC books, which use the standard "A is for . . . , B is for . . . " with a picture to help decode the most unpredictable element, and reliance on the familiar alphabet sequence. A 2-year-old child in Snow's study who cannot read but who is familiar with the format can deal with a new ABC book with ease: "Dis is *I. I* for ice cream" (p. 178).

As Teale (1986) observed, "perhaps [social book reading is] not absolutely necessary for becoming literate, [but] storybook reading has an extremely facilitative effect" (p. 196). Snow and Ninio (1986) examined the role of interactive book reading in children's literacy learning, with the intent of uncovering the routines that the child must master in learning to communicate with

---

[1]Note that the literate interaction Snow described is a case of what is usually identified as an "oral" language mode (i.e., conversation) serving to advance knowledge of "literate" language.

an object (i.e., a book). In order to become literate, children must learn what Snow and Ninio call the "rules of literacy"—rules that are not explicit, nor can they be taught explicitly. Snow and Ninio maintain that the "knowledgeable adult" (p. 116) is a powerful force for development, and joint picture-book reading leads children to internalize the basic skills and concepts important for literacy.

Snow and Ninio (1986) described two ways in which social picture-book reading is different from "true" literacy encounters. First (reflecting the highly integrated drawing/writing relationship discussed in the first section of this review), the text in picture-book reading dyads includes the picture; indeed, in the early stages, it is *only* the picture that is considered, and if the child attends to the text, parents respond in a way that does not differentiate picture from text. Second, picture-book reading is a joint activity, mediated by spoken language. Snow and Ninio hold that tacit *contracts* (basic rules of literacy) about book reading emerge from these interactive sessions that include the child, a knowledgeable adult, and the book.

Several such contracts have been identified by Snow and Ninio (1986), which children need to learn if they are to be successful in book reading interactions, such as:

1. Books are for reading, not for manipulating,
2. Book events occur outside real time,
3. In book reading, the book is in control, and the reader is led.

The child learns that the book is the dominant partner; its role is to control what the reader is to think about (or talk about) while reading.

Summary: Writing and Spoken Language

Children use the symbol system of spoken language to acquire literate structures, such as genre forms and literacy routines. The acquisition of a literate style of language does not wait for formal schooling in a literate society, but begins with the earliest dialogic interactions between child and parent. From the routine of the dialogue grows the child's ability to produce a monologue, or narrative story, and many young children are able to produce dictated stories appropriately as well. The narrative is the young child's preferred form of language (although it is not yet well developed), and is often the learner's path into literacy: most early writing produced by children involves writing a story. This path

is facilitated by social storybook reading, which tacitly teaches children the necessary rules for interacting successfully with written material.

CONCEPTUAL PERSPECTIVES ON EARLY LITERACY

The work of two groups of researchers are illustrative of efforts to systematize research in the field of early literacy.

Harste, Woodward, and Burke: What Young Literacy Learners Know

An influential series of studies conducted by Harste et al. (1984) investigated the patterns of early writing development in preschool children. The studies, which began in 1977 and span 6 years, challenge beliefs about the development of written language among young children, and demonstrate that children are written language users long before coming to school.

Harste et al. (1984) collected "language events" from a broad sample of children. In their first study, begun in 1977, a randomly chosen group of 20 white, middle-class or upper-class children between the ages of 3 and 6 were given four tasks: (a) reading environmental print (e.g., the McDonald's "golden arches" logo or a stop sign); (b) dictating a story and reading and rereading it; (c) writing their name and anything else that they could write; and (d) drawing a self-portrait and writing their name.

The second study, begun in 1978, is a longitudinal study of the 3-year-old children in the original study. The children were followed for 3 years; the original tasks were repeated under the same conditions at 6-month intervals.

In the third (1979–1980) study, the subjects were a random sample of 3- to 6-year-old children from inner-city, lower- or middle-class socioeconomic backgrounds. Additional story writing and letter-writing settings were added to the research tasks. The authors also collected information from their own children and the children of their colleagues throughout the period.

In their studies, the interactions with the children were videotaped with cameras taken to the site. The researchers noted things of interest and evolving patterns in the data; follow-up studies were conducted to verify that the patterns noted were not artifacts of a particular research setting. Once an initial set of categories was determined, the videotapes were reviewed repeatedly and categories were added or deleted until researchers were satisfied that they had accounted for all patterns. The taxonomies thus produced were treated as heuristic devices; once a pattern was confirmed, the literature was searched for other instances of the phenomenon.

"Theory," Harste et al. (1984) argue, "is fundamentally a set of beliefs upon which you are willing to act. It need not be, and most often is not, conscious, explicit, or formal in a hypo-deductive sense" (p.ix). They offer instead a general perspective, the *transactional view*, and contrast it to behavioral and cognitive views (p. 58):

1. Environment → Learner
   Behavioral View: Learning is the result of an S-R bond. Problems in learning are problems in the delivery system. Learner is passive.
2. Environment ← Learner
   Cognitive view: The learner is central. Learning is dependent on assimilative schemas available in the head of the language learner.
3. Environment → ← Learner
   Transactional View: Meaning involves seeing objects as signs which have the potential to signify. Language is an open system.

The researchers describe their extensive data in terms of categories, or major patterns, that characterize children's writing development, including *organization*, *intentionality*, *generativeness*, and *risk-taking*. They conclude that writing is a social action, embedded in a context, and that children are sensitive and attentive to the patterns of literacy and actively seek them out. They then produce a conceptual model (Fig. 1.2) they label the *authoring cycle* (1984, p. 214).

This representation characterizes language learning

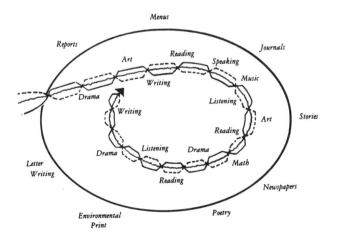

FIG. 1.2. The authoring cycle. From C. Harste, V. A. Woodward, and C. L. Burke. Copyright 1984 by Heinemann. Reprinted by permission.

and the key cognitive processes involved in literacy, as the researchers see them. First, literacy is governed by the search for a *unified meaning*, and one's past history with text is crucial, as suggested by the cyclical nature of the model. Second, literacy is *multimodal*, and includes many kinds of experiences not usually thought of as literacy, such as films and music. Third, literacy is *context dependent*, suggested by the oval surrounding the cycle.

Harste et al. (1984) found no empirical base for an inherent order of acquisition of literacy structures, and their analysis lacks an explanatory mechanism for moving development forward. Instead, they found context so overwhelmingly important that they declared, "There is no sequence to the order. . . . in which the demonstrations [of literacy patterns] are inherently learned. The context in which literacy learning occurs strongly affects the nature and direction of literacy learning" (p. 195).

Ferreiro and Teberosky: How Literacy Learners Come to Know

Research in early literacy grew out of language acquisition research (Teale & Sulzby, 1986). The success of the latter group in identifying developmental sequences prompted some researchers working with developing literacy to look for parallel sequences. Ferreiro and Teberosky (1982), working within a Piagetian framework, employed a quasi-experimental methodology to search for "the path children take to comprehend the characteristics, value and function of written language" (p. 1). By applying Piaget's general theory of the processes of acquiring knowledge to the specific process of acquiring written language, Ferreiro and Teberosky were able to posit a mechanism for development, the Piagetian notion of *assimilation*.

The subjects in their cross-age study are 4 to 6 years old, drawn from lower- or middle-class homes. Like Harste et al. (1984), Ferreiro and Teberosky (1982) believe that the key to identifying the process of early writing development lies in discovering what the children believe they are doing; but Ferreiro and Teberosky go about it differently. They describe their methodology as "an experimental situation, structured but flexible, permitting us to discover the hypotheses children put into play" (p. 21).

The children in Ferreiro and Teberosky's (1982) study were given the following tasks: (a) writing their own name, (b) writing the name of a friend or family member, (c) contrasting drawing and writing situations, (d) writing words traditionally used in beginning school writing, and (e) attempting to write other words that were almost surely unknown. The children read their texts after writing them. The Piagetian technique of the *clinical interview* (an open-ended interview that follows the child's lead) was used to query the children about their responses to the tasks, and the interviews were tape-recorded. The researchers were able to define five successive levels, based on the written responses of the children and the children's comments about their productions:

- At Level 1, the child reproduces the typical features of the writing form. All written strings look alike, although children consider them to be different; writing, however, does not function as communication because children can interpret only their own writing but not that of others. Writing and drawing are differentiated, although children may occasionally express confusion between the two systems.
- At Level 2, the central hypothesis is that to read different things, there must be objective differences in the texts. Graphic progress is discernible in that graphic forms of characters are more defined and more conventional. Children may use the same letters rearranged to make different "words," often the letters in their names. (e.g., in the present study, one child writes *dfoe*, *eofe*, etc., that he identifies once as "Jeff," then later as "eats"). The authors are able to identify this behavior as antecedent to Piagetian combinatorial operations.
- Level 3 finds children using the *syllabic hypothesis*, an attempt to assign sound value to each of the letters, often the sound of the letter name. Some sound values are stabilized; for example, a child writes *Katie* as "KT."
- Level 4 represents the passage from a syllabic to an *alphabetic* method in which combinations of letters stand for a syllable.
- Level 5 represents conventional alphabetic writing.

Ferreiro and Teberosky (1982) believe that conflict between already held hypotheses and novel information drives the child to formulate a new hypothesis that can incorporate both old and new information, that is, the new situation must be "internally reconstructed" (p. 279) to be understood. For example, in their work,

Ferreiro and Teberosky have found that children hold the early (Level 2) belief that a "word" must have a minimum of three letters. The child who writes *Katie* as "KT" with only two letters finds himself in conflict with his prior belief, and must reconstruct his notions about written language, leading him from the syllabic hypothesis toward alphabetic writing.

Ferreiro and Teberosky's (1982) work does not take into account the context or children's spontaneous intentions for writing (the very conditions that Harste et al. found to be crucial). On the other hand, because they based their work on established principles, they are able to make predictions, generate new hypotheses, and expose new observable data through this theoretical framework.

Conclusion

Much of the research reviewed in this chapter has been conducted from the perspective of emergent literacy—the belief that the preschool years are a period of significant development in written language. The work is mostly descriptive, appropriately so, because working out a sound theory requires a solid descriptive base. A wealth of convincing evidence has been accumulated to demonstrate that the so-called "beginner" in literacy is actually a sophisticated written language user; before ever coming to school, the learner has somehow already acquired a great deal of information about writing.

The emergent literacy perspective demands that information be collected in a natural setting. Typically, data are accumulated, described, and classified. But in order to account for the wide spectrum of what actually happens—children interacting with adults and peers in a dynamic process—one must go beyond description and look for an explanatory theory, one which will enable us to make predictions, and test hypotheses.

Foremost are those questions related to development: How can children's progress in acquiring literacy best be explained? What is the mechanism that drives development forward?

Clearly, social context is a crucial part of the story. A theory is needed that can explain a child's developmental progress in literacy and also take into account the powerful influence exerted by the context. The general developmental theory articulated by Vygotsky and expanded by others working in the Vygotskyan tradition is such a theory.

2

THE VYGOTSKYAN PERSPECTIVE

Vygotsky's research and writing career spanned only 10 years. Two years after his death in 1934, his writings were banned in his homeland of Russia and were not published openly for the next 20 years. The Western world knew him as the author of one book, *Thought and Language*, which was not translated into English until 1962. Yet Vygotsky's theoretical vision has been a powerful force in Soviet psychology and has recently become an important influence in the Western world as well. For several years, Western interest in Vygotsky focused on his work in psycholinguistics. The situation changed in the late 1970s when a broader range of Vygotsky's work was translated.

GENERAL THEORY

Two broad themes can be identified in Vygotsky's work: (a) the claim that the defining property of human mental activity is its *mediation* by tools and signs (primarily by speech); and (b) the claim that higher mental functioning in an individual has its origins in social activity. Overall, Vygotsky is a developmental scientist, focusing on mechanisms of growth and change.

Mediation by Tools and Signs

We come to know ourselves and others through the mediation of *psychological tools*. Like material tools that give us control over nature, psychological tools give us control over mental behavior. Vygotsky made a distinction between what he termed *lower* or *natural mental behavior*, and *higher* or *cultural forms of mental behavior*. We share lower forms of mental behavior (the natural, biological kinds) with animals: elementary per-

ception, memory, and attention. The higher forms of human mental functions, like logical memory, selective attention, decision making, and comprehension of language, are products of mediated activity. The mediators are psychological tools, or *signs*. The signs give humans the power to regulate and change natural forms of behavior and cognition. A favorite example of Vygotsky's was that of a knot in a handkerchief used as a sign to help us remember something—the knot augments our natural ability to remember. Through the mediating actions of mental instruments, like the mnemonic device of the knot, natural forms of behavior are transformed into higher, cultural forms unique to humans. Vygotsky called this process *semiotic mediation* (Kozulin, 1985).

Inner Speech

Through social interaction, external signs gradually become internalized and serve as tools for transforming innate biological behaviors into higher, uniquely human behaviors. Vygotsky was especially interested in the mediation provided by signs and in the prototypical mediating system—human language. In Vygotsky's theory, language and thought develop along different lines. Language is a higher human behavior, whereas nonverbal thought (like use of physical tools, e.g.) is natural because it can be found among animals.

Initially, a child's thought is nonverbal (the sensory-motor period of Piaget), and his or her speech is nonintellectual; babbling, crying, and the child's first words are used socially, but not as verbal thought. At the age of 2, the lines of development of language and thought meet: There is a saccadic jump in vocabulary and "speech begins to serve intellect" (Vygotsky, 1962, p. 42). The child actively looks for word meanings, but the word is part of the structure of the object, on equal terms with its other parts; the child must operate with "word as property of object" for a while before attaining full functional use of the sign. Children can use grammatical constructions accurately without really grasping their meaning, as, for example, when they use "because," "if," or "when" without causal, conditional, or temporal relations.

As naive experience accumulates, children use external signs to help solve internal problems. They count on their fingers to add sums, for instance, and in language development, they talk out loud to themselves. Finally, a profound change occurs, and the external operations turn inward: In addition to external speech used to communicate with others, language acquires a second, intellectual function, and becomes a psychological tool for structuring thinking. This notion of soundless language for oneself is the concept Vygotsky called *inner speech*.

In this scheme, language is both the psychological tool and the product that is shaped by the tool, in an interactive and recursive operation. Vygotsky viewed development as more than an ontogenetic unfolding of behavior. Rather, he saw a dynamic process, with upheavals, sudden changes, and reversals. In Piaget's view, development leads learning. In Vygotsky's view, learning leads development, through the gradual internalization of intellectual processes that are activated through social interaction.

Social Origins of Intellectual Processes

The direction of the behavioral transformation is from external to internal, that is, the behavior must exist in the society before it can become part of the internal behavior of the individual. Vygotsky (1978) described this process of *internalization* as a series of transformations:

1. An operation that initially represents an external activity is reconstructed and begins to occur internally. Of particular importance is the transformation of sign-using activity.
2. An interpersonal process is transformed into an intrapersonal one. Every function in cultural development appears twice: first, on the social level, and later, on the individual level; or first, *between* people (*interpsychological*), and then *inside* the child (*intrapsychological*). All the higher functions originate as actual relations between human beings.
3. The transformation of an interpersonal process into an intrapersonal one is the result of a long series of developmental events. The process being transformed continues to exist and to change as an external form of activity for a long time before definitively turning inward (pp. 56–57).

A central point is that every sign-using activity is social in origin, and is gradually transformed into an internal psychological tool that is under the control of the individual. External functioning is transformed into the internal plane of functioning through the general semiotic mechanism of the *emergence of control over sign forms* (Wertsch, 1985).

A major issue that emerges from this analysis is how an external process is transformed (not merely transferred) into an internal plane of functioning: How does an individual come to gain control over sign forms? In Vygotsky's scheme, this occurs through *mediation*: A knowledgeable member of the society mediates the sign system for the initiate during social interaction. "The central fact of our psychology is the fact of mediation" (Vygotsky, cited in Wertsch, 1985).

Regulation

One way to characterize the transformation from external to internal functioning is in terms of the *locus of regulation*. Initially, children are incapable of carrying out a task on their own, and must engage in social interaction to complete the task (Frawley & Lantolf, 1985). Consider a child grasping for a toy beyond his or her reach. The activity is *object-regulated*, controlled by the object the child is reaching for. The child's mother enters and interprets the child's gesture as a request for the toy: a communication, although it is one-sided at this point. The semiotic meaning of the grasping activity is controlled by the child's mother; it is *other-regulated*. In response to the mother's action of fetching the desired toy, the child comes to direct his or her gesture at other adults rather than at the object. The gesture becomes part of the child's mental repertoire, a sign to be used at will. Pointing has become a psychological tool that is under the child's control; it is *self-regulated*. Through meaningful social activity between child and mother, an external behavior that existed in the culture, the pointing gesture, has become internalized within the individual.

THE ZONE OF PROXIMAL DEVELOPMENT

Vygotsky's (1978) theory of development may be thought of as a theory of education, and his most influential concept, the *zone of proximal development*, is of obvious relevance to education (Moll, 1990). In Vygotsky's words, the zone of proximal development "is the distance between the actual developmental level as determined by independent problem solving and the level of potential development as determined through problem solving under adult guidance or in collaboration with more capable peers" (p. 86).

Vygotsky did not go beyond a general prescription in describing the forms of social assistance that constitute a zone of proximal development. He wrote about assisting children "through demonstration, leading questions, and by introducing the initial elements of the task's solution" (Vygotsky, cited in Moll, 1990, p.11). Children internalize and transform the feedback they receive from others. Eventually, they internalize these same behaviors and subsequently use them to regulate their own behavior.

This implies that we must think of the zone as a characteristic, not of the child or of the teaching, but of the child engaged in collaborative activity within specific social environments. The focus is on the social system within which children learn, and this social system is mutually and actively created by teacher and students (Rivers, 1988).

Parents lead children into the zone of proximal development for learning the cultural forms of print, beginning virtually in the cradle, through activities such as social storybook reading described earlier (Snow & Ninio, 1986). Even children in so-called "deprived" environments are surrounded by a wealth of text that they learn to use and manipulate (Taylor & Dorsey-Gaines, 1988). The mediators between child and text are parents, siblings, and later, teachers, who assist in the young learner's gradual transition from assisted to unassisted performance. Teachers, peers, and others in the learning process take on the crucial role of agents capable of driving development and learning by means of providing assisted performance (Tharp & Gallimore, 1988).

A fundamental property of the cultural signs and tools used by humans is that they are social in origin; they are first used to communicate with others. Later, with practice (much of it in schools) these signs and tools come to mediate our interactions with ourselves as we internalize them and use them to help us think.

It follows that a major role of schooling is to create social contexts, or zones of proximal development, within which conscious awareness of these cultural tools may be developed. It is by gaining control over the technologies of representation and communication that individuals gain the capacity for higher order intellectual activity (Moll, 1990).

Change in the Zone of Proximal Development

Change in the zone of proximal development is usually characterized as individual change; in Vygotsky's (1978) words, "What is in the zone of proximal development today will be the actual developmental level tomorrow— that is, what a child can do with assistance today she will be able to do by herself tomorrow" (p. 87).

Vygotsky's writings are insightful, but they are imprecise. His views have been expanded upon by other researchers, notably Wertsch, (1984) who described key concepts that explicitly define and explain what adult guidance and peer collaboration are:

Situation Definition. Situation definition is a critical notion. Situation definition is the way a context is defined by those in it. Not all the people in a context automatically define it in the same way. It is actively constructed and negotiated by the participants in the zone of proximal development; therefore, the situation definition is dynamic and subject to change.

Thus, when the children in the class that is the focus of this study are told they are going to "write a book," the *assignment* (to write a book) and the *task* (each child writing it) are two different entities. The child's definition of the task is the child's actual level of development; however, the teacher's definition (the mature level of development) is not necessarily the child's potential level, even with assistance. The teacher must adjust his mature definition of the situation to accommodate the child, by setting up a third situation definition that is neither the child's nor a mature one. The teacher then uses strategic help to move the child forward. It is essential that both teacher and child alter situation definitions over time if progress is to occur.

As an illustration, consider the revision assignment that is part of the book-writing activity. The direction is to make some kind of change in the book, and during the first revision session, children alter only the pictures. When the teacher asks in a follow-up conference what changes have been made, he expects the changes to be in the picture content: He asks, "How did you make your picture better?" During the later sessions, children begin to alter the story text instead of the pictures, and the teacher's question changes as well, to "How did you make your story better?" Thus the children and teacher mutually change and shape the situation definition, as the children are gradually led to a more mature definition of the revision task.

Intersubjectivity. The "third situation" is referred to as *intersubjectivity* (Wertsch, in Rivers, 1988; Tharp & Gallimore, 1988). When intersubjectivity is achieved, the participants in a situation share a situation definition, and know that they share it. The definition is neither the child's definition nor the adult's, and both child's and adult's definitions change. But the change is asymmetric: The adult accepts the third situation temporarily, but does not give up his own mature concept; in contrast, the child makes a genuine and lasting *re*definition.

The situation definition that is achieved in intersubjectivity is achieved through *semiotic mediation*, typically created by language, in the present study, through the group conferences that accompanied the writing of the books. Because the level of the child's actual development is less than the level he can achieve with assisted performance, the role of the other-regulator (a teacher or peer collaborators) is vital (Rivers, 1988).

A Model of the Zone of Proximal Development

The development of any performance capacity in the individual is also a changing relationship between self-regulation and social regulation. Tharp and Gallimore (1988) developed a four-stage model describing progress through the zone of proximal development, which focuses particularly on the relationship between self-control (or self-regulation) and social control (or other-regulation; see Fig. 2.1).

Tharp and Gallimore (1988) describe Stage I as "where performance is assisted by more capable others" (p. 33). The amount and kind of other-regulation that is required depend on the age of the child and the nature of the task. During the earliest part of Stage I, the child's understanding of goal, task, or situation may be very limited; the teacher (or parent or peer) offers explicit directions or modeling, and the child responds in an acquiescent or imitative way (Wertsch, in Tharp & Gallimore, 1988).

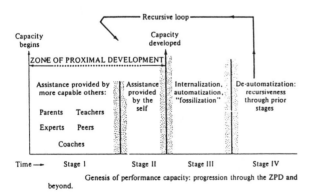

FIG. 2.1. The four stages of the zone of proximal development (ZPD). From R. G. Tharp and R. Gallimore. Copyright 1988 by Cambridge University Press. Reprinted by permission.

I would recast the very earliest part of Stage I as a separate period, an object-regulated stage of operations where the new skill is tried out without connecting the actions with the goal of the activity. That is, the child is outside the zone of proximal development for that particular activity, but uses its forms in an object-like way. For instance, when learning to use written text to tell a story, the child may use a particular text string simply because he is able to write it (his name, for example) and not because it serves the function of advancing the story. A characteristic marker of these object-regulated incidences is that the use of these unrelated forms is not commented on by peers, teacher, or the child herself.

Later in Stage I, the child gradually comes to understand the way the parts of the activity relate to one another, or comes to understand the meaning of the performance. This understanding typically develops through conversation during the task performance. Later direction may come through questions, or further cognitive structuring. This kind of assistance has been described by Bruner's well-known metaphor of *scaffolding* (Wood, Bruner, & Ross, 1976, in Tharp & Gallimore, 1988). The scaffolding metaphor is an apt one in that it implies that the task is held constant, whereas the child's role is simplified by means of gradual assistance. However, it must be remembered that a metaphor has limits: Unlike the uniform nature of scaffolding, the acts of the adults in assisting the child are of qualitatively different natures; that is, the knowledgeable adult structures the situation by providing age-graded manipulatives, selecting manageable tasks, or choosing appropriate tools, for example (Tharp & Gallimore, 1988).

During Stage I, the learner does not need to conceptualize the goal of the activity in the same way the skilled assistor does. In very early writing, the child's goal may be to please the teacher, or to demonstrate that he can write a particular word, or some other motive that the adult may not comprehend (Dyson, 1988). From adult comment on these words ("What does that say?"), questions as to the child's reason for using them ("Does that make your story better?"), and praise for appropriate behaviors, the child is led to writing behavior that more nearly resembles the adult model.

During Stage I, there is a steady decline in the level of adult responsibility for the execution of the task, and a corresponding increase in the child's proportion. In contrast, in Stage II "performance is assisted by the self" (Tharp & Gallimore, 1988, p. 38).

In Stage II, eventually the child himself comes to take over the actual structuring of the task (Lave, 1988a;

Rogoff, in Tharp & Gallimore, 1988). In an example from the present study, during a story conference, Jeff starts to make an off-task remark about his after-school plans, then abruptly interrupts himself with " . . . but that's not in the story," and returns to the topic. Vygotsky called this kind of speech *private speech*; Tharp and Gallimore's term is *self-speech*. The self-guidance effected by private speech is life-long; when learning a new skill adults consistently talk to themselves to assist their performance (consider learning how to drive a car, or operate a computer).

Stage III is "where performance is developed, automatized and 'fossilized,' . . . all evidence of self-regulation has vanished" (Tharp & Gallimore, 1988, p. 38). At this point, the child has left the zone of proximal development. Tharp and Gallimore describe task execution as "smooth and integrated . . . internalized and 'automatized.' Assistance from the adult or the self is no longer needed" (p. 38).

Stage IV represents "where de-automatization of performance leads to recursion" (p. 38) back through the zone of proximal development. Lifelong learning is made up of the same regulated sequences recurring again and again for the development of new capacities. "For every individual, at any point in time, there will be a mix of other-regulation, self-regulation, and automatized processes" (p. 38). To be faithful to Vygotskyan theory, object regulation must be added as well. Tharp and Gallimore conclude that de-automatization and recursion occur so regularly that they constitute a separate aspect of normal development. The "first line of retreat" (p. 39) is usually to the immediately prior self-regulating phase. Thus, when the children write their books, they call on already learned symbol systems to help shape the new writing skill they are learning. In addition to the obvious speech and drawing systems, they call on all of the literacy skills they have learned to date: cultural conventions, storybook reading rules, alphabet letters, and other well-learned written forms. Even gestures find their way into the books: Jeremy draws a representation of a space blast-off that is pure energy, and Todd traces his marker over and over in the same place to produce a "furry" texture.

Tharp and Gallimore (1988) do not mean to imply that the stages they describe are discrete, or that once traversed they are forever behind the child. "Achievement is gradual, with progress occurring in fits and starts" (p. 36). In their diagram of the zone of proximal development, the line between any two stages is represented as a zone itself.

Continuous Access. Stages as described within the Vygotskyan paradigm are very different from Piagetian stages, in that the Piagetian stages represent permanent new states: Once the learner moves into the next higher stage, he does not ever "unlearn" the new concepts and revert back to old beliefs. Vygotsky's scheme is also a developmental sequence, from object-regulation through other-regulation to self-regulation; but unlike Piaget, the three kinds of regulation do not represent finalized psychological states. In Vygotskyan theory, we have continuous access to all earlier states, and often produce behavior from these earlier states when the situation demands it (Frawley & Lantolf, 1985; cf. Stage IV and the Recursive Loop in Tharp & Gallimore's (1988) model). In the present study, the children use drawing and spoken language to carry the message of their books when written language fails them; they fall back upon symbol systems learned earlier and which are more nearly self-regulated than the written language system.

The goal of regulation is control of the self, and all speakers want to be self-regulated in the presence of other speakers; strategies from earlier states are continually available to achieve this goal (Rivers, 1988).

EMERGENT LITERACY RESEARCH RECONSIDERED

Vygotskyan theory holds that human beings are social from the outset, and gradually develop into individuals. This view contrasts with the Piagetian viewpoint that maintains we are initially individuals (i.e., egocentric) who develop into social beings. Thus, individuals are created, in a sense, by society: we have developed from being like everyone else, to being unique.

Ferreiro and Teberosky (1982) define their first "level" (the beginning level of writing where children first produce the forms of writing) as a phase where children can interpret their own writing but not that of others. Within Vygotskyan theory, the same finding can be interpreted, not as children's inability to see others, but children's failure to see themselves as different from others. Rather than being "egocentric," then, these early efforts can be seen as *oversocialized*, with children expecting others to understand what they "write," because of their naive perception that everyone is just like everyone else.

The development of individual cognition from social origins comes about largely through an individual learning to control his environment, primarily through the psychological tool of language. Development into an adult is the systematic transition from the child's cognition being controlled by objects (object-regulation), to the child's cognition being controlled by other people (other-regulation), to the child controlling his own cognition (self-regulation).

The transformation takes place within the zone of proximal development, or more accurately, successive zones of proximal development, as Bruner's (1986) analysis of storybook reading dyads exemplifies: Bruner found that mother and child interactions during book reading consist of regular patterns established by the mother. For example, she might say, "Oh look! What's that? It's a *fishy*. That's right." The child doesn't respond at all at first, but as soon as he responds with any kind of babble, the mother insists on the babble response in the *fishy* spot. Once the child alters his response to a word-sized babble, the mother then accepts only the new, shorter version. When he learns the word, she changes the game once more, to one in which the old and the new are differentiated. In the first pattern, "What's that?" is spoken with a rising terminal stress, and in the new game, it has a falling terminal stress, indicating the child knows the answer. The child responds appropriately, and soon after, mother takes him into the zone of proximal development again, with, "What's the fishy *doing*?" As Bruner says, " . . . she remains forever on the growing edge of the child's competence" (p. 77).

There is a developmental sequence of order, but the sequence is not categorical, it is *dynamic*. According to the concept of *continuous access to earlier phases of regulation*, the learner may at any time produce object-regulated, other-regulated, or self-regulated behavior, depending on the circumstances; control, therefore, is *task-related*, not purely developmental (Frawley & Lantolf, 1984).

The Vygotskyan concept of the *activity*, which was further developed by Leontiev (1978) and others (Kozulin, 1986; Wertsch, 1983), provides an overarching framework for the idea of regulation. In Vygotskyan theory, knowledge is not in the world to be absorbed, nor is knowledge latent in our brains waiting to be awakened. Rather, it is generated and constructed by humans acting in the world. The unit of knowledge is the *activity*, a goal-directed, tool-mediated set of coordinated actions. Inherent in this concept is the notion of the *functional system*. Within a functional system, there is no one-to-one correspondence between a structure

and the function it performs; thus, many different structures can be activated to perform a function (i.e., different methods can be used to get the same results), and conversely, the same structure may participate in many different functions. The feature that distinguishes one activity from another is the *motive*, the objective of the activity. When the goal changes, the task changes (Rivers, 1988).

Research within the emergent literacy paradigm, then, has moved in the appropriate direction with its focus on context. What is missing in many studies is a sense of the activity in which the children are engaged. There is an insistence that the young learners are engaged in actual writing, not in some kind of pre-writing or "pretend" writing. The claim is valid; but although this is an understandable reaction to entrenched views that children only begin to learn literacy with the advent of formal schooling, viewing writing as an undifferentiated activity obscures the inherent order in the development of writing behavior. Early attempts at writing are not the same as later attempts when the sign system of written language is more nearly under the child's control. Children (and teachers) redefine the situation continuously as the children gain more and more control over written text. The goal changes, and therefore the activity changes. Written text forms are produced in an empty way (object-regulated) at first. Later, after practicing the forms interactively with a knowledgeable person who can mediate their meaning (other-regulation), the same forms are used as a vehicle to convey the child's intended meaning (self-regulation). When careful categorization of children's products and processes fails to produce an invariant sequence in the acquisition of the figural aspects of written language, it is not because there is no inherent order, as Harste et al. (1984) maintain. It is because any classification attempt based on form or category must fail, because children can use the same form (and even the same process) for different purposes.

As I demonstrate in the following two chapters, children radically redefine their idea of what it means to "write a book" as they move through the zone of proximal development for this activity, yet the figural aspects of the text forms they produce remain almost the same.

3

METHODOLOGY

SPECIFIC AIMS OF THE STUDY

It is my thesis that Vygotsky's theory, as described in the previous chapter, can serve as a powerful framework for understanding the development of children's writing and, further, that the course of such development can test aspects of the theory. By closely tracking (a) children's emerging writing behaviors, (b) the social and instructional context within which they occur, and (c) the assistance provided by peers and teachers through verbal mediation, it should be possible to identify the phases of development that Vygotsky has described.

In Vygotskyan theory, a child learns to produce written text within a social context, gradually internalizing the task until writing behavior is under his control. The external-to-internal direction of learning is characterized by passage through three states of control, or regulation: (a) *object-regulated* behavior, in which the paramount goal is participation in the activity for its own sake (e.g., in writing, the child copies words and letter forms without regard for their meaning); (b) *other-regulated* behavior, in which the intent of the transaction is controlled by others; and (c) *self-regulated* behavior, when the behavior has become internalized and is under the control of the child (in writing, when the child is able to make the written text convey his or her intended meaning).

In order to explicate the way in which a child progresses from one regulatory state to another, Vygotsky introduced the *zone of proximal development*, a dynamic region of sensitivity in which cognitive development advances. The zone of proximal development is that phase of development in which a child has only partly mastered a task, but can do it if helped by an adult or more capable peers. The tools and techniques of society—such as written text—are introduced to the child and practiced in social interaction with more experienced members of the society in the zone of proximal development.

The boundaries of the zone are defined by the relationship between two levels of development: (a) the child's level of independent functioning, or the child's ability to produce written text on his or her own, and (b) the level where the child can function while participating in social interaction. In the present study, children who cannot read and write conventional text are assigned the task of "writing a book." The teacher provides all the help needed so that the child can carry out the task, such as transcribing the children's dictated stories and helping them read them. Through verbal mediation during public discussions of their books with peers and teacher, the learners move from early uses of letters and words as objects in themselves to more mature uses of written text.

Within the books that are produced, the children include *spontaneous text strings* made up of handwritten letters and letter-like forms, numerals, and symbols. A specific aim of this study is to examine these text strings and the circumstances surrounding their production and use, to determine if the children's products can be categorized into object-regulated, other-regulated, and self-regulated uses of written text. A related aim is to determine if the production of each kind of writing follows the path outlined by the theory; that is, object-regulated writing appears first, then other-regulated text is produced, until finally, writing becomes self-regulated. Expected recursions back to earlier forms (or to earlier-learned symbol systems like drawing or spoken language) should occur when problems arise, and can be accounted for within the framework of the zone of proximal development.

Verbal mediation, during the discussions accompanying the production of the children's books, is the hypothesized mechanism of progress through the sensitive zone. This study seeks to account for the effects of peer and teacher comments by examining the transcripts of the discussions, and relating them to changes in the children's uses of written text over time. Contextual information is examined, to investigate the effects of the classroom background situation on the children's writing behaviors.

Change in the zone of proximal development should be apparent in an individual child, as well as evident in the class as a whole. To determine whether the predicted changes can be observed in a single individual, a case record of one child is examined in detail. To describe the changes in writing behavior of the class as a whole, aggregated data are interpreted.

SUBJECTS

The subjects in this study are the students and the teacher in a class for young elementary children.

The Children

The children—8 boys and 3 girls—are between 5 and 6 years old. The classroom is one of two special classes located within a larger elementary school. (Special education services in this state are provided by an umbrella organization which draws students from a large regional catchment area, but classes are located within regular schools.) The school has a total population of approximately 400 students, with two sections each of grades kindergarten through six, plus the two special classes. The school is located in east central Pennsylvania, and serves a diverse community made up of rural, suburban, small town, and city environments. The children in the study reflect this diversity, and there are children from each kind of community in the class. The children's parents are lower to middle class. Among them are farm workers, truck drivers, small businessmen, white-collar workers, and nurses. Most mothers are housewives, and many of them did volunteer work in the classroom. Ten of the children are Caucasian, and one child is Hispanic.

The children are in the special class because they had all been identified as at risk academically. Nearly all the children had taken part in an early intervention program which provides preschool instruction for at-risk children. When they reach school age, all children who are enrolled in the preschool program are retested by a child-study team to determine appropriate placement in the school system. The class that is the subject of this study is one of the possible placements, and serves young learners who are average or above average in intelligence but who continue to need special services. Most of the children's problems concern speech or language difficulties, and nearly all of them receive weekly speech therapy.

Although these children are considered mildly learning disabled, their academic skills are at age- and grade-appropriate levels by the year's end. Normative testing with the *Wide Range Achievement Test (Revised)* (Jastak & Wilkinson, 1984) and/or criterion-referenced testing with the *Brigance Inventory* (Brigance, 1978) was administered to all of the students in March and May, and all of the children are well within the average range in reading, spelling, and arithmetic skills (Table 3.1). Late in the year, some of the children attended regular kindergarten classes.

The Teacher

The teacher, Neill Wenger, is a young man with a diverse background. Trained as a research psychologist, he entered the classroom with an unusual orientation toward teaching. The teacher treated everything that happened in his classroom as data, that needed to be recorded so that the information could eventually be analyzed and made useful. To that end, he produced detailed notes of each day's events. Children's products were carefully collected and preserved; supplementary information was also saved, including informal and normative testing information.

Wenger taught the special class for young children for four years. The year that he worked with the group discussed in this study was his 3rd year in this position.

TABLE 3.1
Children's Academic Levels in March, Measured by the Wide Range Achievement Test (Revised) and the Brigance Diagnostic Inventory of Early Development

| Name | Age in March | WRAT | | | Brigance | |
| | | Reading | Spelling | Math | Reading | Math |
		(Standard Scores)			(Range in Years)	
Brenton	6.0	108	103	101	6.3–7	5–7
Celeste	6.0	99	90	82	5–6	5–6.3
Damon	5.8	n/a	n/a	n/a	6–7	6–7
Gene	5.6	89	114	94	5–7	6–7
Jeff	6.0	92	95	87	6.3	5–7
Jeremy	6.1	108	98	87	n/a	n/a
Jodi	6.0	105	101	94	n/a	n/a
John	6.0	103	103	104	6–7	6–7
Michelle	6.3	116	117	110	6–7	7+
Todd	6.3	92	103	91	5–6	6–7
Tyler	5.6	111	114	107	6–7	6–7

Teaching across the hall was Carol Avery, who works in the area of early literacy (1988, 1989). She was a source of information and advice for Wenger.

During the year that is the focus of this study, Wenger set up a regime of writing instruction generally based on Graves' (1983) prescription. Wenger (1985) described his view of the process as incorporating six stages. The first two, *prewriting* and *writing*, are engaged in on a daily basis. During prewriting, children make drawings, sing, listen to or read stories, or tell stories to a friend. These activities lead to plans for the actual writing. (During the 3-month period that is the primary focus of this study, the children dictated the text of their stories to the teacher or aide, who transcribed them.) *Conferencing*, the next stage, is a presentation by the author of his work in progress to the assembled group, who listen, ask questions, and critique the piece. The group meeting provides the writer with feedback for the next stage, *revision*, and the writer recreates her work in order to make it more understandable to her audience. The next stage, *editing*, takes up the matter of mechanics (which were of minimal concern at this point because the stories were being dictated). The writer, his peers, and finally the teacher make successive editing changes, until the piece is in shape for the final stage, *publication*. During the time period encompassed by the present study, publication took the form of oaktag-bound classroom books or take-home books.

THE PROCEDURE FOR PRODUCING THE BOOKS

During a period of approximately 3 months (January, February and March) each child completed two books from start to finish. Four story conferences were associated with each book. The stories that made up the text of the books were individually dictated to the teacher or the aide, and then run off on a ditto machine. Stories were typically about four sentences long. The children cut the sentences apart, pasted each sentence on a separate sheet of paper, and illustrated each page. The children had been following a similar routine since early in the school year, and by January, when the book writing commenced, they had already dictated several stories, first as a group, and then individually.

The work of producing the *first draft* of the book was spread over several days. Once the first draft was illustrated and assembled, the teacher made a photocopy of it, before any changes were made, and this photocopy is part of the data record.

The next step in the process was the *writing conference*. Sharing their stories with the class and then inviting their peers to critique their creations was a new experience, and the children were led to the writing conference procedures in a gradual way. When the teacher presented story books, the children sat in a circle in the carpeted area routinely used for play, singing, and story activities. They were encouraged to question and comment about the pictures and the story as the teacher read the book. For the writing conferences, the same physical arrangement was used: The children brought their chairs to the carpeted area, and arranged them in a circle (Fig. 3.1).

Before the first conference with the children's own books, the teacher and the aide modeled a question/critique session; during the early conferences, the teacher modeled appropriate statements for the children, such as "I like that picture of the car," or "Why is your mom's face blue?" The teacher sat at the head of the circle, with an empty chair next to him that would be the author's chair. The teacher chose a student to begin, and the child (assisted by the teacher whenever necessary) read her story to the group. Then the author presented her story page by page, and the group criticized and commented on each page as it was presented.

The teacher typically ended the conferences with a general statement like, "What are you going to do now to make it better?" Although the goal was to encourage the children to use the feedback from the conference to revise their work, there was no rule that they had to do so. The children had to make some kind of change in order to satisfy the task demands, but they were free to make any kind of change they wished. All of the children presented their books during a conference; some of the conferences were lengthy and continued into the following day. Once each child had a turn in the

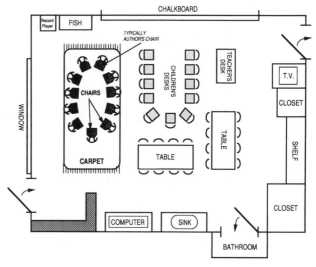

FIG. 3.1. Diagram of the classroom.

author's chair, the class left the circle and moved to the writing table to make their revisions.

After the children revised their first draft subsequent to the first conference, they met again and discussed the changes they had made. The *revised version* of the first draft became part of the data record.

During the conferences, the role of the aide was to record what was said by the children and the teacher during the conferences. Her instructions were to record actual words if possible, with the result that the transcript is near verbatim. The teacher helped in this by what he called "reflecting," or repeating each comment after the child made it; for example, if Brenton asked of John, "What is that green thing?" the teacher would say, "John, Brenton said, 'What is that green thing?'" The repetition served the purpose of slowing down the conferences enough to permit the aide to record the children's words, and it also provided a form of direct feedback to the children about the statements they were making. Because the children were working on language problems in this classroom, the teacher often reflected their words back to them; therefore these interjections do not represent a dissonant element in the conferences. Likewise, the aide frequently worked on papers in the background, and it is not likely that the recording she was doing was noticed by the children.

As the next step, the teacher produced a computer-printed version of each of the books, the *final copy*. Each child received a new set of pages that were blank except for the printed text (the same text as the first story), and made a new set of illustrations. Again, the teacher made a photocopy of the new pages before any changes were made, and this photocopy of the final version is part of the data record.

Notably, the first round of revisions was made to an already existing illustration. The children were making changes to drawings made with magic markers; to delete an element meant coloring over it. This was rarely attempted, and nearly all changes were additions or embellishments of existing elements. When the children were presented with a fresh page with the same text and directed to make a new picture, they were free to delete elements that existed in the first draft version, as well as add new items.

After the new pictures were drawn for the final copy, the author presented his story to his classmates once more, who commented and criticized his work. After the conference the children went back to the writing table to revise the final copy of their books.

Finally, the class met in the writing conference circle for the fourth and last time, to discuss the final copy of the book. As the *publishing* step, the teacher and the aide bound the final copy between oaktag covers; this became the *class copy* of the book, which was kept on the shelf along with the commercial story books.

Both Book I and Book II followed the same routine. Book I was begun on January 9 and completed on February 2. Book II was begun on February 20 and finished on April 2. A schematic representation of the entire process is set forth in Fig. 3.2.

THE DATA RECORD

The data record has three main components: (a) the children's products; (b) the transcripts of the story conferences; (c) and the teacher's record.

Children's Products

The children's products consist of two completed books each, as well as the photocopies made by the teacher of the original work prior to revisions made by the children to illustrations and text. There are two versions of each book, a first draft and a final copy; each page has a photocopy associated with it (four versions of each page). Each book is about 4 pages long; therefore, an individual child's file contains 30 to 50 illustrated pages. Beginning with the photocopies of the child's original drawings and text and proceeding through the four versions of each page, the changes a child makes to her book can be traced through time, from the original version to the final copy.

Transcripts of the Story Conferences

During the story conferences that accompanied the production of the two books, the aide recorded all of the children's and teacher's comments in near-verbatim form. Class sessions in which children discussed ideas for stories were also recorded by the aide. The hand-

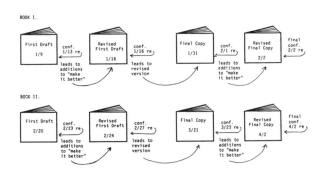

FIG. 3.2. Schematic representation of the steps involved in producing Book I and Book II.

written transcripts have been entered into word-processing files and further reformatted as spreadsheet files.

Teacher's Records: The Datalogs

The teacher kept a journal called a *datalog*, a lengthy and detailed diary with daily notations about each child in the class, plus the teacher's own reflections about those events he considered significant. The aide kept a similar, shorter record which was incorporated into the datalog. Further information about the routine of the class was collected from a set of *objective cards*, on which the teacher and the aide catalogued certain daily activities (e.g., chalkboard practice, computer practice) and comments on individual children's performance. The information on these cards was added to the datalog. Interviews were conducted with the teacher and the aide, and were added to the data record.

Formatting the Data Record

The complete datalog (September through June) has been transferred to an IBM WordPerfect text file, and assembled and printed in both chronological order and by individual child. The datalogs represent hundreds of pages of data. To make it possible to query the data systematically, the datalogs have been reformatted into *hypertext* files. Hypertext files may be thought of as a set of note cards which are linked together electronically. For example, in the datalog set, each child has one note card for every school day, which contains entries from the teacher and the classroom aide. Key words such as *reading* and *alphabet* have been added. The hypertext system permits this large record to be searched rapidly and efficiently in several ways, for example, for specific word strings or key words.

The two books produced by each student have been collected into electronic picture files. Each child's file includes two versions of each book, typically about four pages each, plus a photocopy of each page before any changes were made.

The book pages and the conference transcripts pertaining to each illustrated page have been reformatted so that all four versions of a page plus the conferences for each page are presented simultaneously (see Appendix A). This concise format makes it possible to think about the data as a manageable unit (i.e., a single page that changes over time as a result of specific feedback during the conference). Contextual information is available from the datalogs; specific questions about unclear or ambiguous situations can often be resolved by querying the hypertext datalog files. The children's book covers are presented in Appendix B.

SPECIFIC ANALYSES

It is important to remember that these data are descriptive. The task of this study is to describe phenomena that are intrinsically nonlinear; often, the important event is a singularity. Quantitative aspects are included (a) to indicate the degree of incidence of certain events of interest, (b) to add support to patterns noted in individual case records, and (c) to help identify and clarify the complex relationships that may exist among the various constituents of the data record. Listing the components in a spreadsheet format facilitates multiple sorting of the data, which in turn helps in identifying patterns that might otherwise go unnoticed.

Text Strings

All of the children included handwritten text-like strings of letters, numbers, and symbols in their books (referred to as *strings* hereafter). All of the strings included in both of the books were identified, and collected into a picture file. There were 159 strings. Further, the strings were entered into a spreadsheet (Lotus 123) and coded in various ways:

1. Each string was identified by child, book, and page.
2. Each string was identified as either a *symbol*, *number*, *letter*, *name*, *word/pseudo word*, *convention* (e.g., a speech balloon), or *text*.
3. The strings were coded as *related* or *unrelated* to the story.
4. The transcripts were searched and the strings were coded as *not commented on* or *commented on* by author, peer(s), and/or teacher.

The strings were sorted by each of these criteria, and numerical counts were obtained. The same operation was carried out by an independent rater. Differences were resolved by discussion between the two raters.

Conference Questions and Comments

The conference transcripts were entered into spreadsheet files, and sorted in various ways:

1. Each speaker was sorted out, and her comments were further categorized as (a) comments about

the speaker's own story; (b) comments and questions about the stories of others.

2. The transcripts were searched for remarks related to text strings (described previously) and for all other comments relating to the story and to the printed text. The identified comments were separated by story and grouped into author, peer, or teacher remarks.

3. The teacher's comments and questions were categorized into remarks related to (a) class control, (b) story and text-related comments, and (c) picture-related comments.

The categorizations were obtained independently by two raters, and differences were resolved by discussion.

4

JEREMY'S BOOKS

The children in this study are in the zone of proximal development for learning to use written text to tell a story. The path through the zone must be described as a unity—process, product, and the circumstances of a person engaged in writing. For this reason, I first present an annotated case study of one child, Jeremy. In chapter 5, I show how Jeremy's path through the zone of proximal development is mirrored in the progress of the class as a whole.

JEREMY'S BACKGROUND

Jeremy joined the class in October. We cannot know all of the experiences of written language Jeremy brings with him to his classroom, but we can make some informed assumptions, based on the research in early literacy and the contextural information available in the data record. His knowledge of writing is organized in many culturally determined ways; he knows that text goes from left to right, and top to bottom. The teacher's datalogs furnish some information about Jeremy's literary environment at home:

> Jeremy 10/19 When I [the teacher] read *Where the Wild Things Are*, he said, "I have that book at home."

We can assume that Jeremy has a knowledge of literary genres, including the narrative story, and that he understands the rules for storybook reading; among them, the book is in control and the reader is led, pictures can represent events, and books constitute an autonomous world.

However, when he creates a story himself, it is context-dependent, with a minimally organized structure; to understand it, the reader will need a knowledge

of the context. Jeremy makes a distinction between drawing and writing; although he may not be able to produce conventional text, when he does attempt to write, he intends his marks to mean something.

The datalogs provide background about Jeremy's writing experiences since coming to the classroom in late October. They show that Jeremy, along with his classmates, has been practicing writing his name and the alphabet letters since the beginning of the school year:

> Jeremy 10/27 Board, [writing] first and last name. Good job. Had "Jere" then erased all. Why? "'Cause didn't look right."

> Jeremy 11/9 Nice job! 1st name—last name. Missed letter 2nd time - "Jreemy"

> Jeremy 12/5 a-p [writing alphabet letters] Asked to slow down. Nice job. Knows to recite.

> Jeremy 12/8 board. a-j-z. Super writing. Says all letters.

Each of the children has a name card on her desk, and names are posted in other places around the classroom, such as on coat pegs and charts. Jeremy is interested in the names of others, as well as his own:

> Jeremy 11/29 Asked me to write "David" [for him to copy] . . . nice.

That the teacher believes these tasks to be important is confirmed in the detail with which he records the performance of the children. The alphabet and name-writing practice are often the only scheduled activities on which the teacher comments in the datalog. These tasks are important to Jeremy, too:

Jeremy 11/21 Tracing "Adams" made mistake, erased whole name, looked around, terror on face.

Another daily activity in the classroom is the morning *wake-up* exercise, "How Did You Wake Up?" A large chart in the front of the classroom displays the frame sentence, "X woke up (happy, sad, angry, sleepy . . .)." The matching "face" symbol—happy face, sad face, angry face, and so on—is next to each of the "feeling" words. Using a set of name cards, each child puts his name up on the chart in the appropriate place. The children in the class read the frame sentences that are created (e.g., "Jeremy woke up happy"), talk about them, and use them during reading instruction. Thus, in the datalogs, we see the following:

Jeremy 10/25 "How . . . Wake Up"—[read] 1 line if possible, frame sentence.

Jeremy 10/26 Reading . . . Wake-up. Got "Jeremy," "mad."

The teacher kept a separate notebook in which he recorded the wake-up data. When Jeremy produces spontaneous text strings, these strings reflect the frame sentence, too:

Jeremy 11/30 Wrote *hppy*, under a happy face he drew on the board.

Jeremy 1/3 Wrote *nappy* on the board. "Look, Mr. Wenger, I wrote 'happy'"

The frame sentence also served as a model when Jeremy needed something to put in his *journal*. The journal was begun January 10 (the same time that the first book was written), and was intended by the teacher to be a regular activity. The children were free to put anything they wished into the journal, including drawings, as long as they wrote some kind of text. The teacher hoped the journals would include original ideas from the children's own experiences, but the children typically responded by writing the frame sentence or fragments of it.

The journals have not been saved, and are only infrequently mentioned in the datalogs. The datalog records one of Jeremy's first journal entries:

Jeremy 1/12 In the journal he wrote "W-O-K" (K reversed) - said it was *woke* and drew a picture of a chimney with Santa at the top and Santa at the bottom. He indicated this was the process of Santa going down the chimney.

(Children's use of multiple images as a common way to depict movement is described in Hubbard, 1989.)

Since early in the year, the class had been dictating stories, both as a class and individually. Jeremy had missed participating in most of the group stories because he did not join the class until late October. Most of the individual stories are not part of the data record; we can only know of them from references in the datalogs. These stories are referred to by the teacher as *language experience approach* (LEA) stories, and the process is similar to that described for the books; the teacher refers to the two books that are the focus of this study as LEA stories. The datalogs describe some of Jeremy's experiences with the early LEA stories. There is information about two, one story written 10/25 and another on 11/15:

Jeremy 10/25 Dictated LEA in frame sentence when I said to tell story about how you woke up. Said, "I woke up mad." Then he said, "My brother woke up," and said his brother was watching TV. I said his brother didn't just wake up to the TV, and asked what happened first. He said, "He tied a rope to mommy's leg."

This first story is used for reading instruction for the next few weeks:

Jeremy 10/26 We read yesterday's story and he didn't have a concept of the story line, which is what I expected . . .

Jeremy 11/1 Demonstrated no comprehension of "said," but then he hasn't been in the routine as long as others. . .

Jeremy 11/7 Sat down at table and proceeded to name all the words in his LEA story. Pointing out words and saying "I know . . . " and naming words.

Jeremy dictated the next story on 11/15:

Jeremy 11/15 In LEA story, dictated, "I am sad because I am riding my bike and . . . " trails off. I asked what happened next, and he said, "I fell." I said, "OK, so listen," and repeated what he had dictated—"I am sad because I was riding my bike and . . . what, Jeremy?" He replies, "I fell down."

Jeremy 11/21 Good reading of the LEA . . . he seems to be using initial consonants to decode . . .

Jeremy 11/29 Reading LEA, remembered everything except "was."

On January 3, the children each dictated a story that the teacher assembled into a four-page book, and they made an illustration for each page. These early LEA stories are very similar to the later books that are the focus of this study, but the early books are not shared with the group in public writing conferences as the later books are.

The early books are part of the data record, and we can see Jeremy's low level of organization and context-bound story line. His story reads as follows:

(Page 1) Jeremy said, I love you. (The picture is of a Christmas tree and two stick figures.)

(Page 2) And I slipped on the snow. (A stick figure picture.)

(Page 3) And I go at home. (The only picture is a large "B" shape.)

(Page 4) I ate the spaghettio's [sic] and we ate the eggs too. (The illustration is a colorful "plate of food," surrounded by circles, some of which have wake-up type faces on them.)

Jeremy uses both writing and drawing when he produces the illustrations for this story. Besides the pictures, Jeremy includes several instances of text-like strings: he writes the letters I, L, and U on the cover (perhaps reflecting the text of page 1, "I love you"), and he adds a handwritten numeral 2 near the teacher's 2 on the second page. He also writes a string of alphabet letters, abcde, and the name of a classmate, GeneA.

THE FIRST BOOK: BOOK I

On January 9, the teacher tells the class, "We are going to write a book." When Jeremy is faced with the task of "writing a book," his mastery of writing is far from complete. He knows how to write his name, the names of others (using a model), and the alphabet letters. He is trying to write the words of the frame sentence. All of his experiences with text so far involve direct copies of text in the environment. He does not yet have enough control over written text to enable him to use it as a tool to make meaning. When Jeremy needs to express meaning with a pencil, chalk, or a magic marker, he makes a drawing.

The First Draft

Writing a book starts out just like the familiar language experience stories. After a class discussion about story ideas, Jeremy dictates his story to the teacher, who writes it on a ditto-master. Teacher and students go down to the teachers' room, and the text of the story is duplicated. Back at his desk, Jeremy cuts his story into its four numbered sentences, and pastes each sentence on a separate piece of paper. He draws a picture on each page, and then assembles the pages into a book.

At this point, the teacher makes a Xerox copy of Jeremy's book. So far, Jeremy is on firm ground. Writing a book is just like writing a story.

The First Conference, January 13. With his book in hand, Jeremy takes his place in the writing conference circle. Whereas generating the book has been practiced many times, the "conference" part is new; but it is also familiar. When the teacher reads storybooks to the class, they sit in the same kind of circle. The teacher holds the book up, and after he reads a page, everybody talks about it and asks questions about the pictures and the story.

This time, it is Jeremy who reads the book—his own book. Jeremy leaves his seat in the circle and sits in the author's chair, next to the teacher. The teacher helps, by holding the book and helping out with the words of the story, and they read the book through. For the rest of it, Jeremy is on his own.

Jeremy reads and discusses his story, and the other students comment on it and question Jeremy about his work.

Jeremy reads the text on page 1 (see Fig. 4.1), "I go with lot of people in the house." He himself makes the first comment, "My people is blast off." (*Blast off* is the text of the second page of the story and here on page 1 Jeremy is probably referring to the scribble-like lines around the people.) John and Gene wonder where the house is. "Where's the house?" they both ask. Jeremy's "house" drawing is a simple square and does not include the conventional triangular roof which would make it recognizable as a house. "Santa" is a figure on the rooftop in Jeremy's drawing, ("That's the little guy," Jeremy says) and Jodi points out that "Santa isn't in story." Finally, Jeremy identifies "two Jeremys." Jeremy draws multiple representations of figures in other situations as well (cf. Jeremy's journal entry described earlier, datalogs 1/12), and the datalogs provide a possible explanation. Jeremy is confused about representing relationships verbally, and we can hypothesize that this is reflected in his drawings:

Jeremy 12/15 Jeremy said, "I have two brothers. Jeremy and Adam." [Teacher gives him] whole explanation of Gene isn't Gene's brother, Damon isn't Damon's brother, etc., then, I asked, "How many brothers [do you have]?" "Two. Jeremy is one and Adam is two."

Jeremy said, I go with lot of people in the house.

-1-

FIG. 4.1.   Page 1, Jeremy's Book I, First Draft.

There was no way to get through to him even when I said, "OK, you're sitting at a desk, how many desks do we need for your brothers?" "Two." I pointed out, "Who sits here?" "Adam." "And here?" "Jeremy." "No, you sit here." Every time I asked him, he would include himself.

Jeremy's drawing includes a Santa that is not in the written words of the story, and the house mentioned in his story cannot be identified; both things are commented on by his peers. The other children put pressure on Jeremy to keep the pictures of his story consistent with the words. The children are very competent about this aspect of story books, and they know that the two must match.

Page 2 reads, *Blast Off* (see Fig. 4.2). As the conference progresses, Jeremy's peers continue to look for pictures of his words. The class maintains a sense of the story as a whole, for it is not only the text on page 2 (*Blast Off*) that is considered when the critique of that page starts. As Harste et al. (1984) found, children search for a *unified text*.

When his classmates see his drawing on page 2 (a minimal scribble which is Jeremy's representation of the blast off), they question it in terms of the whole story so far, and many of their questions reflect back to elements mentioned on page 1. They try to make meaning out of what looks like scribble.

John asks, "Where the blast off? Where the house is?" and Jodi asks, "Where are the people?"

Gene asks, "Where's the window?"

Then Michelle asks, "Where's the door?"

Finally, John asks, "Where's *picture*?"

The teacher asks, "What could you do to make it better?" Jeremy replies with the elements of a standard "house" scene that the other children asked about, "Doors, windows, a chimney."

Page 3 (Fig. 4.3) reads, *And the catepillar [sic] come and eat the house.* The picture on page 3 fares no better with Jeremy's critics. The narrated text most likely comes from a film Jeremy has seen, according to the datalog (datalogs 1/12, 1/20), illustrating Harste et al.'s (1984) insight that literacy is *multimodal*. Again, Jeremy's drawing is minimal, just three lines and a dot. The other children cannot find the elements Jeremy has included in the text, and they say so. Michelle asks, "Where's the house?" and John asks, "Where's the caterpillar?" The teacher joins the questioners, "How can a little caterpillar eat a house?" The teacher is challenging the logic of the text, and Jeremy finds a rationale. "He's hungry." The children pick up on the teacher's question. Gene says, "How can a little baby caterpillar eat a big house?" Jeremy assures him it can: "He eats the house." Tyler objects, "'Cept if it's a tem-

ple . . . Temple is too big to eat." Jeff asks about a cryptic element of the drawing. "What's this?" "The body," Jeremy replies. Gene asks, "How can a little caterpillar have a big body?" "'Cause he has to," Jeremy says.

The children are aware that the teacher is the knowledgeable person in the situation. The teacher deliberately tries to act as a participant rather than as the leader of the conferences; yet the children place more importance on teacher comments than on those of peers, and follow up the teacher's remarks with other questions about the same thing in nearly every instance, as in the previous exchange. The children understand who is the authority, who is providing the other-regulation of the story writing situation.

On the last page of the story, page 4, the text reads, *And my little guy has ears* (see Fig. 4.4). The picture is a limbless head and body, with happy face features and two relatively large circles floating on either side of the figure.

The children and the teacher try to make meaning out of the confusing text and minimal pictures. Michelle and John ask about the literal representation of the text. "Where's his ears?" asks Michelle. Jeremy tells her, "The ears are not on the head." The teacher questions why Jeremy drew the ears beside the head, and not on it. "When they're on I hear . . . Blast Offians" kind of noise, Jeremy answers. "How do the noises make you feel?" asks the teacher. "Loud," Jeremy replies. "How do you feel with the ears off?" asks the teacher. "Happy," says Jeremy. "Where are you?" asks John. In answer to John's question, Jeremy identifies the "little guy" figure as *Jeremy*: "Jeremy *is* the little guy." Tyler has been attentive to the text of the story, and observes, "He said 'my little guy.'" There is no way to tell if Tyler has caught the mismatch between the story's words and the identification of the figure, because no one follows up his remark.

There is a great deal of bewilderment about the identity of the "little guy" among Jeremy's classmates, even though Jeremy himself is clear about the identity of his figures. "Is the little guy a caterpillar?" asks Gene. Jeremy says, "No. Little caterpillar is my brother."

Jeff challenges Jeremy's identification. "First time, you said the little guy was *you*."

Jeremy says, "Ain't now. Now I'm Santa Claus."

All the children take their turn in the author's chair. After the conference is over, they go to the writing table and revise their work. There are no constraints on what kinds of things they can change, but the rule is that they have to change something. The children are free to use the feedback from the conference, or not.

FIG. 4.2.   Page 2, Jeremy's Book I, First Draft.

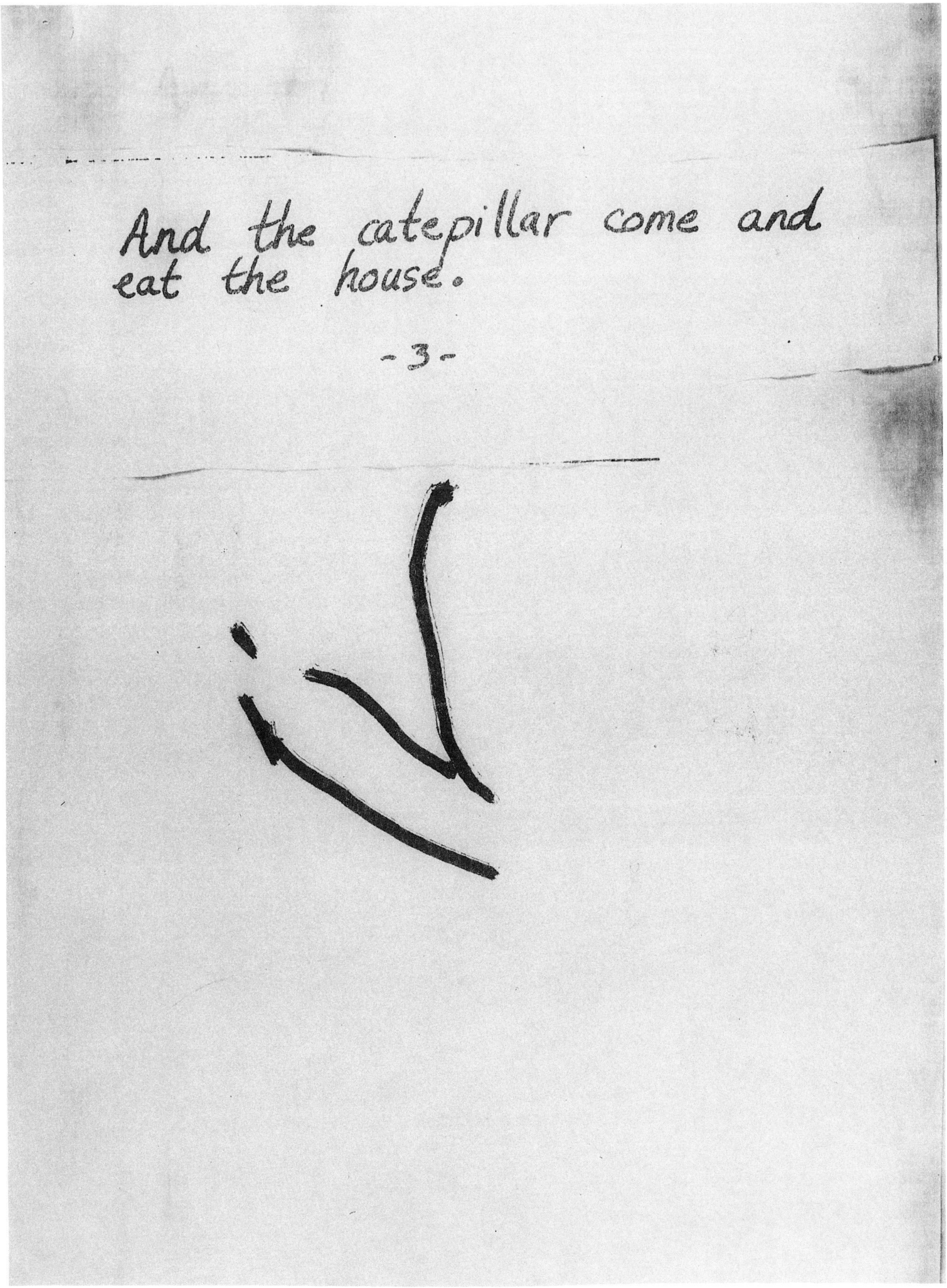

And the catepillar come and
eat the house.

-3-

FIG. 4.3. Page 3, Jeremy's Book I, First Draft.

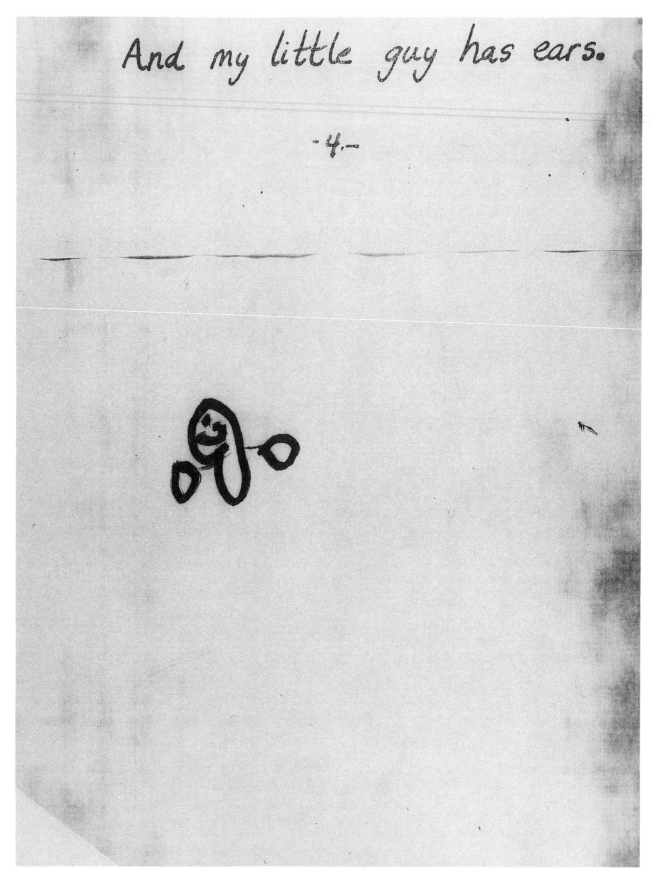

FIG. 4.4.　Page 4, Jeremy's Book I, First Draft.

The Second Conference, January 16. On the afternoon of January 16, the second writing conference convenes. The children sit in the circle and present their stories once again. This time, the teacher asks the authors to tell about what they have changed.

The teacher's expectation is that the children will have made changes to the drawings rather than to the text, as his question to each child indicates: "What did you do to make your picture better?"

The children were making changes to a drawing they had already made, with magic markers. To remove a picture element involved coloring over it. They rarely attempted this, and the changes nearly always were additions. There was no requirement that all of the pictures in the book be changed, even though most of the children made at least a minimal change to every page.

Jeremy presents his revised page 1 to the class (Fig. 4.5). "What did you do to make your picture better?" the teacher asks.

Jeremy indicates a picture element that has not been changed: "These are my friends." His only other revision, which he also mentions, is to the short text string, *J* plus a letter-like mark, which he darkened when he revised his drawing. He identifies it as "my name."

On the second page (Fig. 4.6), Jeremy incorporates the suggestions the teacher and his classmates made at the first conference. "I made a blast off and this is Jeremy sleeping in bed with a ladder," he says. Jeremy has made a "house-like" house on the page opposite the one containing the text. Inside the house is a "bed with a ladder," a picture that had been drawn first by his classmate Brenton. (The "bed with a ladder" motif was widely imitated, and nearly all of the children drew some version of it at one time or another. See Appendix A for many examples.)

Jeremy has made substantial changes to his original picture, adding most of the parts his classmates had identified as missing: a house (complete with chimney), windows and a door, and the blast off.

Gene questions the drawing of the house: "Why a little roof on a big house?" "It's big," Jeremy insists, then switches to another explanation: "I don't want to cover the whole house."

Page 3 (Fig. 4.7), where the caterpillar eats the house, has been duly revised to depict a house, reflecting peer criticisms from the first conference.

Jeremy has also made a revision to the facing page, too: He wrote the text string *Geneupwokohapp*. Notably, this string is positioned in exactly the same place at the top of the page where Jeremy has pasted the printed sentences of the story. No one comments on the addition. The teacher asks Jeremy what he did to

make his picture better. "He made a house," Celeste responds.

On the last page (Fig. 4.8), Jeremy has taken note of the teacher's earlier questions about the detached set of ears, and made a second set of "new ears on his head," because he "wants to hear something."

Jeremy has decorated the back covers of his book, mostly with text strings. The inside back cover has two wake-up-inspired strings, *Genehappy* and *Jeremyhappy*, above a picture of a Christmas tree and presents. (The Christmas tree and other Christmas themes were a frequent motif that appeared on many covers, especially for the first book which was made shortly after the Christmas vacation.) The page facing the inside back cover contains three names, *Gene Jeremy* and *Todd*, both strings enclosed in a sort of cartouche. The text strings on both these pages are in the same position as the sentences of the story.

The outside back cover is clearly a direct copy of the wake-up chart. A sad face hovers over the string *Gene sad*, and the names *Gene Tyler Todd* are followed by a happy face. A lone *J* is in one corner. No one remarks on the covers, neither Jeremy, nor the teacher, nor his classmates.

This first story finds Jeremy using two text strings in the body of the stories, a *J* plus a letter-like mark which he identifies as his name, and a string obviously derived from the frame sentence of the wake-up exercises, *Geneupwokohapp*. He has written five more text strings on the back cover: *Genehappy* and *Jeremyhappy* on one page; *Genesad* (with a sad-face symbol) and *GeneTyler Todd* (with a happy face) on another page; and *Gene Jeremy Todd* on the facing page (see Fig. 4.9).

The wake-up string in the body of the Jeremy's story is clearly an object-like use of text. The string is unconnected to the story and has no semantic meaning. Neither Jeremy nor anyone else comments on its sudden appearance, supporting the object-regulated characterization.

The wake-up strings on the covers can also be thought of as object-regulated for the same reasons. The wake-up strings are most likely a direct copy of classroom print: The frame sentence was available from the "How Did You Wake Up?" chart which was set up in the front of the classroom. Furthermore, it is a successful model for the earlier language-experience stories which precede the book writing, and it works when Jeremy needed something to write in the journals.

Claiming that the wake-up frame sentences are object-regulated uses of text strings is straightforward. The "name" string (the *J* plus the letter-like shape combination identified as "my name") on Jeremy's first page is

FIG. 4.5. Page 1, Jeremy's Book I, First Draft, revised.

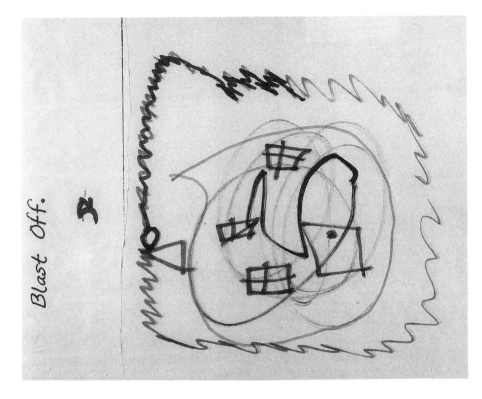

Blast Off.

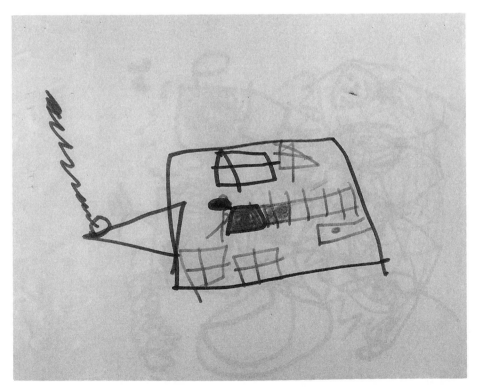

FIG. 4.6.   Page 2, Jeremy's Book I, First Draft, revised.

And the catepillar come and
eat the house.

-3-

FIG. 4.7. Page 3, Jeremy's Book I, First Draft, revised.

And my little guy has ears.

-4.-

FIG. 4.8.   Page 4, Jeremy's Book I, First Draft, revised.

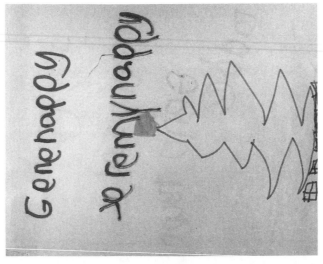

FIG. 4.9. Back cover pages, Book I.

more difficult to think about. Jeremy has embellished the string with more color during the revision, and even though no one else remarks on it, Jeremy has felt it is important enough to comment about when he responds to the teacher's question, "What did you do to make your picture better?"

The use of classmates' names is common, and many children write them, either singly or in combinations. The names are available to copy from several places in the classroom. The children often write their own name on the cover or the first page of their books, and this may be what Jeremy has intended; however, unlike some children who write their names on nearly every illustration, Jeremy rarely does so. Aside from the two-character string he identifies as "my name" on page 1, Jeremy writes his own name only on the back covers, along with the names of some classmates. Jeremy is concerned about his separate identity, and his name-writing may be a symptom of that concern.

Classmates' names (like the wake-up strings) may also be characterized as an object-regulated use of text strings in this first story. The names Jeremy writes are not related to the text of the story; we cannot know why Jeremy wrote them, but they seem to be a decoration, or a demonstration to his peers and the teacher that he was able to write them.

There is a sense that the children know that revision of the writing itself, contrasted to drawing, is a good idea. When someone makes a change that involves writing, they often claim it as an improvement when the teacher asks what they did to made their picture or story better (as Jeremy did with his name string.)

While the spontaneous text strings are ignored, this is certainly not the case with the drawings and the story line. Peers are quick to point out discrepancies between pictures and words, as they actively try to impose meaning on Jeremy's limited text and minimal drawings. Jeremy responds to peer and especially teacher feedback by appropriately changing his story in the only way he is able to, by changing the drawings. He is other-regulated in the drawing task in that he is able to understand and take advantage of the meaning supplied by his audience, and changes his drawings to reflect this meaning.

By the time the first draft is finished, we find Jeremy still outside of the zone of proximal development for using written text to tell a story. Although he writes some text strings, none are related to the story, and no one—peers or teacher—comments on them.

Note that for the skill of illustrating his story, Jeremy is in what Tharp and Gallimore (1988) characterize as Stage I (other-regulated), well into the zone of proximal development, for this aspect of the task. The teacher is

in tune with Jeremy's situation definition of story production. The teacher makes no comments about Jeremy's text strings, although he focuses on the illustrations (his question to the author is "How did you make your picture better?"). Peer questions are also about the pictures, evidence that the class as a whole shares the same situation definition. Jeremy is able to revise his illustrations in a substantial way to reflect his peers' criticisms. The evidence of progress in the story writing task is visible in the improved detail of the drawings after Jeremy revises them based on the criticisms of his peers at the writing conferences.

The Final Copy

The book writing continues. On January 31, Jeremy is given a new copy of the text of his book. This time, the teacher has printed the words across the bottom of the page with a computer. The text has the same words but in a different form—computer-printed—instead of hand-printed by the teacher. The four pages are blank except for the lines of print. Jeremy has to make four completely new illustrations. With nothing on the page but the words of the story, he can consider not only additions that would "make his picture better," but also other kinds of changes.

The Third Conference, February 1. That Jeremy considers the comments of his classmates and teacher is evident. When he redraws the scene for the second version of page 1, Santa is gone (see Fig. 4.10). The house, the topic of so much criticism in the first conference, is so much more house-like that John applauds when he sees it. The drawing is completed by a long row of stylized happy-face people and disembodied happy faces circling the house.

Jeremy says, "This is me—I'm the first one—and all my people." Gene criticizes the disembodied heads. "Why not bodies?" he asks. "Then they have to be dead!"

Jeff is more sympathetic. He too has drawn happy-face people with no bodies, and has been questioned about it. "*I* don't have no bodies," he says.

On the second page (Fig. 4.11), a *house* is not mentioned in the text (the text reads *Blast Off*), but during the first conference the group had insisted on one, with doors and windows; furthermore, the proposed improvements were endorsed by the teacher, the clearly recognized "knowledgeable adult" in the situation. In Jeremy's new picture, the blast off is inside a house, with doors, windows, and a proper, although tiny, triangular roof.

During the January 12 conference, Jodi had asked

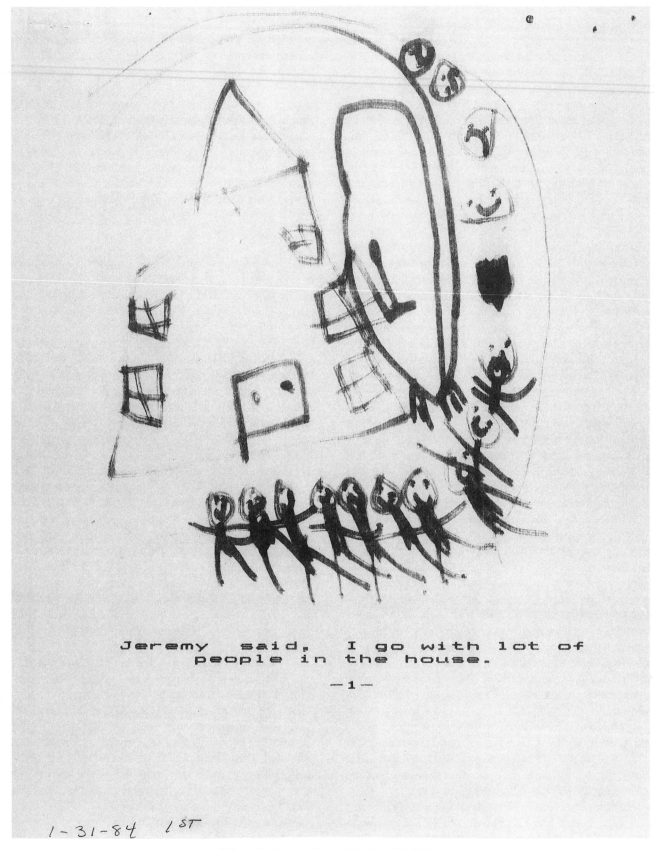

Jeremy said, I go with lot of
people in the house.

—1—

1-31-84   1ST

FIG. 4.10.   Page 1, Jeremy's Book I, Final Copy.

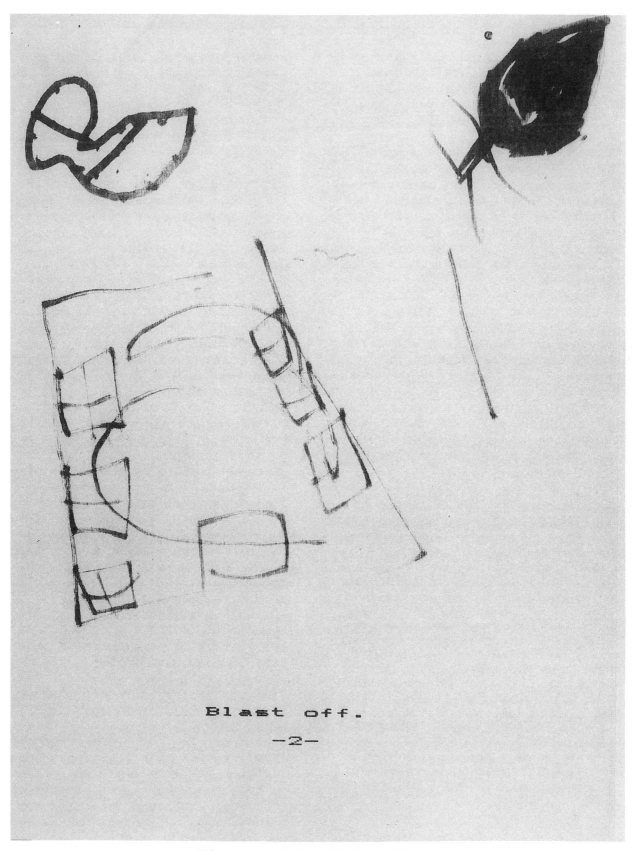

Blast off.

—2—

FIG. 4.11. Page 2, Jeremy's Book I, Final Copy.

where the people were. Jeremy does not include people in his new drawing, but he spontaneously justifies not adding people by explaining that he has added a sun that can eat: "I didn't make people—my sun gonna eat . . . "

The "sun" is not at all the conventional sun the children typically draw. It has a point and limbs. The odd sun does not go unremarked. "Who is that?" asks Gene.

"It's my sun. He's up in the sky," says Jeremy.

"Why do you have a point on it?" asks Celeste.

Jeremy shook his head. "It doesn't have to be round. It looks like fire." Jeremy then spontaneously identifies an irregular shape in his drawing that is positioned opposite the sun. "That's a pretzel in the sky."

On this page, Jeremy develops a secondary theme that is not in the story text. Many of the children weave these second themes into their pictures, often stretching them across several pages (see Brenton's suns in Book II, Damon's war in Book I, e.g., in Appendix A). The second story is carried completely by the pictures, and is separate from the written story. Thus, when the task is challenging, the children move back to an earlier, better learned symbol system, an object-regulated mode, in order to maintain control.

Jeremy draws a "pretzel in the sky." A stick figure that Jeremy identifies as "my sun" floats in the sky across from the pretzel; he says the sun is there to eat the pretzel. A clue to the origins of the odd elements can be found in the datalog entry of 1/26:

Jeremy 1/26 Jeremy told me he had pretzel sticks in his lunch kettle and was smiling . . . excited. We went into the bathrooms, and to hurry him along I told him I was going to eat them as soon as I finished washing my hands. He gave me a smile . . . I went out first and put the pretzels in my pocket. He came out and got his lunch kettle and smiled and said "No one got my lunch kettle, no one opened my lunch kettle." He didn't look inside. [In the cafeteria, Jeremy begins eating his lunch. The teacher joins him, and asks him what he had to eat; Jeremy shows him. Then] I leaned over and said, "I thought you told me you had pretzels." He froze, then started searching his lunch kettle. He even looked under his Baggie. Then he looked at me and said, "You ate them." [The teacher suggests they might be in another student's lunch "by mistake," and as Jeremy goes away to check, the teacher puts them back in Jeremy's lunch kettle. When he returns, the teacher asks] "Why don't you check again?" He started looking and shouted "Here they are! They were hiding! . . . They're *hiding* pretzels."

The presence of these elements in Jeremy's and other children's stories clearly illustrates the context-dependent nature of these early literary efforts. The threads of the story are still very fragile, and contextual elements easily overwhelm the story-illustrating task.

On page 3 of the first draft of the book, the teacher had questioned how a little caterpillar could eat a house, and a lengthy discussion followed about how a "little baby caterpillar could eat a big house." Jeremy meets his critics' suggestions with a tiny, perfectly shaped house and a sky full of caterpillars converging on it (Fig. 4.12).

Celeste says, "There's lots of caterpillars!"

Gene (Jeremy's harshest critic) says, "How are those caterpillars gonna be jumping down on the house, when there is the sky?"

Jeremy says, "Lots of little caterpillars are gonna follow those caterpillars."

The teacher prods, "How can caterpillars eat a house?" Jeremy answers, "It's in my story."

Note that Jeremy is able to provide an *intensional* explanation, an explanation that appeals to the logic created by the *text world*, rather than an *extensional*, or *real-world* factual explanation. He is beginning to be aware of the *metalinguistic* aspects of text, and can talk about his story as a story.

During the first conference, both Jeremy and his classmates were confused about the identity of the figure on page 4, "my little guy" (see Fig. 4.13). This time around, there is no uncertainty: There is only one figure on the page, drawn in bright green. Jeremy begins with the announcement, "I am the green guy."

The ears, which were floating in the first version, are securely attached to the head in the new picture. Ears had been the subject of a lengthy exchange between Jeremy and the teacher in the first conference, and peers zero in on the ears during the second. These conferences were often very lively, and the children did not hesitate to question, or even heckle.

Gene, as usual, starts by saying, "You don't have big ears like him?"

Jeremy responds, "I pulled ears out."

Gene insists, "You don't have big ears."

Jeremy says, "Yes, I do have big ears."

Tyler joins in with "Hey, hey, he's got little ears!"

Celeste says, "No, he have big ears."

Jeremy clearly has a sense of his story *as text*. He is able to talk about the narrative line as a separate entity, with its own logic and reason: In his story, the character *Jeremy* has big ears, and Jeremy the author defends his creation. Tyler and Gene respond as if Jeremy is talking about the real world instead of Jeremy's text world; Celeste is further along in the story-writing task, and is able to respond to the literary *Jeremy* instead of the real Jeremy. This vignette is an obvious example of the

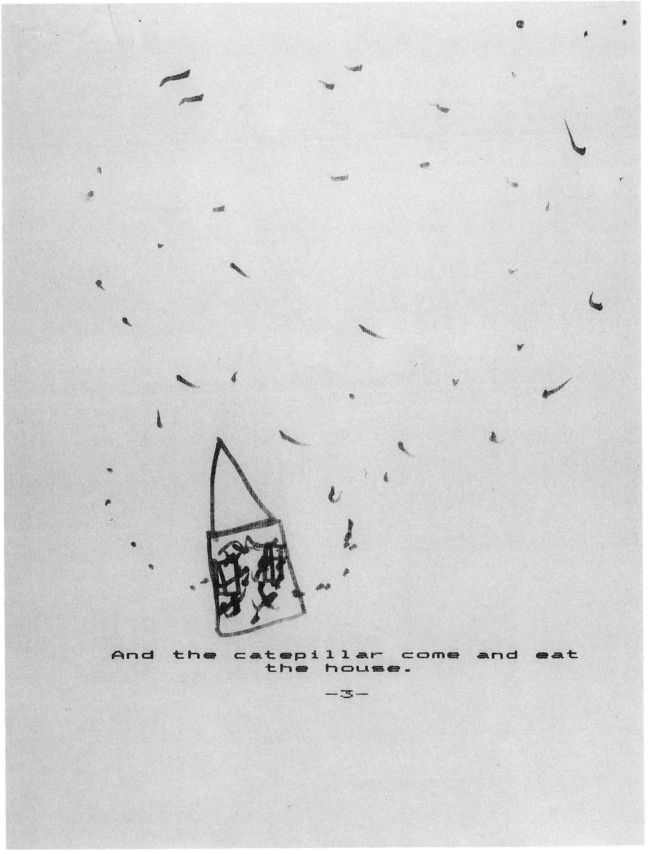

And the catepillar come and eat
the house.

—3—

FIG. 4.12.   Page 3, Jeremy's Book I, Final Copy.

And my little guy has ears.

—4—

FIG. 4.13.   Page 4, Jeremy's Book I, Final Copy.

difference in the situation definitions of the participants in a task. The assignment, "write a book," is the same for all, but each person defines the task differently. Jeremy and Celeste can talk about the story as a story, whereas Gene and Tyler are still bound by the verities of the real world. Most of the class is closer to where Gene and Tyler are, as evidenced by the many misunderstandings that Jeremy encounters when he defends his work from an intensional stance. The teacher, at this point, does not respond to Jeremy's intensional defense of his text, indicating that the teacher's "third definition" of the situation correlates more closely to the level at which most of the class is currently operating. The teacher's question, "How can a caterpillar eat a house?" reflects the kinds of factual questions that most of the children ask.

The last page of the new version of Jeremy's book also includes a conventionally drawn house, even though it is not in the text and no one commented on the absence of one on this page during the earlier conference. The other element that is new is a set of numbers from 1 through 10 positioned above the house. Gene interprets the numbers as being up in the sky, flying, and the Jeremy figure, which is floating halfway up the side of the house, as trying to reach them.

Gene says, "Are you gonna try to get the numbers? How do them numbers fly?"

Jeremy resists the meaning Gene is trying to force upon on his drawing. "They're not flying," he says.

Gene returns, "They're in the sky."

"No," Jeremy repeats.

But Gene persists, saying. "How can you see them up on cloud?"

Jeremy protests once again, "Them not in the sky!"

But he finally yields. When Gene asks, "Where are they?" Jeremy responds, "Up in sky."

A reasonable way to interpret Jeremy's picture is that the numbers are a countdown sequence to his blast off. He has probably drawn the house because of all the comments about the lack of one during the first conference. (There is a house on every page of the second version.) But classmates interpret the house as part of a whole scene and fill in the sky and clouds in the appropriate place. Therefore the numbers have to be interpreted as being in the sky, which makes the numbers "fly." (That Jeremy does not intend an outdoor scene is supported by the take-home version of his story; there is no house on the last page.)

The pictures must be considered as part of the text, because the children's definition (and the teacher's "third definition") of the task, "write a book," is to tell and illustrate a story. The class can all see the "textness" of the numbers in the sky, and they interpret them as

part of the story (i.e., the story must be about Jeremy trying to reach the numbers floating in the clouds). Jeremy, however, sees the numbers as a *comment* on the text—part of the *metanarrative* line—and therefore not in the sky, by his situation definition. Jeremy's ideas are new to him, and he is unsure of himself. He is still tuned to the social aspects of the task, and when pressed by peers about the meaning of the numbers, he gives in to the group.

After all of the children have had a turn in the author's chair, they return to the writing table and "make their picture better." This leads to the fourth conference.

The Fourth Conference, February 2. Back in the conference circle once again, Jeremy discusses the changes he has made. "What did you do to make it better?" the teacher asks. Note that in the second conference, the teacher's focusing question was, "What did you do to make the *picture* better?" In the zone of proximal development, it is necessary for the situation definition of both the knowledgeable adult and the child to change, if progress is to occur, and this is exactly what happens. Note that the teacher's question no longer specifically indicates the picture. His situation definition has changed to incorporate the new behaviors exhibited by Jeremy and some of the others in the class, the recognition of the story itself as an entity.

The most striking change to the drawing on page 1 is a text string adapted from the morning wake-up exercise, *Todd woke up Gene*, written large across the bottom of the page (Fig. 4.14). The string looks like a sentence, and it is located in the appropriate place for text—right beneath the printed text on the bottom of the page.[1] He embellishes the string with a line drawn under it and vertical lines connecting each of the letters in the string to the line below it. Nobody comments on it.

In response to the teacher's question, "What did you do to make it better?" Jeremy points out a door to which he has added stick arms and legs and a happy face similar to the stylized faces of the "people." "This is a door," he says.

Jodi asks, "Who's the first one of the people? What are these faces?"

"That's me and this is daddy, he had a mad face," says Jeremy. "These are scary faces."

The teacher asks again, "What did you do to make it better?" and Jeremy responds, "Wrote *Todd woke up Gene,* and lines from letters. I don't think, I just draw lines. Look like lines." The teacher's repetition of the

---

[1]Note that the written text of the first version of the story was at the top of the page, and Jeremy likewise placed his text strings at the top.

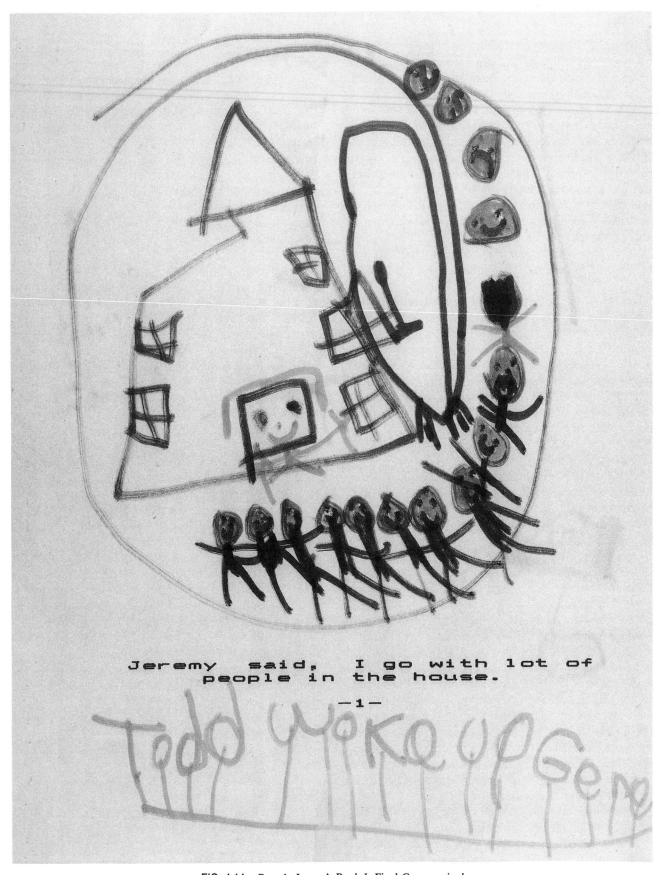

FIG. 4.14. Page 1, Jeremy's Book I, Final Copy, revised.

focusing question is an indication to Jeremy that he did not provide the expected response the first time. The second time around, Jeremy is able to shift to a response indicating the written element, and to refer to the writing in a very abstract way, but he overtly states that he has not assigned the writing a meaning within the narrative; he says, "I don't think, I just draw lines."

As with the wake-up inspired text string of the first version, peers ignore the words Jeremy spontaneously wrote, despite their large size and bright color. Jeremy himself does comment on them this time, although he comments on changes made to the drawing first.

A clue to the origin of the vertical lines and the underline attached to the text string can be found in the datalogs. Jeremy is working hard at keeping his letters on the line:

Jeremy 1/26 Carol [the classroom aide] said she had talked to him about keeping his copy work "on the line."

Jeremy turns to page 2 (Fig. 4.15). The teacher asks what he did better, and Jeremy says, "A sun," referring not to the pretzel-in-the-sky element, but a new element, a small diagonal sun in the left corner of the picture.

"That was already there," replies the teacher, mistaking Jeremy's reference to the new sun as a reference to the previously identified pretzel-sun. Jeremy does not challenge the teacher even though he is in error, nor do any of the children. They are well aware of the identity of the knowledgeable adult in the situation, and respect his authority. Jeremy finds another revision. "This is my car," Jeremy says. The car is an ambiguous drawing in the same position as the text string on the previous page; it is the same color, and there is even a line.

The new "car" drawing is probably object-regulated because there is no apparent connection to either the written story or the secondary pretzel-in- the-sky story. Notably, the datalogs contain many anecdotes that confirm how much some of the boys enjoy playing with toy cars. Jeremy manufactures links between the new elements with the rest of his drawing, when Celeste questions him. "What's the green line?" she asks. "To go up in the house," Jeremy says.

Celeste, mindful of the teacher's earlier correction about the sun, says in Jeremy's defense, "He didn't have that there before."

"I didn't do anything to the picture," he comments about page 3 (Fig. 4.16).

On page 4 (Fig. 4.17), when the teacher asks what he did, Jeremy identifies the numbers as "Letters—how many he has, (fingers) 10."

John is interested in the roof and asks, "Why is the roof there?"

Jeremy replies pragmatically, "We just have a roof on our house."

The teacher asks where the numbers are from.

"I had a book with them," Jeremy replies.

"The computer looks like this," the teacher observes.

"I copied the numbers," Jeremy says.

"From a book or the computer?" questions the teacher.

"Book, page one," Jeremy says.

In this first book, Jeremy is working mainly at the other-regulated level in reference to producing the illustrations to fit his narrated story. Most of his responses, both verbal replies to questions and changes made to drawings, reflect the way he has incorporated the meanings placed on his work by the teacher and his classmates.

Jeremy is beginning to be self-regulated in regard to the story production tasks of telling a story and illustrating it; he could reply to the teacher, "It's in my story" when he was challenged about the caterpillar eating the house on page 2. But the transition is uneven, and social pressures are strong. That the task is sometimes other-regulated is verified by Jeremy's capitulation to the meaning Gene imposes on the flying numbers.

These levels are not progressive, but recursive, as Jeremy's work demonstrates. A few drawings are object-regulated—the anomalous pretzel-in-the-sky, for example. On the other hand, Jeremy is beginning to defend his work from a self-regulated internal stance, as discussed earlier. "It's in my story," he says. He appeals to the intensional meaning and logic of his narrative, rather than to a context-bound, external real-world meaning. He is just beginning to work at this level, and gives way to other opinions if pressed or unsure.

Jeremy's use of the wake-up text strings is still at the object-regulated level. He inserts them in his book, and places them on the page appropriately, but they are not related to the story, and they are ignored by his classmates.

The numbers *1 . . . 10* are a direct copy of the external environment, yet they have meaning in the story if Jeremy is trying to represent a countdown for his blast off. If this is his intent, he is not able to articulate it. He recognizes the numbers as a different kind of element than the pictures—he calls them "letters"—but he is willing to let others provide the meaning, first Gene in the previous day's conference, and then the teacher. We can therefore classify this string as other-regulated.

The final version of Book 1 was bound between oaktag covers and kept in the classroom as the "classroom copy," available for the children to read along

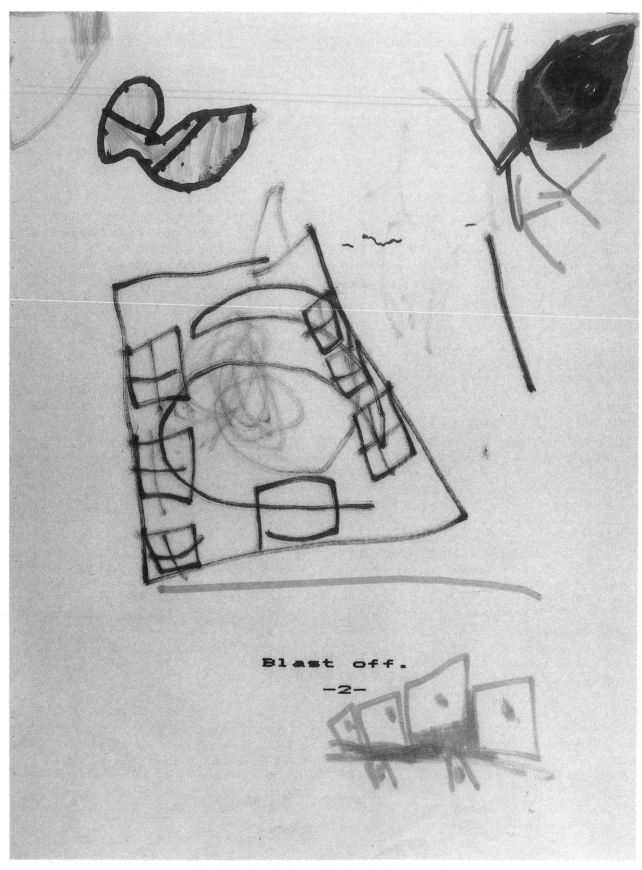

FIG. 4.15. Page 2, Jeremy's Book I, Final Copy, revised.

And the catepillar come and eat
the house.

—3—

FIG. 4.16. Page 3, Jeremy's Book I, Final Copy, revised.

And my little guy has ears.

—4—

FIG. 4.17.   Page 4, Jeremy's Book I, Final Copy, revised.

with other story books. Jeremy really thought of his book in the same category as the commercial story books:

Jeremy, 2/29 - Both recesses read story to me. Little Red Hen, Jack Be Nimble and One Two . . . Shoe. . . . Wanted to read own book to Mrs. S. [volunteer classroom aide and mother] and picked his last story to read (1/9) [Book 1.]

One other version of the story was produced, a "take-home" version. There was no conference about the take-home copy, but the teacher made a Xerox copy of it, and it is part of the data record.

On page 1 of his take-home book, Jeremy drew lines through the computer-printed sentence (*I go with lot of people in the house*) at the bottom of the page, and copied the words *people in*. Although this is clearly an object-regulated action, it is one step closer to meaningfully manipulating the words of the story. Unlike the copies of the wake-up strings and classmates' names, this copied string is the story text itself.

THE SECOND BOOK: BOOK II

On February 22, the teacher announces that "We are going to write another book. Think up ideas for another book." The story ideas are recorded for this idea session, and are part of the data record. Jeremy states that his idea is, "When I was a baby, I rode on a shoe." The aide, Carol, explains the puzzling comment: "Earlier, he showed me a picture in his wallet, of himself as a baby sitting on a toy car shaped like a sneaker. I said to him, 'Oh, you were riding on a shoe.'"

The First Draft

The same process occurs as before. The children each dictate their story to the teacher, a ditto-master is made with the sentences of their story on it, the children cut the sentences apart and paste each sentence on a separate piece of paper (on the bottom this time), make illustrations for each page, and assemble the finished pages into a book. The teacher makes a Xerox copy of the book at this point.

The First Conference February 23. The children gather in the conference circle, and each takes a turn in the author's chair. As before, the teacher helps by holding the book and supplying the words of the story when needed, and the book is read through.

Page 1 reads, *A baby is riding on a sneaker, and Jeremy is riding on a bed* (Fig. 4.18).

Jeremy's second story is hard to comprehend without some background. We know some of the context from the idea session transcripts, and the datalogs give a few more clues to the origin of the story:

Jeremy 2/22—After he dictated his [story] about a "baby" riding the shoe car and himself riding on the bed he asked if he could get his wallet and he referenced the wallet and drew himself on the shoe car.

Jeremy 2/24—The sneaker was a car he had as a baby and had shown and drawn from a photograph in his wallet.

Because Jeremy often drew multiple representations of the same person, we can assume that the drawing is of himself as a baby (copied from his photograph) and also himself on the bed, another demonstration of Jeremy's emerging sense of self.

The other children have a hard time with the two Jeremys. Jeremy reads the page, "A baby is riding on a sneaker, and Jeremy is riding on a bed." Damon challenges him. "No—*you're* riding on a sneaker and the *other* baby rides on a bed." Jeremy stands his ground. "I am riding on sneaker," he insists. At this point, the transcripts remark that there is "confusion about who was on the bed and who was on the sneaker." Jeremy finally says, "I just want to make it that way."

Damon asks about the sneaker. "Where's the sneaker?" Jeremy points it out, "Sneaker, and wheels to ride on."

Jodi comments, "I seen one of those before."

Page 2 reads, *A brother is pushing me off* (Fig. 4.19).

As the conference continues, confusion about just who is who also continues.

"This is my brother," Jeremy announces.

"On the sneaker?" asks Damon.

Jeremy then names all the figures in the drawing: "This is *me*, brother is *here*, Mommy is *here*."

Page 3 reads, *A daddy is doing going to a work* (Fig. 4.20).

Classmates ask about the literal aspects of the picture—a too little door, a too big daddy, the identity of a figure not included in the words of the story.

Gene says, "Why does the car got a little door?"

"That's not a little door," Jeremy explains. "That's his steering wheel to go to work."

Gene (the critic) says, "Where's the door?"

Jeremy says "There's no door on his car," then corrects himself to, "It has a little door."

This does not stop Gene. "'Cept, he's *big*."

Jeremy says, "He was a little baby. Now he's big."

A baby is riding on a sneaker,
and Jeremy is riding on a bed.

1

FIG. 4.18.   Page 1, Jeremy's Book II, First Draft.

A brother is pushing me off.

2

FIG. 4.19. Page 2, Jeremy's Book II, First Draft.

A daddy is doing going to a work.

3

FIG. 4.20.   Page 3, Jeremy's Book II, First Draft.

Michelle asks about the figure unexplained by the story text. "Who's this?" she says.

Jeremy identifies the figure as "Me, I'm saying 'help' because the wheels of the car are not moving."

With the car, Jeremy has introduced a secondary theme, but unlike the pretzel-in-the-sky in the first story, this theme is more nearly related to the written story. After the comments and criticisms of his peers during the first story about unrelated pictures, in the second book, even the "extra" drawings are constrained to have some relationship to the narrative.

Page 4 reads, *A mommy is doing home work* (Fig. 4.21). Jodi repeats the story text: "A mommy is doing." Jeremy's use of the article *a* with *mommy* (and with other words on earlier pages) could be interpreted as either a generic use of the article (i.e., Jeremy means any one of the class of *mommies*), or as a *literary device* to introduce new information or a new character (as in, "A woman entered"). The context of the story indicates that he intends his own mother (not all mothers), and this is the first time she appears in the story; therefore, we can assume that Jeremy is using the article in its second sense—of literary device. Jeremy's growing familiarity with written text suggests that he is aware of the use of the article to introduce new information, but he is overgeneralizing its use, in the same way that children overgeneralize the past tense *-ed* ending and produce spoken forms such as *losted* or *holded*.

The teacher interprets *a mommy* as contextual, not generic, and asks, "Why is your mom doing *your* homework?" Jeremy has a ready excuse: "Because I'm in bed." The figure seems to be holding a paper with the numeral *seven* written on it, but Jeremy volunteers "Mommy fixing sofa."

After the story conference ends, Jeremy and the rest of the class take their books to the writing table, and make their revisions. This time, Jeremy does something different. The datalogs tell the story best:

Jeremy 2/24: Jeremy was the guy who was probably the catalyst. I noticed during his revision work that he had written something under his story line and then crossed it out. I came back later, and when I saw it was lettering I stopped and carefully looked. Under his story line, which said "A mom is doing homework," he had written "And Jeremy is doing." When I asked him to read it to me, he read, "And Jeremy is doing homework." I really praised him and Carol did, too. I talked about what made me like what he had done—he not only made his picture better (revised his picture), but he was the first to revise through his writing, to make his story better through his writing. He was shaking from excitement, and I told him he could have stickers for his book. Some minutes later, he brought me the page again, and this

time he had written "A Gene doing home work." Carol and I again praised him; and a few minutes later he took another page over to her and asked her to help him read it. He had changed "A baby is riding on a sneaker" to "A mommy riding on a sneaker." He didn't stop here— he brought me page two, which said, "My brother is pushing me off"; he had changed it to "A DDDY is pushing me off." I said "That's great, and I know what you mean, but this word is missing a letter." He immediately responded, "The *a*," and walked away and came back with it rewritten, "DaDDY" above the DDDY. He read it, "A daddy is pushing me off."

Later in the day the during the group conferencing he sounded really proud as he asked to read his story first because "I . . . I . . . did the best job."

Second Conference, February 27. The new text reads, *A mommy riding on a sneaker, and Jeremy is riding on a bed* (Fig. 4.22). Jeremy takes the first turn in the authors' chair, and he reads his new sentence. The teacher asks, "What did you do better?" and Jeremy, referring to the figure that has now become his mother, indicates that he has added glasses: "Mommy wears glasses sometimes."

Jeremy has added two new stick figures to his drawing, one with a happy face and one with a sad face. His classmates make no comment about new words or the changed role of the original figure, but Gene asks about the identity of one of the new figures. "Who's this?" he asks.

"Gene," responds Jeremy.

Gene objects, "I'm not in your story."

But Jeremy is not as easy to sway as he was before. "I want to make him sad. I spank you and make you sad," he says. "I just want to make him."

The secondary theme on this page (Gene getting spanked) reflects a bigger theme that is popular with several of Jeremy's classmates. The way this class theme develops is an excellent example of how the children, the teacher, and the text environment interact to produce text. The theme mirrors the plot of a storybook the teacher read to the class, *Pierre* (Sendak, 1962). In the story book, Pierre does a lot of naughty things, then says "I don't care" about his each of his misdeeds. The story is woven into the class's history almost from the beginning of the school year.

In October, Brenton refused to talk one day, and the teacher teasingly called him a bear (datalog 10/12). Brenton kept up the game for a few days (datalog 10/13, 10/18) and a month later he was still a "bear" sometimes (datalog 11/12). A few months later, when reading the story book *Pierre*, the teacher changed "Pierre" to "Brenton Bear." Michelle noticed the similarity to the storybook boy's use of the phrase "I don't

A mommy is doing home work.

FIG. 4.21.   Page 4, Jeremy's Book II, First Draft.

A ~~baby is~~ mommy riding on a sneaker,
and Jeremy is riding on a bed.

1.

FIG. 4.22. Page 1, Jeremy's Book II, First Draft, revised.

care" and Brenton's frequent use of that same phrase: "He always say 'I don't care,'" she said (datalog 1/12). The name stuck— later a classmate referred to Brenton as "Brenton Bear" (Datalog 1/31) and in March, Gene was still referring to *Brenton Bear*.

Many of the books use the *Pierre* theme. Brenton's second book is solidly based on the *Pierre* storybook. In Brenton's story, *Tyler is Bad*, Tyler gets in trouble for telling lies, and is soundly spanked. The story is highly successful (witness Michelle's comment, "I love your story, Brenton Bear!").

There are other *Pierre* spinoffs, each ending with a spanking for the eponymous hero. Tyler's story, *Brenton Was a Bad Boy*, is even more faithful to the plot of the storybook, and Gene's book, *Brenton Bear*, follows a similar story line (see the Appendixes).

There is another aspect to Jeremy's inclusion of a sad-faced Gene getting spanked by a gleeful Jeremy. Besides its communicative function, language has a regulatory function as well; that is, humans use language to control situations (Luria, in Vocate, 1987). Gene is Jeremy's harshest critic in these conferences, and because Gene stays within the rules, Jeremy's only recourse is to put up with it. But Jeremy is learning how to use the new symbol system—writing—to take control. Even though Gene protests, Jeremy has the last word. "I make him sad. I spank him," he says. "I just want to."

Jeremy's conference continues; peers ask the usual kinds of questions: They ask for identification of picture elements that are hard to decipher, and challenge elements they know are illogical.

"What's all the brown stuff?" asks Tyler; Jeremy identifies it as "Grandma's home."

Jodi asks, "Was you really riding on the bed? Were you jumping on the bed?" Jeremy says no, and Jodi then asks, "Did you mommy really ride on the sneaker?"

"Yes," says Jeff.

"She's too big!" says Jodi.

But Gene is still troubled. "'Cept him didn't really spank me," he insists.

Again, we can see the contrast between Jeremy's autonomous text world, and the context-bound reference point of his classmates.

The text on page 2 is new; Jeremy has changed it to read, *A daddy is pushing me off* (Fig. 4.23). Just as on page 1, Jeremy's changed words and the revised role of one of the figures go unremarked by his classmates. The questions refer to the new text as if it had always been that way: "Is your daddy mean?" asks Jodi. "Isn't he mean anymore?" "No," Jeremy answers.

Although the changed text is not cause for comment, the three bright happy face stickers are.

"What's these stickers?" asks Brenton.

"That's three stickers for making my story better," Jeremy replies. No one asks what he did to make the story better.

Peers, and the teacher, ask questions about unclear pictures. The part of the picture that represents the bed is confusing, and the teacher asks, "What's going on here?"

"My bed and all my animals," Jeremy explains.

Brenton asks, "What's this?" and Jeremy identifies it as "a wheel for my bed."

"You don't have a wheel on your bed!" Brenton says, but Jeremy maintains that he does so.

Tyler asks about the "yellow thing," and Jeremy identifies it as a sun. "Hey—not even shining! You didn't make the lines sticking out," Tyler says.

The text of page 3 is unchanged: *A daddy is doing going to a work* (Fig. 4.24). Jeremy has made several additions to his drawing. Reflecting the criticism from the first conference about the absence of doors on the car, he has added two unmistakable doors. A tower-like shape is to off one side, and a line arcs over the car. The figure inside the car is now surrounded by a red field.

After Jeremy reads the text, "A daddy is doing going to a work," Celeste remarks, "Doing his *job*." Note that Celeste (who was able to accept the intensional meaning of Jeremy's "big ears" in the first book) corrects a lexical/semantic element of the written text, rather than a pictorial element.

"I know," Jeremy says, "and this is me [the small figure]."

Jeff asks about the new line that arcs over the car. "What's this?"

"This is a piece of daddy's work," Jeremy answers.

Jodi asks about the car (which had been identified during the first conference.) Jeremy tells her "It's Daddy's car." He indicates the tower and says, "This is a *whole* work. Daddy works in there."

The teacher asks about the name of the place where Jeremy's father works, but Jeremy can only say, "No name."

Page 4 has been extensively revised, and now reads, *A mommy is doing home work. And Jeremy is doing home work. A Gene is doing home work* (Fig. 4.25). Jeremy has colored over all the words of the printed text with his magic marker, and his new words cover half the page. Perhaps in response to the teacher's implied criticism from the previous conference ("Why is your mom doing your homework?"), the revised story has Jeremy doing his own homework: *And Jeremy is doing home work*. The next line is *A Gene is doing homework*. Note the use of the article *a* with *Gene* (another new character). Jeremy's use of the article to introduce new

FIG. 4.23. Page 2, Jeremy's Book II, First Draft, revised.

A daddy is doing going to a work.

3

FIG. 4.24. Page 3, Jeremy's Book II, First Draft, revised.

FIG. 4.25. Page 4, Jeremy's Book II, First Draft, revised.

information (even though it is overgeneralized to include words like *mommy* and *Gene*) indicates that Jeremy has control over the activity of telling a story; that is, of text itself as an object. He is able to perceive text as a discrete entity, autonomous and separate from the context from which it springs.

In the picture, a new, smaller figure has been added, with a text string over the head which is made up of several letters *svdtn*, the numeral *nine*, and some letter-like marks. Jeremy has written the new text strings large and bright, and they occupy about half of the page.

Jodi asks about the words, but her question does not refer to any of the letter strings which are part of the new story text; rather, she asks about "Jeremy doing 'seven'?" Jeremy says, "I just wrote that."

"How did you know to spell 'seven'?" Jodi wonders.

Jeremy explains, "It's on the numbers, like on the board we got at home."

No one asks about the change to the text of the book. Jeremy himself is moving into the other-regulated phase of the zone of proximal development, but the class collectively has not yet begun to attend to text (although there are a few incidences, as noted in Celeste's correction to Jeremy's text, shown previously, "Doing his *job*").

The teacher asks Jeremy again, "What did you do?" But Jeremy still refers to the new picture elements—Mom and the sofa (to which he has added color)—rather than to his expanded story. "I added Mom, and this sofa colored. That's all."

Finally, the teacher asks him directly about changing the words: "What's this called?"

Jeremy does not respond, but Gene, still protesting his role in the story, says, "I ain't doing homework. I wasn't at your house. Except, just at your birthday."

After Jeremy's breakthrough, the teacher discussed what had happened with Carol Avery, who also was a teacher at the same school. (Avery is the author of a number of papers on early literacy.) Avery suggested that the teacher just let the children write whatever they wanted to write, using invented spelling (Read, 1975) and any other conventions they chose to employ. On February 29, the first story using invented spelling was written. The stories are not part of the data record. The children took them home and no Xerox copies were made of them; however, the datalogs reveal the results:

Jeremy 2/29 I was pleased with the writing but had to tell him not to erase, just write what he wanted under the old. I told him I really wanted to read everything he wrote. He did a nice job with decoding and received little help from either of us [the teacher or the aide]:

[Jeremy wrote:] AnD Gen STP frL And FLR W And we LArD And my A d(reversed) am AND Jeremy pAe toS And Gene SToP: WAro We Lard

[He read the story as follows:] Jeremy and Gene stamped on the floor (edited out "and FLR W") and we laughed And my brother and Jeremy play toys. (He wanted to erase this entire line.) And Gene stamped (read at first, "on the floor," but later omitted). We laughed.

He did a drawing that was parallel to Tyler, Page 1 from his 2/20 LEA [Book 2, titled, "Brenton was a bad boy"—see Appendix A] and Jeremy was quite pleased with it as he explained it to me.

Jeremy has successfully and independently used written text to tell a story. The process is almost seamless, growing out of the literacy constructed by the whole class. The *Pierre* theme, filtered through Tyler's book, *Brenton Was a Bad Boy* provides the plot and even the illustration for Jeremy's independently produced story. Jeremy's striving for individualization, evident in the drawings and stories of his books, is demonstrated once again. The story that Jeremy can now tell with written text contains the same difficulty with referencing persons that has shown up in so many of his drawings and stories: "My brother and Jeremy play toys."

Jeremy and the rest of the class write several more stories over the next few weeks. None of the independently written stories are publicly discussed in a conference, as the books have been.

The Final Copy

On March 21, the children are given computer-printed copies of their second book, and the writing conferences resume.

Third Conference, March 23. The figures in the new illustration of page 1 are clear and unambiguous—a large, definitely feminine figure is astride a "sneaker car," and a smaller figure bounces on a bed (see Fig. 4.26). John exclaims, "I see he mommy!"

Jodi continues her line of questioning from the February 27 conference as if there has been no interruption: "Moms can't ride on sneakers!" she says.

Tyler follows up, "They can't fit . . . big people can't fit in little sneakers."

Jeremy holds his ground, "She can when she's little. She's little." Note that Tyler and Jodi adopt the generic use of the article, and interpret Jeremy's text as referring to *all* moms; Jeremy, though, makes it clear that he is

FIG. 4.26. Page 1, Jeremy's Book II, Final Copy.

referring to his own mother, supporting the hypothesis that he is using the article as a literary convention.

The teacher asks if it was a real shoe, and Jeremy says yes. "No," the teacher says. "What did your mom tell me?"

Jeremy begins to describe the toy. "It has stripes, a steering wheel, it was hard, and it had wheels . . . " Finally, he calls it a "sneaker car," and Jodi adds her support, "I know what it looks like, my cousin has a Strawberry Shortcake car." We can hypothesize that the teacher and Jeremy do not have the same situation definition during this exchange: Jeremy seems to mean that the sneaker-toy has a reality independent of his text world; he is responding from an intensional point of view. The teacher, however, is referring to the real-world difference between a real sneaker and a toy sneaker.

The new drawing for page 2 is minimal; the only elements on the page are two nearly identical figures, one with a happy face and one with a sad face (see Fig. 4.27).

Jodi immediately asks about the cryptic text. "'A daddy pushing me off' . . . *what*?"

Jeremy defends his work: "Nothing—just pushing off."

But Michelle insists on substance: "Off the sneaker?"

Jeremy is forced into supplying some meaning for his picture and text. He shifts from one explanation to another: "No, I didn't make it yet"; then, "Pushing me off, but I put the sneaker away." He then repairs his text verbally and returns to the original explanation for not drawing the sneaker: "Daddy is pushing me off the *sneaker*, but I didn't make it yet."

On page 3, the text reads, *A daddy is doing going to a work* (Fig. 4.28). The sentence sounds strange, and it is hard for even adult readers to figure out what Jeremy is trying to say. However, if the first version of the picture is examined (where Jeremy draws dad in a car with "daddy's work" off to one side), and the text of the next page (*A mommy is doing home work*) is considered, the page can be deciphered as a dad, doing "going-to-work," or traveling to work.

Tyler and Michelle attack the text, and Jeremy staunchly defends it. Tyler says, "How is *doing going to a work*—it don't sound right."

"I want it that way," Jeremy says.

"It should say *a daddy is in work*," Michelle says.

Jeremy explains, "I want to mean Daddy in car going to work."

"Should be *a dad going to work*," Tyler advises.

Jeremy persists with his original words. "I want it that way. I forgot to put in. I want that way."

Tyler and Michelle continue to offer some alternate ways to write the text. "You could say *HIS going to work*," Tyler suggests.

Michelle proposes, "*He is in the car.*"

But Jeremy runs into a technical difficulty—"I don't know how to make *car* [the word *car*]."

Jeremy's comment elicits a criticism about the drawing of the car from Gene. "There's just two wheels on car—two in front and two in back—'cept ain't one in back and ain't one in front."

"That's the wheels," says Jeremy.

The commentary in this exchange is almost exclusively about the text *as text*; it is *metalinguistic* comment concerned about the text itself as object. Children discuss how the text will sound, and offer suggestions about how it ought to sound; they discuss what the words of the text mean, and how they should be spelled—Jeremy makes an overt admission that he needs help (i.e., other-regulation) when he says that he cannot spell *car*. The class is beginning to coalesce around a new definition of "writing a book," a definition in which the text strings play a central role. Comments about the text strings are no longer isolated incidents, but occupy most of the conference.

Page 4 in its printed form includes all the new text Jeremy wrote by himself, as well as the original dictated text (see Fig. 4.29). The picture is minimal, consisting of three stick figures that are identical except for size.

Gene's protests about his presence in the story continue, and become even more insistent: "I ain't in this story. I ain't in the story."

Jeff asks who the figures are, and Jeremy replies, "Me, next to mom and Gene—I'm between mom and Gene."

Gene protests, "'Cept you didn't write 'bout me in beginning story!"

Tyler asks, "What's this?" and Jeremy repeats his identification of one of the figures, "My mom."

Gene asks, "Where's dad?"

Jeremy replies, "He's not in my story."

Gene apparently decides that two can play at the same game—if Jeremy can justify the absence of one character (his dad) by citing the text, Gene can appeal to the words of the story to prove that *he* does not belong in it either. "Maybe I ain't in his story, 'cause it says, *A Gene doing work*. It should say, *A Gene is doing work. He's in my school.*" Jeremy has the last word. "I want him in my *home*."

This round of conferences is lengthy, and extends over two days (3/22 and 3/23) before the children finish presenting the new version of their books to the class. After the stories have all been presented, Jeremy and the rest of the class, following the established routine, go over to the writing table and revise their work.

FIG. 4.27. Page 2, Jeremy's Book II, Final Copy.

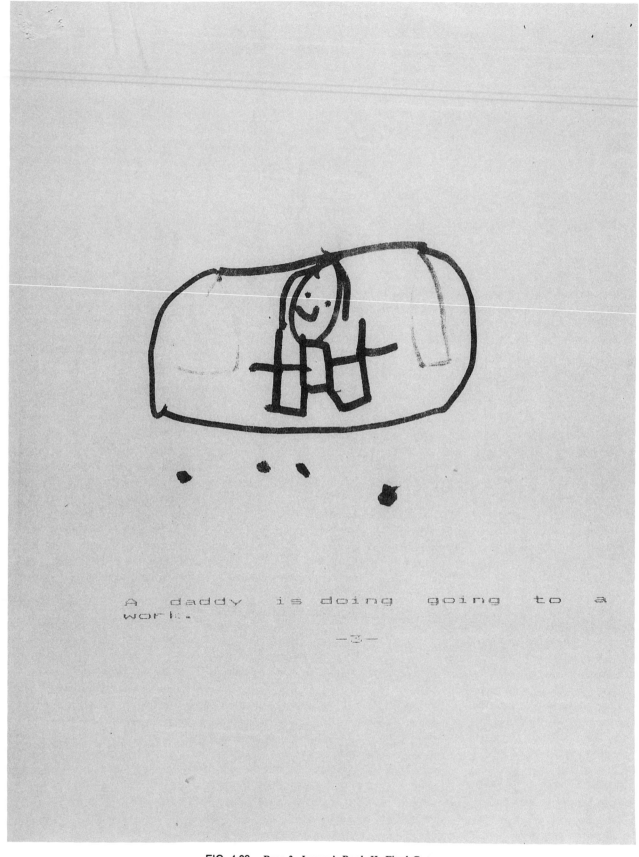

FIG. 4.28.   Page 3, Jeremy's Book II, Final Copy.

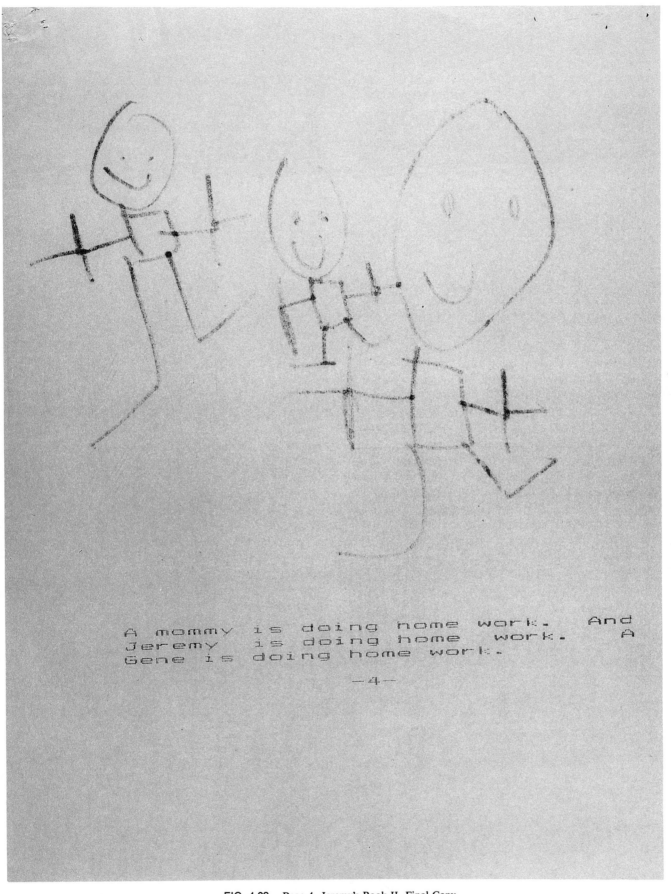

A mommy is doing home work. And
Jeremy is doing home work. A
Gene is doing home work.

—4—

FIG. 4.29.   Page 4, Jeremy's Book II, Final Copy.

Fourth Conference, April 2. The final round of conferences begins on March 27. It is also a long one, and Jeremy does not occupy the author's chair until April 2.

For his revision of page 1, Jeremy has made his picture look more like the photograph he has copied it from, by adding a line around it like those in wallet photographs (see Fig. 4.30). It is not the picture aspect that is commented on, however; the printed text is the salient feature that captures Damon's attention: "I never see picture with words on—unless you write them on."

As shown in Fig. 4.31, Jeremy's revisions to page 2 are also to the illustration, and the changes are a direct response to criticisms from previous conferences. At the first conference, the absence of a sneaker is a problem for Jeremy as well as for his audience; in the revised picture, Jeremy draws a representation of the sneaker positioned underneath the figure of *Jeremy*. And, going back to an earlier conference (2/27) in which Tyler criticizes Jeremy's drawing of the sun ("Hey—not even shining. Didn't make lines sticking out"), Jeremy has added a large yellow sun with lots of rays. Jeremy also has added three text strings: *Gene Love Jodi* across the top of the page; and two names, *Gene* and *GeneM*, one just above and the other just below the printed text.

In a reversal of the events of earlier conferences, no one comments on the new picture elements. To the teacher's query, "What did you do to make it better?" Jeremy indicates his text string, *Gene loves Jodi*. "I just want to make it," he explains.

On page 3, Jeremy has changed the text (Fig. 4.32). It reads, *A dddy is in work*, Michelle's suggested wording exactly. When the teacher asks what has been done to make the story better, Jeremy responds, "Wrote *Daddy is in work*."

Michelle does not question the new text, but she asks, "Where's [daddy's] house of work?"

"Didn't want to make it," Jeremy says; "He's driving in his car."

"Where's the door? How do you get out?" she asks.

Jeremy points out another element, "There's windows here." "But, *no door!*" Michelle repeats.

"He could crawl out a window, maybe," Damon offers.

The text of page 4 is unchanged (Fig. 4.33) Jeremy's peers criticize the drawing mercilessly. Brenton asks, "Where are pants, shirt, shoes, teeth?"

John adds, "Socks?"

"Where's the house?" Michelle demands.

Jeremy ends the conference with, "I forgot to make *everything!*" In this second book, Jeremy's emphasis clearly shifts from picture elements to text, as his final comment eloquently reveals.

During the course of writing Book II (which in this particular classroom context includes story conferences and revising), Jeremy is able to write additional text that expands the meaning of his story. He also changes the existing text in substantial and meaningful ways.

SUMMARY

In January, Jeremy can write a text string that is highly legible and in sentence form: *Todd woke up Gene*. In March, he writes a text string that is superficially very similar (the technical aspects of it are even a little more ragged): *A dddy is in work*. But although the forms look alike, the use Jeremy makes of written text strings has undergone a qualitative change. He has redefined the meaning of written text strings in the context of writing a story.

By following Jeremy's path through successive conferences and revisions, we can see how his progress toward learning to use written text is shaped by himself, his peers, and the teacher in a highly interactive collaboration. Assisted (and often prodded) by the *verbal mediation* of peers, and moved along by the various kinds of assistance from the teacher, Jeremy begins his transit through the zone of proximal development.

In Book I, the text strings are not related to the story, and they are all but ignored by the teacher and Jeremy's peers. The focus of the early discussions is on the illustrations. Within the task definition that the teacher and children have constructed, "writing a story" and "making it better" means making an illustration that is appropriate to the text. Written text strings are not yet part of the task, and are not interpreted as meaningful within the current definition of story writing, although Jeremy is producing spontaneous text strings in an imitative way. The text strings are outside the zone of proximal development for the activity of writing a story and no one talks about them. They are object-regulated.

The assignment in Book II remains the same: "We are going to write a book." But the situation definition has changed: "Writing a book" is beginning to mean something different from drawing pictures, and text strings are beginning to be used as something more than an object included in the book.

The agent of change in the zone of proximal development is the interactive feedback of the participants in the situation. During the course of the second book, after Jeremy's discovery that he can use written text to alter the story itself, peers and teacher begin to comment on the text strings; indeed, some of the conferences are almost entirely given over to talk about text, for example, the March 23 conference about page 3.

FIG. 4.30.   Page 1, Jeremy's Book II, Final Copy, revised.

A daddy is pushing me off.

-2-

FIG. 4.31. Page 2, Jeremy's Book II, Final Copy, revised.

FIG. 4.32. Page 3, Jeremy's Book II, Final Copy, revised.

A mommy is doing home work. And
Jeremy is doing home work. A
Gene is doing home work.

—4—

FIG. 4.33. Page 4, Jeremy's Book II, Final Copy, revised.

The discussions address the grammar and semantics of Jeremy's sentences—the *metalinguistic* aspects—and not their perceptual aspects: "That don't sound right," and "I want it to mean, daddy is going to work" are some of the comments.

The teacher provides many kinds of assistance to Jeremy during this other-regulated period of the sensitive zone. The teacher has structured the situation, and provided the technical help Jeremy needs to get the book together—transcribing, printing, and duplicating the pages of the book, as he did with Book I.

But the teacher also does something that is different from the things he did during Book I: He talks about the text strings. When Jeremy changes his text, the teacher praises his act to the whole class, gives him sticker rewards, and as the teacher puts it, "reinforced it to the hilt" (interview, June 1990). During the conferences, the teacher asks Jeremy directly about the words that are changed: "What's this called [changing the words]?" he says, when Jeremy fails to elaborate on his new text (Book II, p. 4, version 1).

Jeremy's hold on the new ideas is still tenuous. During the last conference, Jeremy has added a string, *Gene loves Jodi*. The teacher asks the focusing question, "What did you do to make your story better?"

Jeremy knows that indicating a text string, rather than a picture element, is a good idea. "I wrote *Gene loves Jodi*," he responds. But he also is beginning to realize that the string is different from the others he has written in Book II; this one is not part of the story. Unprompted, he offers an excuse for the unrelated string. "I just want to make it."

Jeremy's overgeneralized use of the article *a* with words like *Gene* and *mommy* is an indication of his growing control over text itself as an object. He is able to use a literary convention—use of the article to introduce a new element—and he practices it on nearly every page of his second book.

Jeremy's emerging sense of himself as an individual is clearly evident, in both the first and second book. In Vygotskyan theory, humans are social beings initially. Through social interaction, we come to know ourselves as individuals; we learn to react to ourselves in the same way that we see others react to us. Thus, the individual develops out of the social self. (In contrast, consider Piaget's view that humans are egocentric beings at first, and only later come to recognize others as different from the self; in Piagetian theory, the social self develops out of the individual.) Rather than being seen as egocentric, Jeremy's writing may be viewed as overly socialized (Zebroski, 1982); that is, Jeremy produces minimal pictures and narrative with the expectation that his peers will understand his meaning because everyone thinks the same way. When Jeremy recognizes that his peers do *not* understand—his pictures at first, and later, in Book II, his text—we can see his struggle to make the writing act his own. "I want it that way," he says, again and again. His sense of himself as a separate individual grows from Book I to Book II. In Book I, he often gives way to group pressure—the blast-off numbers are "in the sky," he concedes when peers question his explanation. In Book II, he is much more able to stand his ground, and he insists on the integrity of the text world he has created. He is willing to accept peers' and teacher's suggestions, but only within the framework of his own narrative line. He changes the odd-sounding *A daddy is doing going to a work*, but, as he says, "I want to mean a daddy in the car going to work."

Note that he can defend his intended meaning vigorously when the medium is spoken language—a psychological tool that is more nearly under his control. When he moves into the use of written language, he yields to the meaning that his classmates have imposed, and the semantic message of his text is altered to reflect the other-regulation they provide. In the final copy, *a daddy is in work*, not on his way to work.

Jeremy is beginning to understand that the text strings he uses must be constrained to the words of the story. Even as he begins to realize this aspect of written text, the teacher starts to push him gently into the next zone of proximal development, the use of conventional forms of written language. When Jeremy writes *dddy*, the teacher says, "That's great, and I know what you mean, but this word is missing a letter," and he sends Jeremy off to change it (datalogs, Jeremy, 2/23).

5

GROUP RESULTS

Jeremy does not make his journey through the zone of proximal development all by himself. Jeremy's growing knowledge about the nature of written language is constructed by the interactions of the members of the classroom society — Jeremy, his peers, and the teacher. The change is remarkably homogeneous, as the group data demonstrate.

As explained in the methodology section, the data analysis focused on two main areas: (a) text strings — the children's handwritten letters, numbers, symbols, and letter-like forms; and (b) conference records — the transcripts of the children's and teacher's discussions of the stories. The changing definition of written text from object- to other-regulatedness is reflected by changes in the ways the class used and talked about spontaneous text strings. Numerical counts support patterns noted in individual case records, and help elucidate the often complex relationships that obtain among the various components.

TEXT STRINGS

As the children enter the zone of proximal development for learning to use written text to tell a story, the forms of the activity — written text strings — are produced, in an imitative or acquiescent way, but the forms are empty and are not perceived as connected to the goal. The children produce what look like conventional forms of written language, but this activity is not treated as part of "writing a book." The children include some well-learned written units in their early books (like their own names, or Jeremy's wake-up strings, e.g.), but do not interpret them in the context of the task of book writing.

Driven by the verbal mediation of peers and teacher,

the learners' definition of the situation changes, moving gradually nearer to the mature model. The later books find children using written text in a way that is appropriate to its mature use, to change the meaning of their stories.

All of the children include handwritten text-like groups of letters, numbers, symbols, or some combination of these conventional forms in their books (referred to as *strings* hereafter). There are 159 such strings altogether, in all copies of both books (including the take-home copies).

There are more text strings in the second book than the first: 55 in Book I and 104 in Book II. Children include text strings more often, then, as they gain experience in writing their stories.

Of even greater interest is the kind of text string that is produced. If the class as a whole is being led from using text as an object, to finding story-related meaning in their writing, then this should be reflected in the changing use of text strings from earlier stories to later ones.

The strings have been sorted into three groups: (a) unrelated to the story, (b) related to the story, and (c) part of the story. An example of an unrelated string is the wake-up sentence Jeremy writes in Book I, *Geneupwokohapp* (p. 2, First Draft). Related strings include those strings that are related to either the text or the illustration, for example, labels (such as Jody's label, *foot*, on her drawing of her father in Book I, p. 2, Final Copy). An example of a string that is part of the story is Jeremy's change from *baby* to *mommy* in Book II, p. 1, Final Copy. The results are presented in Table 5.1.

Of the 62 strings that could be classified as related to the story or part of the story, 81% were in the second book. In contrast, the amount of unrelated strings was nearly stable over both books (44% and 56% in Books

TABLE 5.1
Number of Spontaneous Text Strings Categorized as
Unrelated to, Related to, or Part of the Story

	Book I	Book II	Total
Unrelated to story	43	54	97
Related to story	12	29	41
Part of the story	0	21	21
Total Text Strings	55	104	159

I and II, respectively). All of the text strings that added to or changed the text of the story were in Book II. Therefore, the children were not simply writing more text strings; instead the increase represented text strings that had meaning within the context of the task of "writing a book."

The presence of the unrelated strings in Book II is consistent with the notion of progress within the zone of proximal development; transit through the zone is not smooth, but is characterized by recursions back to earlier forms (i.e., the quality of *continuous access*) when support is needed or problems are encountered.

FIGURAL ASPECTS OF WRITING

Consider the following two number strings, one produced by Jodi and one by Jeremy. Both are from Book I. The number strings are an excellent example of the need to use a *functional* scheme to analyze early writing efforts (see Fig. 5.1).

Jodi produces two number strings on the front cover of her first book. No one comments on them, and the strings are unrelated to the story. Perhaps she is practicing writing numbers, or demonstrating that she can write them, or just decorating the cover. But the strings can clearly be categorized as object-regulated writing, writing done for the sake of doing it, rather than writing to advance the written story.

Jeremy writes a very similar-appearing string of numbers. But in the context of the story, a tale based on a science fiction film he has seen, the numbers fit the text: "My people is blast off," he writes. "Blast Off!" Jeremy's use of numbers as a countdown to a blast off is quite different from Jodi's, even though the strings are superficially similar. Peers and teacher comment on Jeremy's number string, and Jeremy even changes his description of the numbers as a result of the remarks. His use of the string is other-regulated.

All of the children include handwritten text-like strings of letters, numbers, and symbols in their books. These strings can be categorized by their form; however, as Jeremy's and Jodi's number strings illustrate, within

each category of similar-appearing strings we may find different levels of use. Four categories of forms—names, wake-up sentences, *X loves Y* sentences, and word-like strings—illustrate how children use nearly identical forms in very different ways.

Names

Forty-eight of the text strings are names, and 32 of these are the child's own name. The child's own name influences the development of the forms of written language almost from the beginning. Harste et al. (1984) present evidence that suggests the kinetic organization of the strokes of the first letter of a child's name influences the way writing and drawing are initially differentiated; Ferreiro and Teberosky (1982) characterize the child's own name as "a model of writing, as the first stable written string [endowed with meaning] and as the prototype of all subsequent writing" (p. 212).

We know from the datalogs that the children in this class practiced their names on a daily basis, and the teacher and the aide carefully monitored and recorded their performance. The children were aware of how important the task was. The datalogs show this:

Brenton 10/17 Happy about doing last name.

Celeste 11/2 Really excited—"I thought I couldn't do it [write last name] but I *did* it!"

Jeremy 11/21 Tracing last name, and he erased whole name. Looked around, terror on face. I [the aide] asked if he'd like me to write model again. Relief—-"Yes!"

The task was emphasized at home, as well. Celeste says, "My mommy told me to put my name on every picture I draw" (Celeste, Book II, p. 3, version 2; see Appendix A).

The children make use of name strings in both Book I (28 name strings) and in Book II (20 name strings). However, the perception and use of the name strings changes over time. In Book I, 27 of the 28 strings are unrelated to the story (as Celeste says, she puts her name on every picture); 23 of the 28 were not commented on. In Book II, 5 name strings are used that are actually incorporated into the text of the story. (e.g., Tyler adds *Brenton* to his narrative, "I played computer." The new text reads, "I played computer [with] Brenton"). Half of the names that appeared in the later book were occasions for comment.

Ferreiro and Teberosky's (1982) classification scheme for writing development is based on the degree of sound–symbol correspondence the child is able to demonstrate. However, when one examines the context

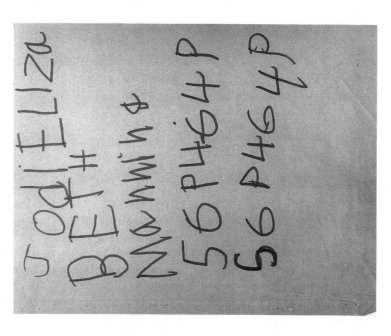

FIG. 5.1. Jodi (a) and Jeremy's (b) uses of number strings.

within which name strings are produced, it becomes clear that names are not a unidimensional category that children get better and better at writing and decoding. It is more reasonable to group name strings according to their *metacognitive function*, as object-regulated, other-regulated, or self-regulated uses of writing.

The datalogs document that name strings are well-known to the children; models are available in the classroom environment and the children and the teacher believe practice in name-writing is important. The use of name strings in the early books seems object-regulated—writing something because one can—with the (nonwriting) goal of pleasing the teacher, or demonstrating competence, rather than advancing the story line.

The name strings are not remarked on in the first book; it is not until later during the second book that the other children and the teacher take note of the name strings as written text. Thus, in Book I, Jodi can write her whole name—first, middle, and last—on nearly every page, in large, bright letters, and no one (including Jodi) mentions it. In Book II, a far smaller and shorter string, *Jodi* alone, gets commented on three out of five times: "Jodi wrote her name on there," John says. In the second book, peers begin to remark on the presence of names, and the name strings start to become other-regulated as written text.

"How Did You Wake Up?"

Besides names, another important word string in the children's environment in this particular classroom is the "How did you wake up?" sentence. There was a large chart in the front of the room, with the sentence, "I woke up" printed on it, along with a set of cards with the children's names and a set of "feeling" words (happy, sad, sleepy, mad, etc.) with an appropriate matching face.

Every morning, as part of the daily routine, each child told how he woke up. The task was to speak in a complete sentence, using the frame, "I woke up [happy, mad . . .]." The sentences formed in this way were transcribed (with the appropriate child's name inserted, as "Jeremy woke up mad"), and used as reading lessons. For example, the datalogs report:

> Jeremy 10/26 Reading . . . Wake-up. Got "Jeremy," "mad."

The children practiced wake-up words in other ways as well. There was a set of wake-up words in an envelope, which the children used to make sentences; also, the teacher had programmed the wake-up words into a matching-type game on the classroom computer. The datalogs describe the classroom:

> Brenton 10/18 Chose to remain at seat and create sentences with the *How did you wake up* cards. He'd read them to me and was visibly pleased. I would read "I woke up sad," and then he'd say to me, "I didn't know you woke up sad!" which was the same thing I was doing to him.

> Jodi 1/18 While she was waiting for the bus, she played the *Concentration* game on the computer, on which I had programmed the wake-up words.

Additionally, the teacher kept a daily record of how each child reported feeling each morning. Thus, the wake-up words had many of the same attributes as names: They were practiced frequently, valued by the teacher, and there were many models available in the classroom.

The wake-up words appear often in the children's spontaneous writing:

> Jodi 10/24 During free time this morning she was copying the words *happy, scared*.

> Jeremy 11/30 Wrote *hppy*, under a happy face he drew on the board.

In January (about the same time that the book-writing began) the teacher started the class writing daily journals. The journals were not saved and are not part of the data record; however, there is mention of them in the datalogs. The teacher reported that the only rule for the journal entries was that the children had to write; they could write anything—letters, numbers, words—as long as it was writing. Pictures could accompany the writing, but some kind of text string had to be present. The children responded to the task by writing wake-up frame sentences or fragments of them. There are many examples in the datalogs:

> Jeff 1/10 In his journal he copied some wake-up words.

> Jeremy 1/12 In the journal he wrote "W-O-K [reversed]" and said it was "woke."

The faces (happy faces, sad faces, mad faces, etc., from the wake-up chart) accompany the wake-up sentences in every kind of circumstance where the children write the sentences. The faces appear in the journals, they are included in spontaneous writing and drawing on the chalkboard, and there are many examples of the faces in Book I (cf. Jeremy's cover for Book I; see p. 36).

Twelve wake-up strings appear in Book I; there are none in Book II. (When the children stop producing wake-up strings, they stop producing the faces as well. There are no wake-up faces in Book II.) Over half the children write wake-up strings (6 of 11 children). When the strings appear, they are ignored by the teacher, peers, and the authors themselves. It is almost as if they are invisible. The only peer comment in the conferences that refers to the wake-up strings ignores the wake-up part of the string altogether and focuses on the name: Brenton writes the string *Brenton woke up Jeffrey* on the cover of his book. Jeffrey remarks, "He wrote 'Jeffrey' on the back [sic]." (See Appendix B.) Jeffrey's definition of the task of *writing a book* at this point includes telling the story and illustrating it. He views the page as text, with the pictorial elements and the text string as undifferentiated from each other, except for the only unit that is meaningful to him, his own name.

All of the wake-up strings are unrelated to the story. Because they are unrelated to the story and ignored by the children, it is clear that the wake-up strings are object-regulated as written text; they are outside the zone of proximal development for the activity of using written text to produce a story. Like the name strings, the children write them because they can, not because they are part of the story. The children produce the forms of written text, but they do not interpret the strings. Thus, when Jeremy adds *Todd woke up Gene* to his illustration with large green letters, it goes unremarked by his peers and the teacher.

"X Loves Y"

In Book I, Michelle wrote the (story-unrelated) string, "I love John" on her cover. There are 11 instances of love strings in the second book, and many of them are quite long; for example, John writes, *Todd/Tyler Love/ Brenton /Jodi Love Todd/Michelle* (p. 2, Final Copy) which he "reads" as "Todd love Tyler. Brenton love Michelle. Jodi love Todd. Todd love Michelle."

Whereas the wake-up strings are clearly a copy of the text available in the classroom environment, the love strings are more like an evolved classroom convention. Their history can be reconstructed from the datalog entries. Most of the children had been in a preschool program the year before, where Michelle already was using "I love you" oral sentences. She reminds her classmates of former times:

> Michelle 10/25 Michelle said, "Remember last year when I loved you (to Tyler) and I changed my mind to John?" She said it two times, then said, "I think he's the best."

Notably, Michelle wrote the only love string in Book I, "I love John."

X loves Y strings found their way into the daily journals early (the daily journal writing commenced January 10, the same time that Book I was started). A reasonable explanation for their presence may be found in Brenton's datalog entry of 1/11, the second day of the journal writing. Brenton wrote coupled names, and the teacher paid a great deal of positive attention to Brenton's act:

> Brenton 1/11 In his journal he combined two kids' first names and a word from the cigar box [in which the magic markers were kept]. It wasn't intentional, until I read his list of words out loud, and all the kids got excited, and hooped an hollered. Then he did even more systematic combinations. Later he called my attention to the board where he had written "JodiTodd," and drew two stick figures and a heart. He explained that it meant that Todd loves Jodi.

Brenton's invention appears in several places afterwards. In a similar construction, John's journal entry for 1/16 is " . . . a figure," (nicely done) and "I [heart] you" (datalogs, John, 1/16).

The motif is used in the dictated stories: Page one of Todd's first book reads, "I love you," and includes three large hearts above the figures in his illustration (Todd, Book I, p. 1). In another situation, the covers of Gene's Book I are decorated with a heart with the almost-word *LOVD* written on it. The datalogs report still another application:

> Jeremy, 2/1 Jeremy made a picture of a heart that said, "I love you Gene," and had hearts and people drawn on it [which he presented to Gene].

All of the children used the X loves Y form. The datalogs catalog X loves Y journal entries for 7 of the 11 children in the class, and 7 of the children included them as spontaneous text strings in their books.

Even though all of the love strings are similar in appearance, the uses to which they are put are very different. Many of the love strings appearing in Book II seem to be object-regulated; that is, the children write them to show they can write them. The children have seen these kinds of strings produce a strong favorable reaction from the teacher; it can be hypothesized that (because most of the strings are unrelated to the story line) they are included in their books as things (objects) to please the teacher.

But unlike the wake-up strings in the earlier Book I which were not remarked on by the class, the love strings in Book II are often cause for comment. Of the 11 love strings in Book II, only 4 go unremarked. The remaining strings are commented on 5 times by the author, 9 times by peers, and once by the teacher. For example, John's deciphering of the string (*Todd/Tyler Love/Brenton* etc., discussed earlier) is in response to Michelle's question, "What's that say?" After he reads the string for Michelle, the teacher follows up with, "Was that in the story?" ("No," John replied.) Therefore, we are able to classify many of the X loves Y strings as other-regulated.

The love strings, although they never become part of the story text, are beginning to be integrated into the illustrations as written words with some relation to the story line. Tyler's drawing on page 1 of his second book depicts Brenton falling down, and his mother nearby. A word string, *I love you*, runs across the top of the page. The first question is about the text string.

Gene asks, "What does that say?"

Tyler answers, "It's Brenton saying 'I love you' to his mommy."

In this example, we can see the beginnings of self-regulation of written text; that is, the ability to use written text as a tool to convey the writer's intended meaning.

Letters, Pseudowords, and Words

The children include 34 strings in their books that could be described as either letters, pseudowords, or words. Disentangling these strings by type is often problematical. Jeff writes *ptdly*; when asked what it says, he says, "Don't know." John writes *FOE* and says it is "Jeff." Jeff challenges John, insisting that it is not his name, and John changes his reading of the word to "eat." Todd writes *MARKette* (copied from his magic marker); when queried, he reports that it says "Nothing." Yet he writes *PRODUCTOEL* (copied from the cigar box in which the markers are kept) on a dinosaur picture and says it is the name of a dinosaur.

Seven of the words are labels; however, not even the labels can be considered a homogeneous category. Consider Damon's use of the label, *TOYS*, which he writes on a picture of his toy box (arguably object-regulated because it is part of Damon's drawing of the toy box) contrasted with Jodi's other-regulated use of a label to solve a pesky problem of identification of a story element (Book I, p. 2): Jodi draws her father with a hurt foot, but the foot is strangely shaped. During the course of two conferences, her classmates ask, "Where are the feet?" Jodi revises her book, and at the next conference, her father's foot is neatly labeled. When asked what she did to make her story better, Jodi replies, "I put *foot*" (see Fig. 5.2).

Except for the labels, none of the strings is related to the story or picture in the first book. The only peer comment this kind of string elicits is a request for Damon to identify an ambiguous mark in his picture. "That's a *g*," he responds (although there is nothing in the picture that can be readily identified as the letter *g*).

In the second book, even though most of the strings are unrelated to story or illustration, the appearance of a word-like string is usually noticed and remarked on; there are 16 comments from peers, and children comment on their own strings 10 times. Jeff's cryptic pseudowords (*DFOE, FOFE*) go unremarked in the first book (two instances). But in the second book, all three occurrences of similar strings (*EOFOBP/TOF/hohPH, FOE,* and *EOF*) are met with peer questions and comments, typically the remark, "What's that say?"

The strings in the second book are more clearly other-regulated uses of text strings. Children are consciously trying to use the written text to mean. Their peers are joining in the collaboration by questioning and commenting on nearly every string that looks like a word. The remarks address not only the what the words might spell, but also the reasons for including the word strings. Damon (Book II, p. 1) writes *Cheeky's Michelle*. "What's that spell?" asks John. "Michelle's cheekys," Damon responds. "I just added it to make the story sound funny." The children are beginning to think about what is appropriately included as written text.

STORY TALK

The mechanism of change in the zone of proximal development is the *verbal mediation* provided by the conference discussions. Luria (in Vocate, 1987) maintains that spoken language is both the initial influence and the determining factor in the acquisition of other higher mental processes, including written language. Thus, in the present study, the psychological tool of spoken language (which is more nearly under the child's control) is used to shape the developing tool of written language.

All of the children contributed fairly equal amounts of talk to the discussions. A gauge of the quantity of each child's contributions has been obtained by sorting the conference comments by individual; each child's transcripts have been further separated into comments about his or her own work and the peers' work. The amount of talk has been estimated by simply counting the number of words in each of the files thus obtained. The average transcript is between 7 and 8 pages long; the comments a child makes about her own books are about 3 pages long, and comments about the work of others fill nearly 4 pages. The transcripts range from less than $5\frac{1}{2}$ pages to 10 pages.

We might not go because my
daddy's foot started to hurt.
. -2-

FIG. 5.2. Jodi's use of a label.

The conferences about the second book were longer than those that accompanied the production of Book I. Of all the talk, 30% was from Book I, and 70% from Book II. The classroom aide provided part of the context for the increased talk during the later conferences: When the conferences first began, she reported that the children were somewhat fearful and reticent about displaying and discussing their work; by the second set of conferences, things had changed—the children were comfortable with the format, and discussions were lively and even a bit contentious at times (cf. the interplay between Gene and Jeremy in the last conference of Book II; interview, Carol 6/90).

As with the text strings, what the children are saying is more interesting than how much they are saying. Jeremy's case characterizes the flavor of the change in the discussions over time. By the end of the set of conferences about the second book, the children talk about the text far more frequently, and far more knowledgeably, than they do at the beginning.

To quantify the magnitude of the change, as well as to determine whether the change involved all of the children or just a few, the conference transcripts have been sorted, first, into separate files for each child. The individual files were further sorted into two files each: (a) talk about text and story, and (b) other talk. Included within the first category were exchanges such as that between Gene and Jeremy (Book 1, p. 4, Final Copy), when Gene queries Jeremy about the number string, "How do them numbers fly?" and the discussion (Book II, p. 3, Final Copy) about Jeremy's phrasing of his text, *A daddy is doing going to a work*—"It don't sound right," Tyler says. A word count has been obtained for each file, and the percentage of talk devoted to each category was calculated.

Figure 5.3 recapitulates the change from Book I to Book II by individual child. The data show that the children are talking more about words in the later book than in the earlier one. The amount of talk focused on text string elements increased from approximately 8% percent in Book I to nearly 20% in Book II. Furthermore, every child in the class, without exception, increases the amount of talk focused on text and story from Book I to Book II. The range for Book I is 2% to 14% with a standard deviation of 4.0 percentage points; for Book II the range is between 10% and 26% with a standard deviation of 4.6 percentage points.

Talk About the Text Strings

The way the children respond to the spontaneous text strings is of special interest in relation to the concept of the zone of proximal development. If spoken language during the discussions about the books is driving the children to change the way they use text strings from Book I to Book II, then the story conferences should reflect an increase in direct remarks about the strings (i.e., *metalinguistic remarks*) from the first book to the second.

Each of the text strings has been coded to identify whether no comment was made, or if teacher, peer, or the author him or herself remarked on the text string. The results have been tabulated, and are presented in Table 5.2. There are two striking changes in the children's talk about the text strings from Book I to Book II. First, the "not commented on" category of strings is far greater in Book I; in Book I, over two thirds of the text strings pass unremarked. In contrast, in Book II, only one fourth of the strings are not commented on.

TABLE 5.2
Percentage of Spontaneous Text Strings Categorized by
Who Commented on Them During the Story Conferences

	Book I	Book II
Not commented on	68%	26%
Author comments	21	26
Peer comments	9	42
Teacher comments	2	6
	100%	100%

This supports the hypothesis that many of the strings in Book I are object-regulated: The text strings are made for some reason other than advancing the story and are outside the zone of proximal development; therefore the children largely ignore them when they are discussing the story. This analysis is further supported when symbols (like hearts and happy-type faces) are considered; the 12 symbols that appear in Book I are commented on nine times by peers. Because the symbols are meaningful (e.g., they are within the child's zone of proximal development) they are noticed and commented on. Word strings have no meaning within the story and go unremarked.

The second major change in the class's responses to the text strings is in the amount of peer comment in the two books. In the earlier book, peers treat the text strings almost as if they are invisible; only 9% of the text strings are commented on. In the second book, peers remark on 42% of the strings, supporting the hypothesis that the use of text strings has become other-regulated.

There is a change in the quality of the peer comments from Book I to Book II as well. The change is illustrated clearly in the transcripts of Jeremy's conferences. In Book I (other than Gene's query about the blast off number string, which is related to the illustration, "How do them numbers fly?"), there are no peer comments about the spontaneous word strings Jeremy includes. In contrast, in Book II, there are many sophisticated references to text. For example, the long sequences in the March 23 conference accompanying page 3 of Jeremy's second book include remarks about the grammar of the statement ("How is *doing going to a work*—it don't sound right"), suggestions for alternate ways to phrase the idea ("It should say *a daddy is in work*"), and recognition of the pragmatic meaning of the phrase within the context of the story (Jeremy says, "I want to mean Daddy is in the car going to work").

Most of the comments are of the type "What's that word?" or "What does that say?" but there are also many examples of peers' shaping and coaching in specific ways in Book II. For example, Celeste (Book II, p.

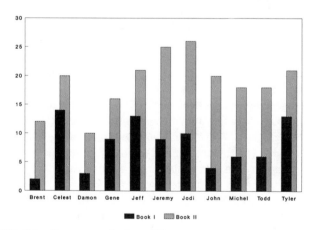

FIG. 5.3. Percentage of talk specific to text and story, by individual child.

1, version 2) writes a long string, *Jodi loves Celeste loves John*. Tyler says, "That's not in her story. It doesn't make it better." Brenton asks Celeste, "Does that make the story better?" "No," she says, suggesting that she is aware the string is not part of the story text. "Then why did you write it?" Brenton asks. "I just like to," she says. "She could wait until recess and write it on another piece of paper," Gene adds helpfully.

Teacher Talk

The teacher is a participant in the conferences, at the same time that he is acting as the *metacognition* for the children in the new activity. One of the limits of the familiar *scaffolding* metaphor is that scaffolding suggests a uniform kind of assistance. The acts of assistance provided by the adult in the zone of proximal development, however, are of qualitatively different kinds. "Sometimes, the adult directs attention. At other times, the adult holds important information in memory. At still other times, the adult offers simple encouragement" (Griffin & Cole, 1984, cited in Tharp & Gallimore, 1988, p. 34).

Rogoff (1986, cited in Tharp & Gallimore, 1988) described *structuring situations*, where the knowledgeable adult assists the child by setting up the task and providing appropriate materials. The children in this class can use the conference discussions so effectively because the teacher has carefully prepared and structured the situation. The procedures associated with making the product (the language experience story) have been practiced since early in the school year. The teacher has also provided practice with the routine of a discussion group, by conducting social storybook reading sessions in a group discussion format that is similar to the one used during the writing conferences; and before the children publicly discuss their books, the teacher and the aide make clear what is expected of the children by explicitly modeling the conference situation for them.

The teacher consciously tries to limit his role in the actual conferences to that of a participant, as much as possible, and he succeeds very well—the amount of the teacher's talk (exclusive of *reflecting*, or repeating of each statement, and not including the opening "How did you make . . . better?" question) is about 8%, exactly average.

Examples of different kinds of assistance provided by the teacher during the conferences are evident in the transcripts. Each child's conference begins with a focusing question from the teacher, "How did you make your story (or picture) better?" Some teacher remarks are directed at maintaining attention and control; for

example, Damon starts off on a tangent about "lightning bug poopoo," and he is stopped immediately—"Maybe you can rest face down" (Book II, pp. 2–3, version 2).

In order that the flow of the conferences remain child-directed as much as possible, praise and encouragement are more often left to the actual writing times, as the datalogs document. (Jeremy's breakthrough and the teacher's public reinforcement, described in chapter 4, is a good example.) Many of the teacher's comments are directed at helping the children find the constraints of what may or may not be appropriately included in their books. Comments like "That's not what you told us last time" (Damon, Book II, p. 4); "What does the story say?" (Michelle, Book II, p. 3); "Did it help your story?" (Gene, Book II, p. 3) are some examples.

Within the zone of proximal development, knowledgeable adults and naive learners co-construct a state of *intersubjectivity*—a situation definition that is neither the child's definition of the task nor a mature adult's. During the transit through the sensitive learning period, both the child's and the adult's definitions of the situation change. The change is not symmetrical. The data indicate that the children are growing in knowledge about written text, and are able to talk about and use text strings in a more meaningful way in their later books. The teacher's knowledge of written text does not change, but his expectations of what the children can do in the task are different in Book I and Book II.

In Book I, the teacher directs most of his remarks to the pictorial elements in the children's work. "What makes you look big in the picture?" he asks Damon about an extremely long-legged figure (Damon, Book I, p. 1); he comments about an odd color choice for John's drawing of his mother, "Your mother is blue" (John, Book I, p. 2). A telling indication of the teacher's emphasis is the focusing question that begins each child's discussion in the early conferences: "What did you do to make your picture better?"

The conferences about the second book begin with, "What did you do to make your story better?" Questions and remarks within the conferences change their focus also. The teacher points out the additions and changes children have made to the story text, for example, "Damon made the story longer" (Damon, Book II, p. 4); and "Jeff added sentences and changed the story" (Jeff, Book II, p. 3). He calls attention to the way the written text constrains the illustrations in the story; for example, Celeste (Book II, p. 1) abruptly shifts to an indoor scene that does not match the story text. "The story says they're outside," the teacher reminds her.

The teacher's change in emphasis mirrors the changes

that are occurring within the children's books. When Jeremy begins to concentrate on the text of his story, he pays less attention to the drawing. "I forgot to make everything!" he exclaims of the picture on the last page of Book II. When Damon adds a new page to his story (Book II, p. 4), his typical illustration style changes dramatically. Damon includes an enormous amount of background detail in most of his illustrations—furniture, appliances (complete with plugs, outlets, and lines to represent heat and light), and unusual machinery such as air compressors, leaf vacuums, and various war machines. But the illustration for his new handwritten page is spare, and includes only essential elements. Like Jeremy, Damon is working at carrying the meaning of his communication with the new symbol system, writing.

To quantify the changes in the focus of teacher's remarks during the conferences, the teacher's comments were collected into a file, and were identified as belonging to Book I or Book II. The comments were coded into three general categories: (a) remarks pertaining to control and teacher concerns; (b) comments and questions about pictures; and (c) remarks about story and text. An example of the kind of remark that was coded as a teacher concern is a comment made in response to Jeremy's (Book II, p. 1) story, *A mommy is doing homework*. "Why is your *mommy* doing your homework?" (instead of Jeremy, who should be doing his own homework). Remarks about the picture content were typically requests to identify an ambiguous picture

TABLE 5.3
Percentage of Teacher's Statements During Story
Conferences Categorized by the Subject of His Comment

	Book I	*Book II*
Control and teacher concerns	32%	31%
Comments about pictures	50	26
Comments about story and text	18	43
	100%	100%

element, for example, "Where's your face?", "Who's this?", and "What's the thing on the bottom?" Story and text comments were of three kinds: (a) remarks about the logic of the story ("Is that a real story?"); (b) comments about spontaneous text strings ("Damon made the story longer"); and (c) comments about the printed text (Jeff colors over the printed words of the story, and the teacher asks, "Why did you do that?").

The tabulation of this data is presented in Table 5, 3. The shift in emphasis from pictures to text is clearly evident. The amount of "control" type comments is almost the same in both sets of story conferences. But remarks about story and text increase considerably from Book I to Book II, from 18% to 43%; at the same time, the amount of teacher talk about the picture content decreases, from 50% to 26%. The teacher's shift in emphasis from pictures to text mirrors the children's growing focus on the text elements of their stories, and illustrates the reciprocal nature of learning in the zone of proximal development.

6

CONCLUSIONS
AND IMPLICATIONS

This study investigated beginning writing behavior of a class of 11 5- and 6-year old children and their teacher over a 3-month period from January to March. The particular focus of the study was a set of two "books" each child produced during this period and the discussions that accompanied their production.

Using the notion of progress through the zone of proximal development as a framework, I developed the case study of one child, Jeremy, in depth. I chose Jeremy because he provided the singular event that catalyzed the class and moved them into a new awareness of written text. Based on Jeremy's case, predictions were made and confirmed about the rest of the class. The text strings they were writing became more related to the story line, and the conference talk focused more on the text and story.

THEORETICAL IMPLICATIONS

I have used Vygotskyan theory as a framework to structure and interpret an analysis of children's developing writing. Although Vygotsky's theory is a general one and he wrote little about beginning writing behavior, his ideas have been expanded by the work of others who articulated the general theory in more specific terms (notably, Rivers, 1988, and Tharp & Gallimore, 1988).

With the concept of a *zone of proximal development* that was divided (or graduated) into object-, other-, and self-regulated phases, I was able to take a different approach to the topic of developing literacy. The forms of writing, when viewed through the window of the zone of proximal development, are seen to be secondary to the way the forms are used—the same form may be used as object at one time, and as written text at another. *BrentonGeneJohn* is a decoration on a cover, whereas *Brenton is Bad* is text.

Following Vygotskyan theory's emphasis on the goal-directed process that underlies the manifestation, I based my interpretation of the text strings on the nature of the activities that the children indicated, rather than on the form of the text string. I was able to find a stable sequence of development in the data, from object- to other-regulated use of text strings (with a few hints of the self-regulation to come), and to support the pattern with whole-class data. Related text strings are far more likely to be produced in the second, later book. Unrelated strings are found in nearly equal amounts in both, which can be explained within the concept of the *zone of proximal development* as recursions back to better-known, more comfortable forms when problem situations confront the young learners.

Using Vygotskyan theory, I have hypothesized about explanation—the nature and operation of the mechanism that advances the developing literacy learner through the sensitive learning zone. The hypothesized agent of change—verbal mediation and feedback in social interaction—can be seen operating in the prodding and prompting that characterize the verbal interchanges during the writing conferences and the children's reactions to the remarks. The hypothesis is supported and strengthened by the patterns of talk during the conferences; object-regulated text strings are far more likely to pass unremarked, whereas later strings are cause for increased comment as the class moves into the sensitive zone.

IMPLICATIONS FOR RESEARCH INTO
CHILDREN'S WRITING

The idea of *teacher-as-researcher* has become more influential as studies in the area of early literacy continue to clarify the important role of context in beginning writing. The emphasis on naturalistic research demands a nonintrusive research method, which is ideally realized in the person of the teacher/researcher. Unfortunately, most efforts at "kidwatching" (Goodman, 1989) are unsupported by theory, and result in a plethora of descriptions that are merely catalogs of writing products. When the descriptions are informally interpreted, results often resemble those quoted here:

"Intensive writing conferences probably shouldn't begin until second grade . . . the writing conference isn't begun immediately with all children, but rather *when children are interested in discussing their writing*" (italics added; Manning, Manning, Long, & Wolfson, 1987, p. 38).

Such work, while well intentioned, is clearly wrong. In the classroom that is the focus of the present study, the prekindergarten children could not have been more interested in discussing their writing; they were in the sensitive zone for just this activity. Learning to write is built on talking about writing. To truncate the sequence, and not resume talking about writing for 3 or 4 years, is irresponsible and is certainly poor pedagogy.

Even researchers who collect data carefully and describe it meticulously can overinterpret the data record if not guided by theory. Harste et al. (1984) searched for patterns in their data record, and characterize children's beginning writing as having a number of properties (e.g., intentionality, generativeness, etc.). To support their characterizations, the researchers make rich interpretations of writing events: Beth, a 5-year old who has received no formal literacy instruction, is asked to "write a story." She draws a sun and a minimal mandala-house, then writes her name. "I can write my name another way," she announces, and she does, this time with a lower case *e*. After this success, she announces the name of her brother, *David Dansberger*, and writes that, too, almost perfectly. She tries to write *Jeff* (another brother) but the *J* is not satisfactory: "That doesn't look right!" she says, and abandons the task.

Harste et al. (1984) credit Beth with writing a story that is "intentionally orchestrated and placeheld via a highly ordered set of in-process markings" (p. 115). They view her story as beginning with a setting (the mandala-house and sun), followed by the introduction of characters (Beth and her brothers).

The findings of the current study force a reinterpretation of Beth's work as follows: Beth draws the scene—sun and mandala—because they are the only figures in her range (this hypothesis is supported by her inability to draw human figures, which appear developmentally after the mandala and sun; Beth draws circles to represent people [Kellogg, 1970]). Her own name and her brother's name appear to be object-regulated uses of text strings; she has been assigned the task of "writing a

story," and it is not unreasonable to suppose that she writes out her repertoire of well-learned strings in order to demonstrate her competence, as an object to please the attentive and appreciative researchers (cf. Dyson, 1988).

Harste et al. (1984) assume that Beth's definition of the task, "writing a story," is the same as the researchers' definition of the assignment. Beth may indeed intend her written marks to have meaning, but the intent of the meaning appears to lie outside the zone of proximal development for the use of written text to tell a story.

IMPLICATIONS FOR INSTRUCTIONAL DESIGN

Children begin school believing they are able to write. When schools teach only the letters, what children learn are the *constraints* of written language. All the wealth of knowledge about writing that children acquire before entering the classroom is set aside so they can center on the arduous task of learning the letters. The children's beginning attempts can only be called errors or mistakes; their work is "wrong." When the zone of proximal development is sidestepped, learning has no point from which it can be pushed forward. Children have no "first line of defense" to revert back to when meaning in the new system is threatened. They learn that they cannot write, after all.

Jeremy learns something different. He learns that he is an author. Jeremy believes he can write and, with the teacher's assistance, he does. The letters and words he practices so carefully on the chalkboard are gradually and seamlessly integrated into his books via the spontaneous text strings, until these letters and words finally become the actual text of the stories.

Vygotskyan theory provides the framework for the developmental view of beginning literacy that has been amplified in this study. The general theory that underlies this specific application to beginning writing is characteristic of how humans acquire higher mental functions; therefore, in one sense, there is no classroom that is not a "Vygotskyan" classroom. What is implicit in the theory, particularly the concept of the zone of proximal development, is that curriculums and classrooms can be structured to take advantage of the primary mechanism of learning—verbal mediation—as in the classroom described in this study; or classrooms can be designed to stifle and suppress, as in conventional classrooms with their rules of silence and "no copying."

Jeremy's teacher, Neill Wenger, provides a setting where the processes that operate in the zone of proximal development are clearly visible. The teacher follows the principles of the concept intuitively, and in the process illustrates an example of what good pedagogy can be. Wenger makes use of Graves' (1983) framework of the writing conference as an arena where the vital exchanges among children and teachers can take place. The idea of peer conferences within a "writer's workshop" approach has been developed by others (cf. Calkins, 1986; Newkirk & Atwell, 1988), and the open verbal communication inherent in these approaches makes it easy to perceive the function of verbal mediation.

But Vygotskyan principles do not operate only within the emergent literacy or *whole language* paradigm. "Code-emphasis" need not be thought of as "an unenlightened commitment to unending drill and practice" (Adams, 1990, p. 26). The core notion here is *learning within the sensitive zone*—the zone of proximal development—driven by the mechanism of *verbal mediation*. Instruction must make use of the principles of the zone of proximal development by fostering active verbal interaction among peers, assisted and guided by the knowledgeable adult, the teacher. It does not matter whether the instruction is motivated by whole language goals, or if the goal is to teach conventional spelling and phonics skills. A successful phonetic-skills learning program that incorporates verbal mediation is *The Writing Road to Reading* (Spalding, 1986). In this program, students learn sound–symbol relationships and a distinctive marking system by quizzing each other and helping each other to practice. But the program goes one step further. Once students are familiar with letter sounds and how to mark diphthongs and exceptions, *as a group* they mark their spelling words (which includes words from mathematics or history or science); they discuss possible marking systems, and argue about discrepancies. The children themselves make the decisions about how to mark and pronounce a disputed word. In lively and spirited discussions, they talk about why words are spelled as they are, and why they sound they way they do. They use the process of *verbal mediation* to learn about basic phonics. It is an effective program (Aukerman, 1984).

Beyond the borders of writing, in the area of education in general, a group of instructional models that incorporate the principles of the zone of proximal development are the *cooperative learning* models (Johnson & Johnson, 1986; Slavin, 1990). Cooperative learning models emphasize collaboration among peers as a key concept. "Collaborative activity among children promotes growth because children of similar ages are likely to be operating within one another's proximal zones of development, modeling in the collaborative group behaviors more advanced than those they could perform as individuals" (Slavin, 1990, pp. 14–15).

Within a cooperative learning classroom, children work in heterogeneous groups, discussing learning tasks among themselves and helping each other learn. Instruction is designed so that students take as much responsibility as possible for their own learning, and each member of the group assumes responsibility for what the group produces. "You are not done until everyone in your group is done" is one of the tenets of cooperative learning classrooms. The teacher is a facilitator who provides guidance and supplies needed resources.

Use of cooperative learning methods has increased during the last decade—"mushroomed," according to Slavin's (1990) reckoning, and the numbers of cooperative learning classrooms "are certainly in the hundreds of thousands" (p. xi). Research documenting the effectiveness of cooperative learning methods is continuing, and the effects of cooperative learning on achievement are clearly positive. Noncognitive outcomes are less clear and the evidence is not conclusive; but overall, cooperative learning enhances variables such as self-esteem, peer support for achievement, and cooperativeness (Slavin, 1990).

Vygotskyan theory is being used to design and structure an entire educational environment. The concept of the *zone of proximal development* is an explicit guide for the practice of teaching implemented in a large-scale educational research-and-development program aimed at educationally at-risk, ethnic-minority children, the Kamehameha Elementary Education Program (KEEP), described by Tharp and Gallimore (1988) in their book, *Rousing Minds to Life*. Wenger's insight produces a classroom environment that is remarkably consistent with the philosophy of the KEEP program. Teaching in the KEEP program is redefined as *assisted performance*: Teaching consists of assisted performance, and teaching is occurring when performance is achieved with assistance. The teacher's task is to provide for collaborative interaction, to achieve intersubjectivity, and to provide assisted performance—an *activity setting*—within the context of a goal-directed action. The teacher is crucial, for it is the instructing voice of the teacher that eventually becomes self-instruction. "The teacher acts as the voice of the learner in transition from apprentice to self-regulated performer" (Tharp & Gallimore, p. 57). The teacher's voice gradually becomes the child's *private speech*, the vehicle of self-regulation (Frawley & Lantolf, 1984). Listen once more to the story conferences, as Jeff starts to talk about what he will do after school, "Next, when we are done, when we are done . . . " He pulls himself up short. "But that's not about the story," he reminds himself, and returns to the task at hand.

Appendix A:
Book Pages and
Writing Conferences

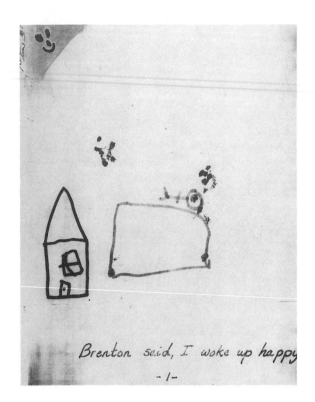

Book I, First Draft, Page 1
Conference 1/13/84

John	Where is you?
Brenton	In house, in bed.
Jeremy	Whose that blue?
Brenton	Him.
John	What is purple?
Brenton	Came through paper. [Purple splotches that seeped through the paper from the cover drawing.]

Conference 1/16/84 A.M.

John	Where are you?
Jeremy	On bed.
Jeremy	How can Brenton be blue?
Brenton	Don't know.
Gene	Why bed out of house?
Brenton	'Cause can't put it in house.
Celeste	Too big.
Gene	How gonna get up if too big?
Brenton	Make a ladder.

Book I, First Draft, Page 1 revised
Conference 1/16/84 P.M.

Teacher	What did you do to make your picture better?
Brenton	Ladder. Wheels on bed [Celeste pointed out].

Book I, Final Copy, Page 1
Conference 2/1
Tyler There's "happy" in it.
Jeff Brenton wrote my name on back.

Book I, Final Copy, Page 1 revised
Conference 2/2
Teacher What did you do to make it better?
Brenton That red stuff.
Jodi What's that?
Brenton Colors on my bed.
Jodi I never see color beds.
Gene I see.
Todd I have E.T. sheets colored.
John I—I—I—I have E.T. sheets!
Brenton Drawed that brown stuff. Chimney.
Teacher Why a square brown chimney?
Brenton 'Cause I wanted to.
Teacher Because of what people said?
Brenton Yes.

I ride my bike.

-2-

Book I, First Draft, Page 2
Conference 1/13
John   Where bike?
Celeste   He green.

Conference 1/16 A.M.
Jeff   Brenton is green bike.
Jeremy   Brenton green and bike green.
Tyler   How be blue and green?
Brenton   Don't know.
Michel   Maybe he colored it green.
Gene   Maybe colored himself.
John   What blue?
Brenton   Chimney.

I ride my bike.

-2-

Book I, First Draft, Page 2 revised
Conference 1/16 P.M.
Teacher   What did you do to make your picture better?
Brenton   Smile face on sun. Mommy.

Book I, Final Copy, Page 2
Conference 2/1

Jeff   Black?
Brenton   Yes.
Michel   You are black in picture—you don't have black body.
Tyler   No—brown, brown person.
Gene   Why you got round chimney?
Brenton   I don't.
Gene   Well, you drawed on here!
Tyler   How don't you have round now, if you drawed it on for real house?
Brenton   I just made it.
Gene   Why house skinny?
Brenton   I want to make it like that.
Tyler   Why roof bigger and skinny?
Brenton   It's not.
Michel   Why green and purple house?
Brenton   I wanted to make it.

Book I, Final Copy, Page 2 revised
Conference 2/2

Teacher   What did you do to make better?
Brenton   Did "X" across house. 'Nother square chimney and that brown [color] around sun.
Celeste   He made hair.
Brenton   That was done.

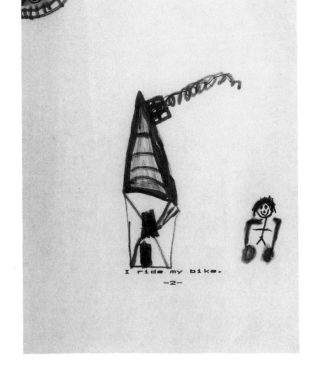

I like it.

-3-

Book I, First Draft, Page 3
Conference 1/13
John   Where you?
Jeremy   In red?
Brenton   [That's] Daddy.
Jeremy   What are they thinking of you riding bike?
Brenton   Don't know.

Conference 1/16 A.M.
Gene   How you be red — first blue, green, now red?
Brenton   I drawed it.

I like it.

-3-

Book I, First Draft, Page 3 revised
Conference 1/16 P.M.
Teacher   What did you do to make your picture better?
Brenton   Sun. [added blue and purple borders]

Book I, Final Copy, Page 3
Conference 2/1
Todd　　Big sun.
Brenton　I don't care.
Michelle　Still have black, brown chimney.
Brenton　I don't care.
Michelle　He always say "I don't care."

Book I, Final Copy, Page 3 revised
Conference 2/2
Teacher　What did you do to make better?
Brenton　Drawed black stuff on house. Made 'nother square chimney.

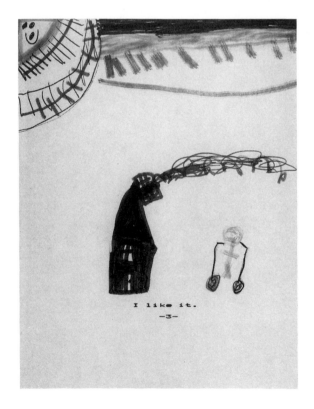

Book I, First Draft, Page 4
Conference 1/13
John   Jumped-up purple things?
Brenton   Toys.
Gene   I thought they were toys.
Jeremy   They ARE toys!

Conference 1/16 A.M.
Gene   How you can be brown?
Tyler   How Brenton blue and green?
Brenton   I ain't.

Book I, First Draft, Page 4 revised
Conference 1/16 P.M.
Teacher   What did you do to make your picture better?
Brenton   House—was there before. Drew chimney and smoke.

Book I, Final Copy, Page 4
Conference 2/1
Gene What's them round circles?
Brenton Toys.
Celeste What's triangle? It looks like a diamond.
Brenton I don't care. Toys.
Todd How smoke red and blue?
Brenton I drawed it that way.

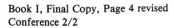

Book I, Final Copy, Page 4 revised
Conference 2/2
Teacher What did you do to make better?
Brenton That blue stuff around sun.
Teacher Why?
Brenton I wanted to.

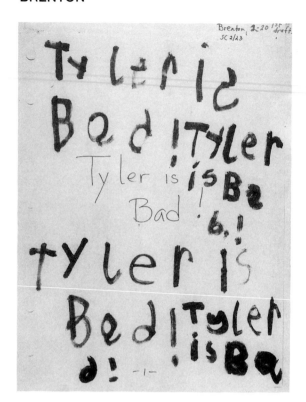

Book II, First Draft, Page 1
Conference 2/23
[No comments.]

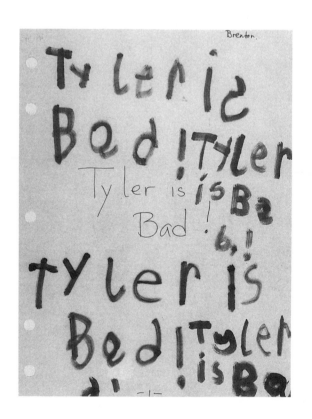

Book II, First Draft, Page 1 revised
Conference 2/28
Brenton   I wrote "Tyler is bad."

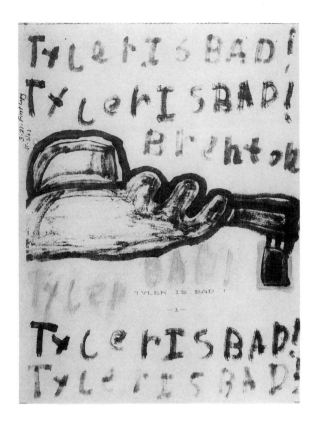

Book II, Final Copy, Page 1
Conference 3/23

Jeremy   Look at that hand!

Brenton   That's Tyler's fat hand.

Jodi   What's he holding?

Brenton   That his big thumb.

Jodi   What's that thing?

Brenton   His fat fingernail.

Jodi   What's that thing?

Brenton   He hanging a box on it. Only got one hand—broke his other hand.

Teacher   Why draw a hand on the title page?

Brenton   I want it to look nice.

Book II, Final Copy, Page 1 revised
Conference 3/26

Teacher What did you do to make better?

Brenton Wrote "Tyler is Bad, Tyler Bad."

Book II, First Draft, Page 2
Conference 2/23
[No comments.]

Book II, First Draft, Page 2 revised
Conference 2/28
Teacher   What did you do to make it better?
Brenton   I draw purple, and under purple to make it brown, and colored windows in and door.
Jodi   What's that?
Brenton   Chimney.
Michelle   A triangle chimney?
Brenton   I want to make it triangle.

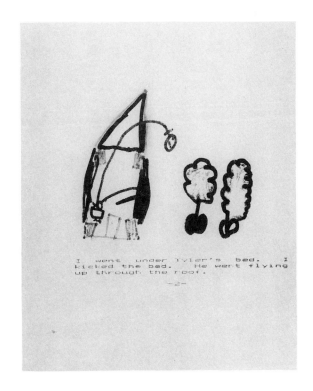

Book II, Final Copy, Page 2
Conference 3/23
Michelle I love your story, Brenton Bear!
Tyler He—someone say "I don't care"—Brenton say "I don't care" when Michelle said that.

Book II, Final Copy, Page 2 revised
Conference 3/26
Teacher What did you do to make it better?
Brenton Put pants and hair on, and there's pants and hair.
Celeste What about shirt?
Brenton I already did shirts, right there.
Jodi What's brown thing?
Brenton My big foot—I kick him up.
Jeff What round thing?
Brenton Them roots.

He landed on his mother.
His mommy give him a spanking.

— 3 —

Book II, First Draft, Page 3
Conference 2/23
Jodi   Who said that?
Brenton   Tyler.
Jodi   You're in the closet?
Brenton   Nope, I went out under bed.
Celeste   He lying—mom gave spanking.
Tyler   Lickin' and spankin' same thing.

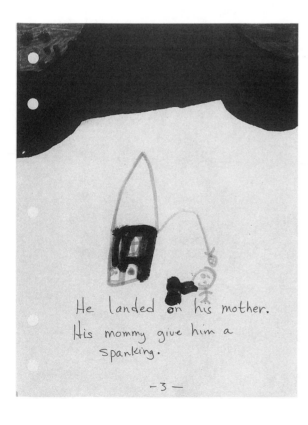

He landed on his mother.
His mommy give him a spanking.

— 3 —

Book II, First Draft, Page 3 revised
Conference 2/28
Teacher   What did you do to make better?
Brenton   Did color-in [of the house], draw paddle, Tyler sad-face.
Tyler   Face happy!
Brenton   I make it sad.
Tyler   This mom, and this me happy
Brenton   No—that you sad.
Celeste   You didn't write the chimney.
Brenton   Not 'nough time.
Jodi   You say that, then you have to do it! [A reference to the teacher's rule.] Who said that?
Brenton   Tyler.

Book II, Final Copy, Page 3
Conference 3/23

Jeremy   Whose this house?
Brenton It's where she [his mother] works—here's flour coming out.
Teacher Like, to make bread?
Jeremy   Yes.
Jodi   Who's people?
Brenton Me. Tyler. And Tyler's mom giving him a spanking. Line drawed where I kick him up and then Mom spank. He sad, and he bawling.
Gene   Old sun and new sun.
Brenton Yeah, old sun going down. New coming up.
Damon   Why Tyler mom bald?
Brenton I draw her bald.
Tyler   NOT my mom. YOUR mom!
Jodi   Where's his mom—she tied to a rope?
Brenton No—line where I kicked Tyler.
Damon   How come Tyler bald too?
Brenton His hair didn't grow right.
Tyler   You're bald too!
Brenton I ain't in picture.
Tyler   Yes.
Brenton So?
Jeremy   Who's that?
Brenton Tyler, getting 1,000 paddles.

Book II, Final Copy, Page 3 revised
Conference 3/26

Brenton I draw old sun falling down and going with other suns, and draw a new sun. And put hair and pants and shirt.
Jodi   What's the thing on house?
Brenton Flour—where Tyler's mom works.
Damon   Sun never fall down, 'cause it's a big ball of fire and never turns old.
Brenton Well, this one does.
Damon   Made out of fire.
Brenton So?
Damon   When I draw sun it will never be old.
Jeremy   My sun don't fall down.
Celeste What's that?
Brenton Ty landed on mother, and she gave him spanking.

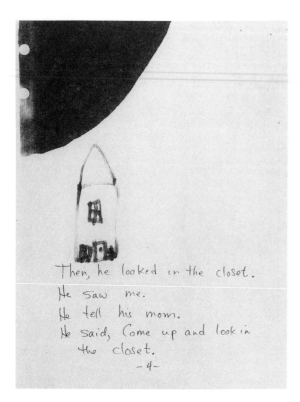

Then, he looked in the closet.
He saw me.
He tell his mom.
He said, Come up and look in
the closet.
—4—

Book II, First Draft, Page 4
Conference 2/23
[No comments.]

Then, he looked in the closet.
He saw me.
He tell his mom.
He said, Come up and look in
the closet.
—4—

Book II, First Draft, Page 4 revised
Conference 2/28

Teacher What did you do to make it better?
Brenton Drew black. This is the old sky and this new sky. That part [in between old and new] gonna fall down. And this his mommy looking in the closet.
Tyler I am at the window.
Teacher What time of day—new sky—old sky—?
Brenton Summer. Sky is all rusty.
Jodi Sky not rusty.
Brenton I want to make it that way.
Tyler It not in your story. It not in your story.
Brenton You already say that.

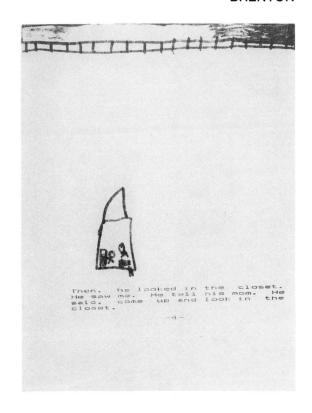

Book II, Final Copy, Page 4
Conference 3/23

Tyler   I didn't say that—he said that—he got a spanking.
Jodi   What's that toy?
Brenton No toy.
Jodi   Gingerbread boy?
Brenton No! It's Tyler's Mom downstairs. Tyler looking in— windows open and run in. I didn't make a door.

Book II, Final Copy, Page 4 revised
Conference 3/26

Teacher What did you do to make it better?
Brenton There the sun, and the new sun in case it fall down. It will fall on the box—suns are in the box—they the ones that fall down.
Celeste Why did new suns fall down?
Brenton New sun *ain't* falling.
Celeste You said them new suns fall down.
Brenton When *old* it will fall down.
Jodi   Looks like old sun too because lines are crooked like this.
Brenton Them ain't crooked.
Jeff   Why old sun falling down?
Brenton Because it's old.
Jeff   I make my sun yellow.
Brenton I make mine blue.
Damon   I make mine red hot.
Jodi   Sky is blue, so could have blue sun.
Tyler   Two skies—blue and green.
Jeff   What's this blue thing?
Brenton Sky.
Gene   What are these?
Brenton Flowers.
Gene   Flowers ain't big.
Brenton Uh-hunh.
Damon   Why lines in sky?
Brenton I wanted to make like that. I saw lines in sky when airplane went.
Damon   Oh—I'm gonna draw lines and jet in my picture!

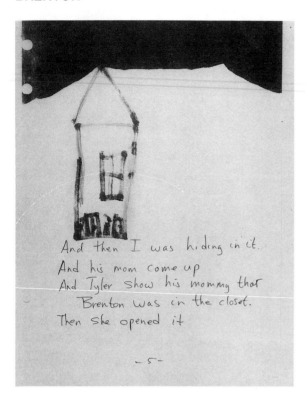

Book II, First Draft, Page 5
Conference 2/23
[No comments.]

Book II, First Draft, Page 5 revised
Conference 2/28
Teacher   What did you do to make it better?
Brenton   Drew me. And flower and green, and there him mom opening, and there Tyler.
Celeste   And nobody there and she smacked him!

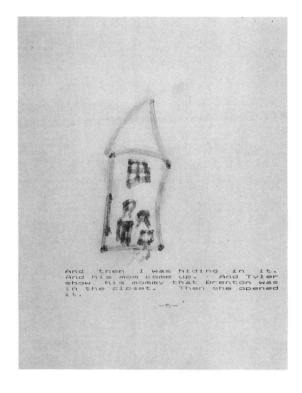

Book II, Final Copy, Page 5
Conference 3/23

Teacher   What's blue thing?
Brenton   The other bed where Tyler sleeping.
Jodi   Somebody on crutches?
Brenton   No. Tyler's mom, me under bed. And Tyler.
Tyler   And you ain't got any arms.
Brenton   I stuff 'em in my pockets.

Book II, Final Copy, Page 5 revised
Conference 3/26

Teacher   What did you do to make it better?
Brenton   Drew new sun and old sun falling down.
Jodi   What are they?
Brenton   I already told you, them suns.

Book II, First Draft, Page 6
Conference 2/23
Tyler   Hey, you said bad word—"You lying."
Damon   What two blue things?
Brenton   Suns.
Gene   Whole bunch of suns.
Tyler   New York gots a sun. California gots a sun.
Todd   Ever hear name of the place your mom and dad go?
Brenton   St. Croix.
Tyler   Hey, St. Croix have a sun too.

Book II, First Draft, Page 6 revised
Conference 2/28
Teacher   What did you do to make it better?
Brenton   I drew that [house] and there's a paddle and Mom spanking. That little guy is Tyler.
Tyler   Who's this house?
Brenton   That's the orange shed, the barn, and spanking him there so no one can hear him.
Tyler   Yes you can hear getting spanked—out the window.
Brenton   No windows—that's a door.
Tyler   Yes, is too a window.
Brenton   No.

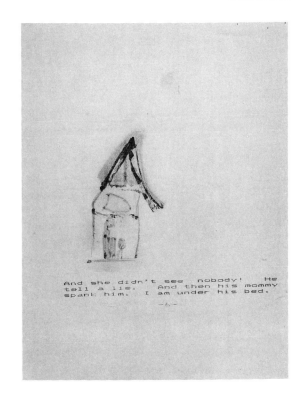

Book II, Final Copy, Page 6
Conference 3/23
[No questions.]
Tyler No pants.
Brenton So what—neither do you or your mom.
Tyler No underpants on.
Brenton Neither do you.

Book II, Final Copy, Page 6 revised
Conference 3/26
Teacher What did you do to make it better?
Brenton Draw sun, and that, and that [old and new sun].
Damon Why Ty tell a lie, why Ty tell a fib?
Brenton He didn't tell a fib, he tell a lie—he say I in closet and I not.
Teacher What's the difference between a lie and a fib?
Brenton I don't know.
Jodi I know when you tell a story it's a fib.
Teacher What's a lie then?
Jodi When you do something and tell Mom. Like my brother, when Mom tell Steve to put clothes in dresser and Steve put them on the floor and he told Mom they were on dresser—Mom say that a lie.
Damon I tell fibbers at home and at school I tell lies. Like when we have talks about them [the teacher had what were called "talks" when he reprimanded the students]—that the only time I lie. Just fibbers at home.
Gene Where's the chimney?
Brenton I didn't want to make one.

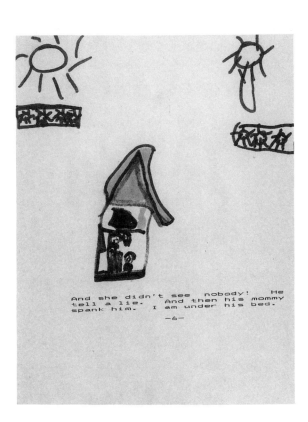

BRENTON

Book II, Page 7, First Draft
Conference 2/23

John   Silly Tyler.
Todd   Silly Brenton.
Jeff   Silly both.
Jodi   Look down 'fore you get out of bed. Might be fox bite your feet off!
Tyler   Nuh-uh—windows are all shut. I gonna tell some story 'bout you.
Brenton   I'm gonna write a bear one 'bout you.
Jodi   'Cept he's not a bear, Brenton the bear.
Brenton   BAD Brenton story.

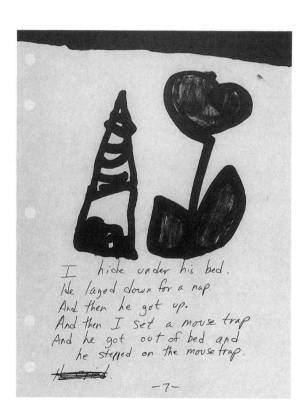

Book II, First Draft, Page 7 revised
Conference 2/28

Teacher   What did you do to make it better?
Brenton   Colored black stuff in, and made a BIGGER mouse trap. There's him getting out bed, and he step on trap and—OW!
Jodi   What's that?
Brenton   Flowers.
Tyler   That bigger than your house.
Brenton   I put a lot of seeds in.
Tyler   But hey, seeds don't grow that high.
Brenton   I just want to make it.

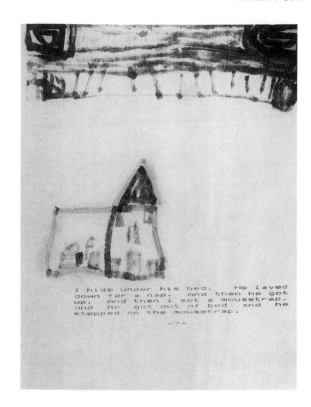

Book II, Final Copy, Page 7
Conference 3/23

Jodi   He went one /illegible/!

Brenton   No, he got a fat, piggy toe and couldn't wear no socks or shoes—had to go barefooted.

Todd   What's that?

Brenton   Me. I set a mousetrap right here, and there Tyler.

Celeste   Where he big toe?

Brenton   Then toe turned black and blue.

Gene   What these?

Brenton   That's the sky. New sun—old sun—the little line where it's falling down.

Damon   It's like a millipede (little line).

Book II, Final Copy, Page 7 revised
Conference 3/26

Teacher   What did you do to make it better?

Brenton   Suns, pants, hair and shirt, and stuff on windows.

Damon   I touched a mouse trap at home and at Grandfather's—I snapped it at my balloon but it didn't break it.

He cried.
His mother told him to stop it.
~~And~~ She give him a spanking

I was laughing!

The end.
— 8 —

Book II, First Draft, Page 8
Conference 2/23
[No comments.]

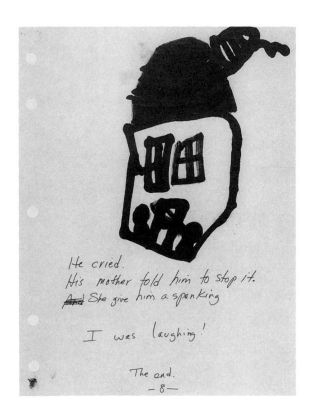

He cried.
His mother told him to stop it.
~~And~~ She give him a spanking

I was laughing!

The end.
— 8 —

Book II, First Draft, Page 8 revised
Conference 2/28
Teacher What did you do to make better?
Brenton Colored part house in, made 'nother window, made paddle.
Jeremy Who's that?
Brenton That's his mother spanking that little guy Ty.
Michelle What's this?
Brenton The door.

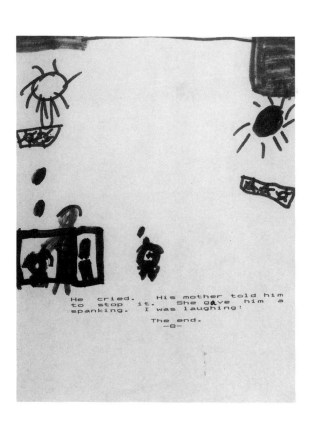

Book II, Final Copy, Page 8
Conference 3/23
No questions.

He cried. His mother told him
to stop it. She give him a
spanking. I was laughing!

The end.
-8-

Book II, Final Copy, Page 8 revised
Conference 3/28

Teacher What did you do to make it better?
Brenton Pants, hair and shirt.
Teacher Who's this?
Brenton Ty's mom giving him spanking. That the window, door. Gene tell me to make Ty and snow falling down Ty's pants.
Michelle Gene not in story.
Teacher Where are you?
Brenton Not in—I forget to draw.
Gene Where is house?
Brenton Right there—ain't got no roof.
Jeremy Why Ty's Mom as big as the house?
Brenton Because if I draw a chimney she wouldn't stick out her hand. She grew a lot.
Damon If she fall down chimney she would be burned up and if she have no pants on she would be cold.

He cried. His mother told him
to stop it. She gave him a
spanking. I was laughing!

The end.
-8-

Book I, First Draft, Page 1
Conference 1/12
John   Where's bed?
Jeremy   Red bed.

Conference 1/16 A.M.
John   Where she bed?

Book I, First Draft, Page 1 revised
Conference 1/16 P.M.
Teacher   What did you do to make your picture better?
Celeste   The spring came out of bed and went all around.

Book I, Final Copy, Page 1
Conference 2/1

John   Where your sister?
Celeste She went to tell Mommy. Celeste still sleeping, didn't have time to draw.
Jeremy   What's yellow stuff?
Celeste Springs.
Jeff   What round thing?
Celeste Springs.
Gene   What's *springs*?
Celeste They come out of bed where white rips, and gray thing is spring.
Todd   Spring makes bed go up and down.
Jeff   Maybe it's a water bed. We went shopping, and play on water bed. Not mommy—just C., J., and D.

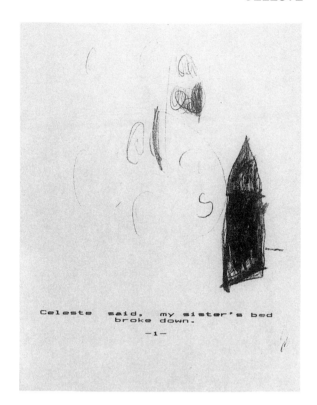

Book I, Final Copy, Page 1 revised
Conference 2/2

Teacher What did you do to make better?
Celeste The spring. The baby.
Brenton What green stuff?
Celeste Already said yesterday. It the spring. Brown, soft spring.

Her didn't broke the bed down.
Her tell my mommy.
-2-

Book 1, First Draft, Page 2
Conference 1/13
John   Where you?
Celeste   Ain't in story.
John   Where's mommy?

Conference 1/16 A.M.
John   What that?
Celeste   Her feet, my mommy's.
Brenton   What's that?
Celeste   Hand.

Her didn't broke the bed down.
Her tell my mommy.
-2-

Book 1, First Draft, Page 2 revised
Conference 1/16 P.M.
Teacher   What did you do to make your picture better?
Celeste   Made a yellow face. Spring of bed came in kitchen.

Book I, Final Copy, Page 2
Conference 2/1
Jodi   What's that?
Celeste Sister and mommy. Them went outside to talk about it. Not really—I just make it up. Snow around.

Book I, Final Copy, Page 2 revised
Conference 2/2
Teacher What did you do to make better?
Celeste That outside. It a star.
John   Where you?
Celeste I didn't have time to draw sister. That when her hurt that foot.
Brenton What's that?
Celeste Bed.
Tyler   What's this?
Celeste My house.
Tyler   You not even in it.
Celeste We ain't done talking. It's far, far away.
Tyler   Then your sister sleeping outside house far away. Bed here.
Celeste When them get to house, go bed.
Tyler   You said green the bed.
Celeste Not enough room in here. This I made from Brenton show me [the star].

My sister was mad.

-3-

Book I, First Draft, Page 3
Conference 1/12
Jodi   Mad, sad, mad.
John   Where sister?

Conference 1/16 A.M.
Michelle Why she mad?
Celeste   Her wanted play Barbie.
Michelle I thought she mad about bed.
Celeste   She think about bed and play Barbie. Forgot to make 'nother leg.

My sister was mad.

-3-

Book I, First Draft, Page 3 revised
Conference 1/16
Teacher   What did you do to make your picture better?
Celeste   Wrote "my sister." Pillow and bed all fixed. And made headboard and number "5." Triangles go up—was gonna make a lot—not enough time [a version of the bed-ladder].

Book 1, Final Copy, Page 3
Conference 2/1

John	Where are you?
Tyler	There's "mad" [the word] inside of the reading.
Brenton	What's this?
Celeste	Clouds.
John	Clouds white—not orange.
Gene	And others can be gray, blue, orange, red.
Todd	When sun go down, clouds can be red.
Jodi	Far far away.
Tyler	My mom and dad say them are rainbows. Pink and all kind of colors.

Book 1, Final Copy, Page 3 revised
Conference 2/2

Teacher	What did you do to make better?
Celeste	Two middle sisters—Staci and Jeanie.

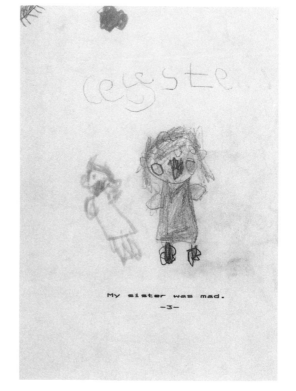

And her play Barbie with me.

—4—

Book I, First Draft, Page 4
Conference 1/12
Michelle Where's Barbie?

Conference 1/16 A.M.
[No comments]

And her play Barbie with me.

—4—

Book I, First Draft, Page 4 revised
Conference 1/16 P.M.
Teacher What did you do to make your picture better?
Celeste The spring broke again and come right to here. Went here and all these spots. Hit sister on nose.
Teacher Did the spring really hit her?
Celeste No, just a story.

Book I, Final Copy, Page 4
Conference 2/1
Michelle Todd says he hate Barbie.
Celeste I didn't have time to write "Barbie."
John Who's that?
Jodi Sister.
Michelle Where's Barbie?
Brenton What's that?
Celeste Part of name.

Book I, Final Copy, Page 4 revised
Conference 2/2
Michelle Where Barbie?
Celeste *You* know.
Teacher What did you do to make the story better?
Celeste Suns. Snow.

Book II, Page 1, Version 1
Text: Celeste, Michelle, and Jodi's sister Amy all went out to take a walk.
Conference 2/23
Brenton   Went out to take a walk.

Conference 2/27
Teacher	What did you do to make the story better?
Celeste	Made hair. This is Jodi and mommy I made—
Tyler	Her gots mad face.
Celeste	Happy, 'cause this up.
Jeremy	Jodi's mom don't have red face.
Celeste	I just want to draw it red.
Jeremy	What's that?
Celeste	Her hand, arm, and finger.
Jeremy	I don't see head.
Celeste	Here. Her mad. I went like this—made a big thing. Forgot to make other part of mad face.
Jeff	Why's Jodi's Mom happy?
Celeste	Her proud of me 'cause I'm at her house.
Jeff	Who's mad then?
Celeste	Michelle.
Tyler	What's this thing?
Celeste	Face. Her nose.
Gene	What's this thing?
Celeste	Feets and toes-ies.

Book II, Page 1, Version 1
Conference 3/23

Celeste	And I made these big hands by Michelle. Michelle's big hand.
Jodi	What's that green?
Celeste	Michelle's hair sticking up—her didn't comb it. Her comb it a little.
Jodi	Why my "GE"?
Celeste	Was going to write "Jodi loves Celeste," was gonna write "GENE."
Todd	What's that say?
Celeste	"Celeste."

Conference 4/2

Teacher	What did you do to make your story better?
Celeste	Michelle combed hair now.
Damon	How come she has straggly hair?
Celeste	She don't, her combing her hair.
Damon	I think it's funny 'cause her head like this (tilted).
Brenton	Where's her comb?
Celeste	Forgot to draw.
Brenton	Why one big foot—one little?
Celeste	They're both same.
Brenton	Don't look same.
Celeste	Here is—
Teacher	Answer the question.
Celeste	Don't know—didn't want to make same.
Brenton	Why don't you want to make same?
Celeste	Didn't want to—wanted to make one big—one little.
Brenton	Why blue legs?
Celeste	Her pants—forgot legs.
Brenton	Where socks?
John	Why say same, and now say one big—one small?
Celeste	This is the baby.
Damon	What's her name?
Celeste	Jodi's sister Amy.
Brenton	Why pointy feet? Where shoes?
Celeste	Socks—her have shoes on.
Brenton	Where's shirt, pants?
Celeste	Her getting dressed.
Michelle	Where's house?
Celeste	Them inside.
Teacher	Story says outside.
Celeste	Well, them dressed and now out. Above words is inside—below is outside.
Michelle	You should make a line.
Celeste	Would get in my hair.
Gene	What's this—"John loves Jodi"?
Tyler	Not in her story—doesn't make it better.
Brenton	Does that make story better?
Celeste	No.
Brenton	Why you write it?
Celeste	Just like to write it.
Gene	She could wait 'til us have recess and write on another piece of paper.
Celeste	I was gonna write GENE but you [teacher] said "Listen up."

119

Book II, Page 2, Version 1
Conference 2/23

Damon	What is that?
Celeste	Our ladder.
Gene	To what?
Celeste	To our bed.
Jeff	What is that?
Celeste	Ground. (purple color over words)
Tyler	What is this?
Celeste	It our squeaky toy.
Brenton	Why does she have a triangle nose?
Celeste	Everybody have one.
Brenton	Why purple, yellow green, orange, black hair?
Celeste	Because. Didn't have any colors to make it.
Michelle	Could use yellow.
Brenton	Could use brown.
Celeste	I want to make purple.

Conference 2/27

Teacher	What did you do to make the story better?
Celeste	Made them hands. This little baby doll and this one.
Jeremy	What's that?
Celeste	Michelle. This Jodi. No. Michelle and Jodi.
Teacher	Jodi's not in story.
Celeste	I know. I forgot to make Jodi's sister. This me, this Michelle, forgot to make Jodi's sister.
Damon	What's that?
Celeste	A ladder. Told you yesterday.
Tyler	What purple stuff that covered words?
Celeste	[Illegible]
Gene	What's that?
Celeste	Ladder. Just told Damon. That is Michelle's house. First to Jodi's house—then Michelle. Jodi ain't in story.
Todd	What is these?
Celeste	Squeaky toy.
Tyler	You said little worm before.
Celeste	It a squeaky snake toy.
Jeff	You said floor last time.
Celeste	It is a rug on the floor.

Book II, Page 2, Version 2
Conference 3/23

Jeff	What are those letters down here?
Celeste	[copied] Words in story.
Jodi	Who's that?
Celeste	Jodi.
Teacher	Jodi's not in story.
Celeste	She in house, come out—so in other story. I just want to make Jodi.
Michelle	I'm not in story.
Celeste	Yes, you are. That's you and me and Amy.
Tyler	What's that dot?
Celeste	Doorknob.
Jeff	What's that?
Celeste	Smoke.

Conference 4/2

Teacher	What did you do to make your story better?
Celeste	I drawed Jeremy's down there and Jodi's sister and I forgot to draw me. These flowers and roots down here.
Brenton	Hey she copied me too! She make old sun. New sun and line going down.
Gene	What's that?
Celeste	The hair.
Tyler	What's that?
Celeste	I'm inside.
Tyler	Hey, you forgot to draw yourself. Hey, you forgot to draw yourself—You said!
Celeste	Well, I forgot to draw me outside.
John	What's blue?
Celeste	Nothing.
Gene	She said they outside playing baseball and she inside. So—where's baseball?
Celeste	They forgot to get it—them play with 'nother toy.
Jeff	Where's toys?

CELESTE

Book II, Page 3, Version 1
Text: I stayed inside, them went outside.
Conference 2/23

Gene   What dots?
Celeste   Snow.
Gene   'Cept ain't snowin'!
Celeste   When them went out it snowin'.
Brenton   What's that?
Celeste   Michelle!
Michelle I don't have red hair.
Todd   Don't matter, Michelle.
Celeste   I make purple hair.
Michelle Where Amy?
Celeste   She stay inside.

Conference 2/27

Teacher   What did you do to make your story better?
Celeste   Made these dots colored in. Made mouth. Jodi's sister.
Gene   What's that?
Celeste   Mouth. Bugs coming down in Michelle's hair.
Damon   What are these?
Teacher   We just told you. Why ask?
Damon   Is a bug.

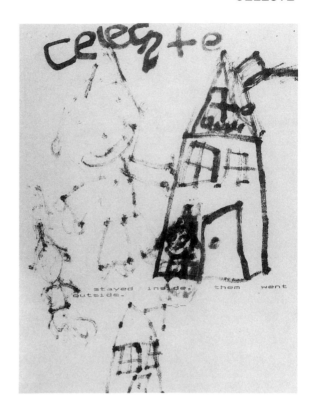

Book II, Page 3, Version 2
Conference 3/23

John   What's that, that, that?

Celeste I came out with them too, then came back inside—I'm sitting on a chair.

Todd   What's that word?

Celeste CELESTE!

Jodi   Who has hat on?

Celeste Michelle—I mean Jodi.

Michelle She's not in story.

Celeste This Amy. This me. This Michelle.

Jodi   She's not little. She's 7.

Brenton Why got a pointy hat?

Celeste She thinks it her birthday. No—this Jodi sister. I'm just gonna pretend it her birthday and Michelle have little tiny hat on. This hat Michelle wearing.

Tyler   Who's house? [little one]

Celeste Jodi's house.

Conference 4/2

Teacher What did you do to make your story better?

Celeste I drawed a monster.

Brenton Why a blue nose?

Celeste I wanted to.

Brenton Monster ain't in story.

Celeste Him down in ground.

Brenton That don't make her picture better.

Celeste I want to draw it. I put "Celeste" on. My mommy tell me to put my name on every picture I draw.

Brenton My mom didn't tell me that.

I went to eat and them went to eat.

4

Book II, Page 4, Version 1
Text: I went to eat and them went to eat.
Conference 2/23
Celeste   Everybody go to eat when I went.
Gene   What's this?
Celeste   Food. Cereal — bowls, chairs.
Brenton   Got too much people in there. Only 5 in my family.
Celeste   Not mine.
Brenton   How many?
Celeste   Dad. Mom. Baby, brother. Me, Janie, Staci, forgot Michael.

I went to eat and them went to eat.

Conference 2/27
Teacher   What did you do to make your story better?
Celeste   Made Mikey point. Made Jodi.
Tyler   Who Mikey?
Celeste   Our baby. We have two babies and Mikey growing.
Tyler   Mikey have funny name.
Todd   Me and Tyler have funny name.
Celeste   Made Mikey, and I forgot 'nother people. I didn't say Darryl, I forget Darryl.
Jodi   Why have faces for plates?
Celeste   Them ain't.
Jodi   Then why does it look like that?
Celeste   It them cereal.
Tyler   That don't look like cereal, just raisins around.
Celeste   Well, what about them brown things, like Capt'n Crunch. It's all brown.
Tyler   We only cook like oatmeal and stuff. That only cereal we have. Have one kind of cereal — remember rainbow on TV — Lucky Charms — I have that when I stay at Brenton's house and I eat his cereal.

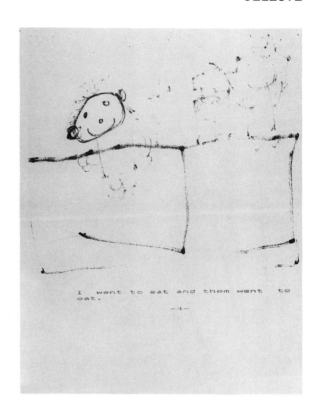

Book II, Page 4, Version 2
Conference 3/23

Jeff   What's that? [Two things]
Celeste   That's to hold up the tables. Other side of table. Other people didn't want to eat yet.
Jodi   What's them names?
Celeste   Celeste. Amy. Michelle. And Staci—I mean Ralphie my brother.
Jeremy   What's this?
Celeste   Them were thinking of, like, if them buy a car or if . . . [means they're thinking.]
Jodi   What's that thing?
Celeste   My fingers.
Gene   What's that?
Celeste   The other page.

Conference 4/2

Teacher   What did you do to make the story better?
Celeste   Make monsters playing. Spoons them picking up.
Brenton   Monsters ain't in story.
Celeste   I want them in.
Jeremy   What are these?
Celeste   Monsters.

Damon said, I like to turn a lamp on. ~1~

Book I, First Draft, Page 1
Conference 1/13

John	Where lamp?
Damon	Here it is.
John	Red?
Damon	Oil, kerosene in bottom. That's me when I'm BIG boy. Can't turn on now, I get burned.
Teacher	What makes you look big in picture?
Damon	Me looking like my daddy.
Teacher	Because of the long legs?
Damon	Yes.

Conference 1/16 A.M.

John	Why you blue?
Damon	Because I did get oil spilled on me. My grandma did it.
Tyler	Now you telling us a story.

Damon said, I like to turn a lamp on. ~1~

Book I, First Draft, Page 1 revised
Conference 1/16 P.M.

Teacher	What did you do to make your picture better?
Damon	Made sense. Made it right. Clock with wind-up. Made new lamp and new oil in it. Splashing around 'cause Mom just put it in. All green stuff is heat around room.

Book I, Final Copy, Page 1
Conference 2/1

Celeste	What's all that stuff?
Damon	That's all part of my room, and that's all my toys.
Celeste	What's that?
Damon	Thing they burn trash in at school. Toy in my room. Heat coming out burned me up. No fire. Night-time light my mom turns on. Lamp for play. [Little blue rectangle] is my sister— no—is my sister's heater. She's out—turning mommy's lamp on. This is incinerator. I see one on my bus and made one for my room.
Todd	I see one at Mt. Joy school.
Michelle	That's Pre-first—that not Mt. Joy. That Riverside.
Todd	I mean Manheim. I went last year. You not go with me.
John	What's that?
Damon	Sister's fan. 'Cause she break fan blades off and she cut cord off.
Teacher	Who showed her how?
Damon	No—only story. Inside bunk beds are teddy bears. I sleep with teddy bear.

Book I, Final Copy, Page 1 revised
Conference 2/2

Teacher	What did you do to make better?
Damon	Make my toys—army tank.
Celeste	I see an X not there [in the first version].
Damon	Black X to tell if incinerator real heavy. I could hardly lift it when I bought it. I don't really have one—I just draw one—I really have a radiator in my room. Pipe is for water to go in my mom's bathroom.

Book I, First Draft, Page 2
Conference 1/13
Damon   Lamp under the story. Flame off.
Jodi   You draw good.
John   Where's bed?
Tyler   Big bed.
Jeremy   How are you getting down?
Damon   I'm drawing a ladder on today.

Conference 1/16 A.M.
Michelle   How you get down?
Damon   Didn't draw [a ladder]—I jump.
Gene   'Cept maybe you break yourself.
John   Where are you?
Jeff   I know way [get down]. Make ladder from dresser.
Damon   Can't walk on dresser. I get spanked.
Brenton   What's that red? [Red color that has bled through the paper.]
Damon   On 'nother side. Blood. Blood from sister's foot.

Book I, First Draft, Page 2 revised
Conference 1/16 P.M.
Teacher   What did you do to make the picture better?
Damon   Ladder, plug for plug on light bulbs.

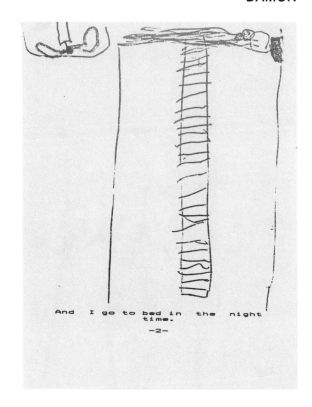

Book I, Final Copy, Page 2
Conference 2/1

Damon	There's my heater, 'cept my mom turned it off. My incinerator to warm me up.
John	What's that?
Damon	My ladder 'cause I have big bed. Two light bulbs—in my light.
Michelle	What's that?
Damon	Incinerator. My mom's gonna take me to Garden Spot to see one. They're metal.

Book I, Final Copy, Page 2 revised
Conference 2/2

Teacher	What did you do to make better?
Damon	Army tank bombing the bed down.
Tyler	No—bombing *leg* down.
Damon	Leg too.
Gene	It gonna fall down on you little heady-by too.
Damon	Army tank not really bombing bed down. Bombs falling in front of bed.

My mommy turns my lamp on.

~ 3 ~

Book I, First Draft, Page 3
Conference 1/13
Damon   There's flame in lamp.
Jeremy   No foots?
Damon   Here they are. Mommy put different color oil in [the lamp] — yellow.

Conference 1/16 A.M.
John   Where's lamp?
Jeremy   Yellow flame. Flame.
Tyler   What this?
Damon   Pillow.
Todd   Him could walk down bed, climb down.
Jeremy   What's cross?
Damon   Dresser.
Brenton   What's that [purple dot]?

My mommy turns my lamp on.

~ 3 ~

Book I, First Draft, Page 3 revised
Conference 1/16 P.M.
Teacher   What did you do to make the picture better?
Damon   Drew another clock and heater.

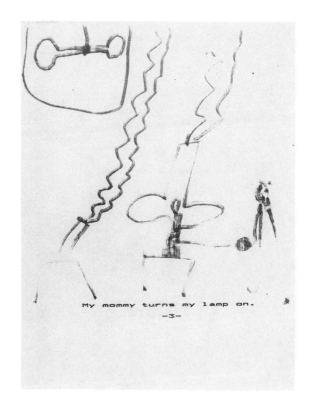

Book I, First Draft, Page 3
Conference 2/1

Damon   My mommy's lamp. I don't know where my bed is 'cause on other side, not enough room [to draw it].

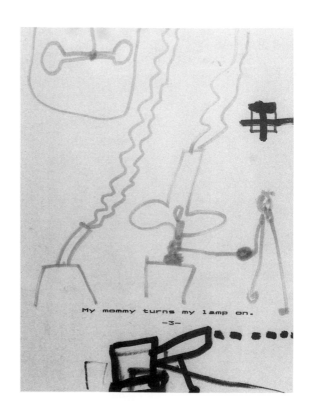

Conference 2/2

Teacher   What did you do to make better?

Damon   Look at this silly army tank with wheel on the gun. No—I just want to draw one, like Gene in his story. Window.

Teacher   What's the black [across the window]?

Damon   That's dark, from night time. That night, there gonna be a thunderstorm. I out in boat and big, big storm come and I hide under a towel.

Gene   You mean you fall asleep under the towel.

131

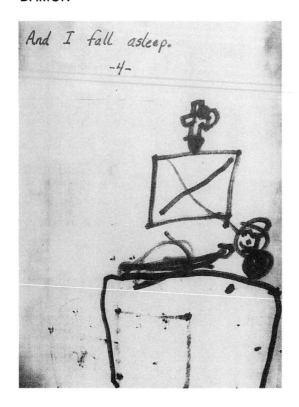

Book I, First Draft, Page 4
Conference 1/13
Michelle Damon didn't go to sleep.
Damon Eyes are open. Sleep with eyes half open.

Conference 1/16 A.M.
[No comments]

Book I, First Draft, Page 4 revised
Conference 1/16 P.M.
Teacher What did you do to make the picture better?
Damon Drew ladder.

Book I, Final Copy, Page 4
Conference 2/1
Tyler   Oh boy—I see a cannon.
Damon   That's my toy one I took to school one day.
John   What's that?
Damon   Heat coming out my incinerator pipe.

Book I, Final Copy, Page 4 revised
Conference 2/2
Teacher   What did you do to make better?
Damon   Toy box—wrote "T-O-Y-S" on box. New lights with red light
bulbs in it.

Book II, First Draft, Page 1
Conference 2/23

Damon Air compressor. Cold air going in to pipe to keep cold. This Barbie. I didn't have time to draw myself.

Todd What's this?

Damon Tank that Cokes in. That [is a] tree, that lantern, that chair.

Todd What's this? [dots across the top of the page]

Damon Just testing marker to see if works.

Book II, First Draft, Page 1 revised
Conference 2/27

Teacher What did you do to make the story better?

Damon Make some more tanks. To make air—hot air.

Gene What's this?

Damon Smoke.

Jodi What's this?

Damon That's Barbie.

Jodi Doesn't look like Barbie.

Damon That's her big bold tongue cause she's sticking tongue out, she's hungry.

Gene Where are you?

Damon Forgot to make myself.

John What's that?

Damon Smoke.

Brenton What's that?

Damon Lightning bug.

Jeremy Lightning bug not black and red. Lighty bugs are yellow.

Damon Some are. I see red, yellow, green.

Gene What's this?

Damon Tank—heater tank.

Brenton What's this?

Damon Dot—poop coming out of lightning bug.

Teacher That's not what you told us last time.

Damon Test, see if marker works.

Celeste What's this?

Damon Boo-boos.

Book II, Final Copy, Page 1
Conference 3/22

Teacher	Damon made story longer.
John	Barbie—Yee, yee!
Damon	This a mad face.
Jodi	Who's that?
Damon	That's just to scare bad people away.
Celeste	What's that?
Damon	Coke air compressor.
Jeff	What's that?
Damon	Hose, dirt, compressor, sweeper and hose.
Gene	What's that?
Damon	Air compressor—me.
Tyler	What's that line?
Damon	Tree.
John	What's that spell [the words]?
Damon	"Michelle Cheekys." Just added to make story sound funny.
Tyler	What's that word?
Damon	"Michelle."
Gene	What's that word?
Damon	I don't know what he meant. Barbie.

Book II, Final Copy, Page 1 revised
Conference 4/2

Teacher	What did you do to make the story better?
Damon	Colored in chairs and draw that ["mad" face] to scare bad people away.
Todd and	
Tyler	That was before.
Teacher	[turns page] This is the new one [on Page 2]. What did you do [on this page] that's new?
Damon	Tree—no—there before.

Book II, First Draft, Page 2
Conference 2/23
Damon And first page—my air compressor—this man's at party serving food.
Todd What's this?
Damon Letter "g."
Todd What's this?
Damon Lantern—see flame in it?
Celeste What's that?
Damon 'Nother tank. I forgot to draw hose in and forgot to draw bottom.

Book II, First Draft, Page 2 revised
Conference 2/27
Teacher What did you do to make the story better?
Damon Made sweeper get poo-poo out.
Celeste How do you spell "sweep"?
Damon "S-W-P."
Celeste How spell "sweep the kitchen out, sweep"?
Damon "T-H-E."
Celeste How spell "Sam-I-am"?
Brenton What's this?
Damon Red poo. One pooped on my head this summer. No—I didn't really see that. I just saw lightning bug poo on grass.
Gene What's that?
Damon Poo-poo. . .
Teacher [Stopped the "poo-poo" sequence.]
Damon Part of tank.

This is a new drawing, and it was not discussed. However, the text was added to the Final Copy.]

[The Xerox copy made before any revisions is not available for this page.]

Book II, Final Copy, Page 2
Conference 3/22

Damon	Look at "mad" face again.
Jodi	What's that?
Damon	Lightning bug.
Gene	What's that?
Damon	Air compressor—you know, you saw me draw picture. That's just paper and I drew mad face on and tongue made of cotton.
Michelle	Who's this?
Damon	My mommy, happy face on.
Jodi	That her skirt?
Damon	Yes.
John	What's that?
Damon	That's the bright.
Jeff	What's that?
Damon	Air compressor.

Book II, Final Copy, Page 2 revised
Conference 4/2

Teacher	What did you do to make the story better?
Damon	Draw my grandfather mad, because mad at these bad people.
Celeste	His tongue sticking out.
Damon	That's how you get mad.

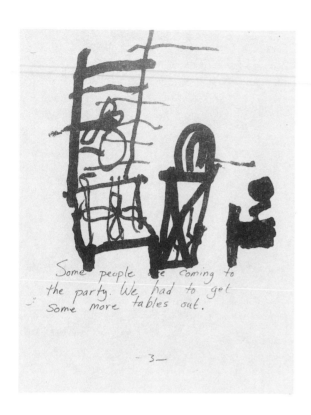

Some people are coming to the party. We had to get some more tables out.

—3—

Book II, First Draft, Page 3
Conference 2/23
Damon More tanks.
Gene What's this?
Damon Lantern—hurricane in it. Hurricanes protect you—you don't get burned. There's lightning bugs.
John What's that?
Damon Tree. Real bright coming out of lantern. Three bugs.

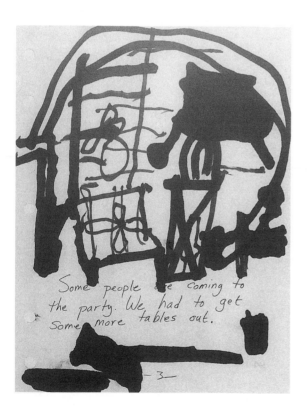

Some people are coming to the party. We had to get some more tables out.

—3—

Book II, First Draft, Page 3 revised
Conference 2/27
Teacher What did you do to make the story better?
Damon Drawed tanks and machines to blow me and air compressor away. That me, goin' up through hose.
Jodi What's this?
Damon Tank, tired of telling you!
Teacher Maybe you can rest face down.
Damon No.
John What's this?
Damon Fan.
Celeste What's that?
Damon Tank. You heard me.

Book II, Final Copy, Page 3
Conference 3/22

John	What's that?
Damon	Air compressor.
Michelle	What does that say?
Damon	"Air compressor."
Jeff	What's that?
Damon	Rain and lightning.
Jodi	What's that? Are bugs?
Damon	Lightning bugs.
Jodi	They inside?
Damon	They don't care if they get struck because they're lightning bugs. Party outside.
Teacher	Remember the tree—is the lantern on?
Gene	What's that?
Damon	That's the hole for them—lightning bugs.
Gene	What's that?
Damon	Their scratchy feet did that when they walked in.
Gene	'Cept they fly.
Damon	They wanted to walk.
Michelle	I see one walk. I pick one up and he walk up my hand and I get him and put him in my basket.
Damon	He was dead. When you put them up at night, in morning they're dead. You need lightning bug for light in your house.
Todd	I get lightning bug and pick up and keep him and next morning still alive and then disappear. Dig hole in attic and never come back again.
Damon	I had lightning bug in jar with real big holes in lid, and night-time flew out and scared me. My eyes were open and I see and say "Mommy, get 'nother jar and put holes in" and Mom say "I will and hope he doesn't die—I'll put a fan in for him."
Teacher	That's a fibber!
Damon	[smiles]
Gene	Someone give ME bug.
Damon	I'll tell you something else I NEED to tell you guys—I slept outside with my sister—lantern on tree and we see lightning bug, and get and put in jar.
Michelle	We were SLEEPING in a swimming pool—no water in. Opened my mouth and lady bug went in my mouth—I'm making story up. I swallowed and went under water.

Book II, Final Copy, Page 3 revised
Conference 4/2

Teacher	What did you do to make the story better?
Damon	Drawed that—when gets dark the lights shine on dirt.
Brenton	What's this?
Damon	I trying to make page sticky like Todd's [rubbing the marker over the same place repeatedly].
Teacher	Does that make story better?
Damon	That's the ground.
Tyler	What are these bugs?
Damon	Lightning bugs.

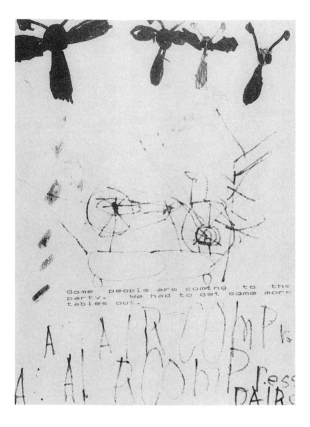

Then the lantern turned really bright. The people could see lightning bugs.

— 4 —

Book II, First Draft, Page 4
Conference 2/23
Damon I put tables away with my air compressor — in my garage. Air compressor real strong — BLEW tables in.

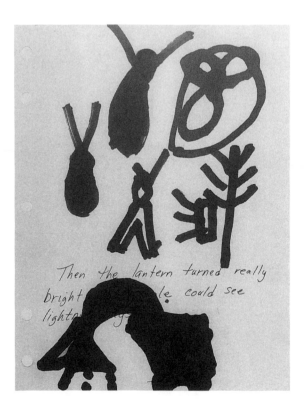

Then the lantern turned really bright... le could see lightn...g...

Book II, First Draft, Page 4 revised
Conference 2/27
Teacher What did you do to make the story better?
Damon Lightning bugs eating.
Teacher What's that?
Damon Came through page [where he was rubbing the marker].
Gene What's that?
Damon People with antennas on their head.
Teacher That's not what you told us before.
Damon They're lightning bugs. Holes in their heads so they can breathe.
Jeff What's that?
Damon Lightning bug house. They're eating.
Brenton What's that?
Damon Dirt. Sweeper sucking dirt up.
Celeste What is this?
Damon Tree stump.
Celeste What 'bout things coming down in ground?
Michelle Something's missing.
Damon Forgot tables.
Teacher No.
Damon Roots — forgot to draw them. Next time I'll draw the roots.
Gene What's that?
Damon Lantern.

Book II, Final Copy, Page 4
Conference 3/22

Gene   What's that?
Damon   Big table, big chair.
Jodi   What's that?
Damon   Lantern.
Jeff   What's that?
Damon   Lightning bug.

Book II, Final Copy, Page 4 revised
Conference 4/2

Teacher   What did you do to make the story better?
Gene   Where's bugs? Where's other ones?
Damon   Here—other ones on page 3.
Celeste   What's this?
Damon   Gonna be a wind storm.
Gene   What's that?
Damon   Cereal.
Michelle Barbie can't eat cereal.
Damon   It's a real Barbie. It can eat cereal. In this story Barbie real. If I
              get a kid I'm gonna name it Barbie.
Brenton   Where's other people?
Damon   [turns to page 5 in response to the question]

Book II, First Draft, Page 5
Conference 2/2
[No comments.]

Book II, First Draft, Page 5 revised
Conference 2/27

Teacher	What did you do to make the story better?
Damon	Draw some people.
Jeremy	Had people. Yes you did!
Teacher	What did you do?
Damon	Draw tank and lightning bugs eating underground.
Celeste	What's that?
Damon	Hair.
Celeste	Them have little bit—everybody have a *lot*.
Damon	I forgot.

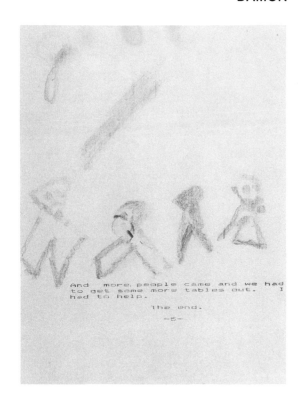

Book II, Final Copy, Page 5
Conference 3/22
Celeste What's that?
Damon Lightning bug. That's a dig. Yeah—that pirates dig on island.
Gene What's that?
Damon That's a dig.
Jodi What's a dig?
Teacher Is that in your story?
Damon No.
Jeff What's that?
Damon On another page.
Jodi What's that?
Damon People.

Book II, Final Copy, Page 5 revised
Conference 4/2
Teacher What did you do to make the story better?
Damon Drawed big steel fans.
Tyler Where's tables? Where's all tables?
Damon I forgot to draw them.
Tyler He didn't forget—he got 'nough time to do it.
Damon You [the teacher] said "Listen up, we're gonna do things."

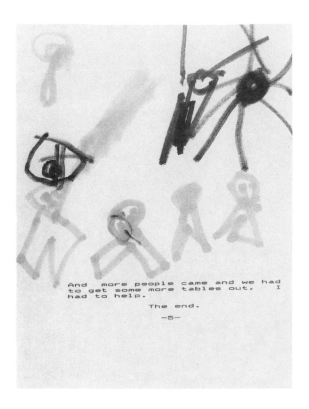

Book I, First Draft, Page 1
Conference 1/12
John   Where's sun? Where you? Where grass?

Conference 1/16 A.M.
Jeremy   "Sun" laugh.

Book I, First Draft, Page 1 revised
Conference 1/16 P.M.
Teacher   What did you do to make the picture better?
Gene   Made 'nother sun.

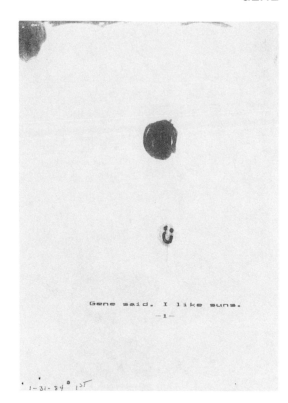

Book I, Final Copy, Page 1
Conference 2/1

John   Where suns?
Todd   Just one sun — just one sun.
Gene   I made three — I made three!
Jeff   What brown thing?
Gene   Sun too. Purple is sky.
Tyler   Could be your clouds 'cause you don't have any clouds.
Jeff   Why not draw me?
Gene   Because.
Celeste It's not in story.
Jeff   I play with you.

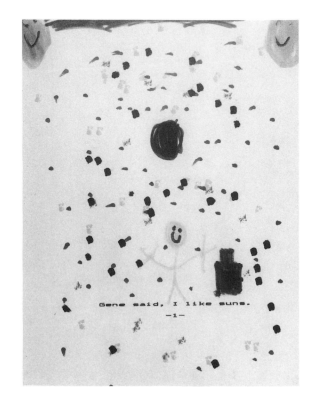

Book I, Final Copy, Page 1 revised
Conference 2/2

Teacher What did you do to make it better?
Gene   Made house and snow.

Book I, Final Copy, Page 2
Conference 1/12
John   Where's house?

Conference 1/16 A.M.
Celeste It [house] black.
Gene   'Cept really white.
Teacher Why make it black?
Gene   I want to color it in.
Tyler   Does house have a black chimney?
Gene   Don't know. Us don't have attic.

Book I, Final Copy, Page 2 revised
Conference 1/16 P.M.
Teacher What did you do to make the picture better?
Gene   Drew Santa Claus and Rudolph.

Book I, Final Copy, Page 2
Conference 2/1
Celeste What's blue things?
Gene People—mommy and daddy and me. Ohh—Rudolph!

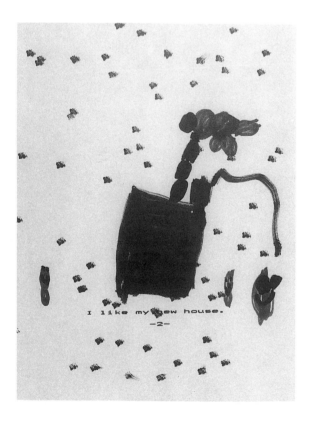

Book I, Final Copy, Page 2 revised
Conference 2/2
Teacher What did you do to make it better?
Gene Made snow, Rudolph, and Santa.
John What's that?
Gene My chimney.
Jeremy Rudolph has eyes—I don't see his eyes.
Gene I didn't make.
Brenton What blue things?
Gene Mommy and dad and me. Added faces.

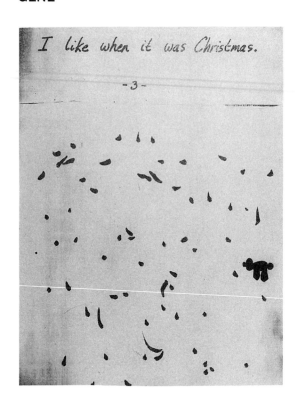

I like when it was Christmas.

- 3 -

Book I, First Draft, Page 3
Conference 1/12
Michel   Rudolph's here.
John   Where you?
Jodi   Where house?
Celeste   Where Rudolph?
Tyler   Don't you see his red nose?

Conference 1/16 A.M.
Celeste   Only Rudolph.
Jeremy   Said it was him. Where are horns?
Gene   When snows out, all horns fall off reindeer. Saw on TV.

I like when it was Christmas.

- 3 -

Book I, First Draft, Page 3 revised
Conference 1/16 P.M.
Teacher   What did you do to make the picture better?
Gene   Drew whole lot of Rudolphs and my house and draw Santa.

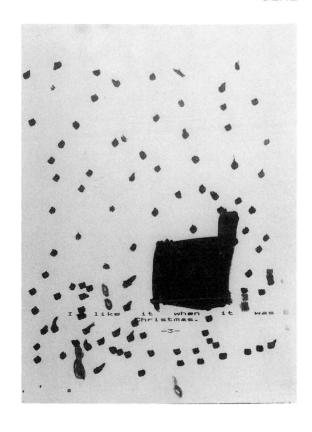

Book I, Final Copy, Page 3
Conference 2/1
Jeremy   Black snow!
Jodi   You can't see the words.
Tyler   Yes you can.
Gene   Yes you can.

Book I, Final Copy, Page 3 revised
Conference 2/2
Teacher   What did you do to make it better?
Gene   Made stars and made moon and snow and house and 'nother house. Made Santa.
Teacher   Santa was there.
Gene   Put face on him.
John   What's that?
Gene   Moon.
Tyler   Who are two people?
Gene   Elves [green and orange].

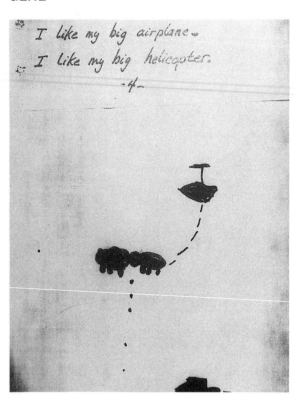

I like my big airplane.
I like my big helicopter.
_—4—_

Book I, First Draft, Page 4
Conference 1/12
Michel   What's this one?
Gene   Airplane. Helicop-up. Little dots bombs. Little army tank, I just make that.

Conference 1/16 A.M.
John   Where helicopter?
Jeremy Where plane?
Gene   I already told you. When mommy and daddy come in, me take in my helicopter and my plane. 'Cept don't know when.

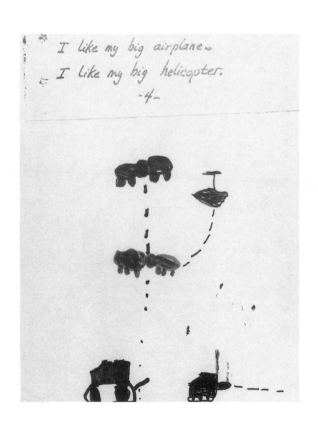

I like my big airplane.
I like my big helicopter.
_—4—_

Book I, First Draft, Page 4 revised
Conference 1/16 P.M.
Teacher What did you do to make the picture better?
Gene   Drew 'nother airplane and army tank.

Book I, Final Copy, Page 4
Conference 2/1

Celeste	What black things?
Gene	My tank what I got for Christmas.
Celeste	Why it not shooting?
Gene	'Cause it really don't.

Book I, Final Copy, Page 4 revised
Conference 2/2

Teacher	What did you do to make it better?
Gene	Made snow.
Jeremy	What green thing?
Gene	Christmas tree.
John	What's that?
Gene	Me.
Damon	What's this on army tank?
Gene	Guns.
Damon	Then, why not a cannon?
Gene	'Cause it's a tank.

GENE

I was staying overnight at Brenton's, and I hide under the bed.

Book II, First Draft, Page 1
Conference 2/23

Jeremy	Where's bed?
John	What black thing?
Gene	Brenton's mommy.
Jodi	What's thing at top?
Gene	Brenton.
Jeremy	Where's Gene?
Celeste	Under bed goin' like this. [Punching]
Jeff	What's black thing?
Gene	Mom.

Book II, First Draft, Page 1 revised
Conference 2/28

Teacher	What did you do to make better?
Gene	Colored in all this.
Tyler	I see more.
Gene	I made pillow and blanket.
Jeremy	It was there.
Gene	No.
Teacher	What else?
Gene	Drawed birds.
Jodi	What's that?
Gene	Brenton's mom.
Jodi	Is she a snowman?
Gene	No.
Jodi	What round thing?
Gene	These her hands, her legs.
Teacher	Who's this?
Gene	Me. Brenton in air.
Jeff	What are these?
Gene	I was gonna make something.
Jeremy	I show him how make my name.
Celeste	What's that?
Gene	Chimney smoke coming out. Brenton's hand.
Michelle	What's that?
Gene	That's door.
Celeste	What about doorknob?
Gene	I color over it.
Jodi	What's that?
Gene	The window.
Jeremy	What that?
Gene	Brenton's mommy.
Jeff	What blue stuff?
Gene	The floor.
Tyler	What's that?
Gene	Part of cover hanging down—big brown pillow and blanket. His fingers.
Jodi	Fingers on his *head*?
Gene	No—ain't on his head.
Brenton	What's that line?
Gene	That your bedroom wall.
Jeremy	1, 2, 3 [fingers].
Todd	Him have 9 fingers.
Brenton	No I don't, I got 10!
Todd	[Denied he said nine, insisted he said 10; all in circle heard 9.] I just say that.

Book II, Final Copy, Page 1
Conference 3/22

John	Me know that a heart.
Jeff	What's that?
Gene	Bird and smoke.
Jodi	What's that?
Gene	That's steps, and this bedroom. That's Brenton kissing his mommy.
Jodi	What's heart for?
Gene	To make him kiss Mom—so you know he's kissing Mom.

Book II, Final Copy, Page 1 revised
Conference 3/27

Teacher	What did you do to make the story better?
Gene	Draw Brenton['s] little brother's bedroom. Colored in steps.
Brenton	Where's my basement steps?
Gene	I didn't make.
Jodi	What's this?
Gene	The steps.

GENE

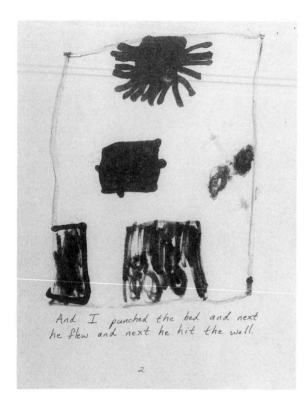

And I punched the bed and next he flew and next he hit the wall.

2

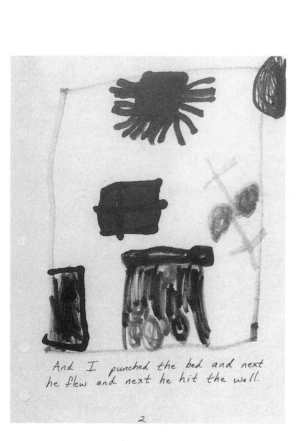

And I punched the bed and next he flew and next he hit the wall.

2

Book II, First Draft, Page 2
Conference 2/23

Jeremy	Who Brenton?
Todd	This is Brenton.
John	Is that—
Celeste	Green thing [is] Brenton.
Damon	What is that?
Gene	Door for bedroom.
Tyler	Don't you know what doors look like?
Michelle	Where is Brenton's bed?
Brenton	Then where is Gene's bed?
Gene	Don't have no room to draw.
Celeste	Where is pillow?
Gene	Didn't draw.
Celeste	'Posed to lay on pillow.
Todd	My mom don't.
Jeff	I don't.
John	I don't.
Brenton	I don't lay on pillow.
Gene	You have pillow.
Brenton	Tyler does too. I at his house—he does.
Damon	I always do.
Todd	My mom don't like pillows but likes blankets.

Book II, First Draft, Page 2 revised
Conference 2/28

Teacher	What did you do to make better?
Gene	Drawed sun.
Jeremy	That's not in house.
Gene	It's outside.
Jeremy	I see *inside*.
Gene	That's the light.
Michelle	You say that [is the] sun, yesterday.
Jeremy	Uh-huh, you say sun.
Gene	It the light from the light bulb.
Jeff	What's that?
Gene	Window.
John	What's that?
Gene	Brenton hitting the wall.
Brenton	What's that?
Gene	Me and my smile. I'm laughing at you 'cause you hit the wall.
Brenton	You only got one nose in there.
Gene	Only *have* one nose.
Brenton	No eyes, no mouth. Don't got any ears.
Gene	No room to make.
Brenton	No hair. People have hair—and where's your clothing on?
Gene	Yes—there my pjs.
Brenton	No socks and shoes.
Gene	You can't sleep in socks and shoes.
Brenton	Well, afternoon in this page.
Brenton	I see it—the sun is there.
Gene	So—I just made the sun.
Michelle	What's that?
Gene	My feet.
Michelle	Why no feet on Brenton?
Gene	Right here—little feet.
Todd	What's that?
Gene	Window.

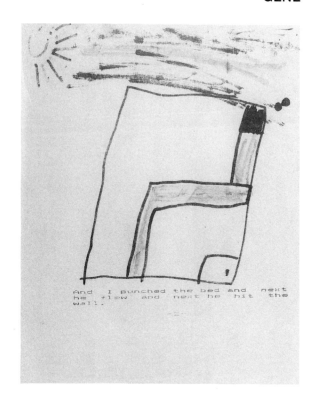

Book II, Final Copy, Page 2
Conference 3/22

Tyler	"And next" and "and next he hit the wall." It don't rhyme. "Next" don't rhyme. [Note: The storybook on which this story is derived, *Pierre*, is written in rhyme.]
Teacher	How would you like [it to be]?
Tyler	"Then he hit" instead of "next."
Gene	Don't want to write that.
Jodi	What's that?
Teacher	What my question?
Jodi	How does it sound?
Teacher	Right.
Jeff	Maybe make Brenton felt sad, maybe.
Gene	I don't know.

Book II, Final Copy, Page 2 revised
Conference 3/27

Teacher	What did you do to make better?
Gene	I draw sky, drew grass, and here him falling down.
Teacher	You told me [that was] your dog when you were drawing.
Gene	Yes—I don't want dog in story.
Teacher	So what's this?
Gene	My dog. Scooby. I change my mind.
Jodi	Who's thing like this?
Gene	Brenton. His brother. Me.
Jeremy	What yellow thing?
Gene	Sky.
Jodi	You said that sky, and you kicking him out of sky?
John	Why Brenton here and here? [Two Brenton figures.]
Gene	When I kicked him out—he *here*—then I kick him out and he's *here*.
Jodi	How can he do that? He's here—he kick this way and he goes out other way.
Gene	Well, I kick him around first.
Jodi	He can't go through sky. He can't get out like that. Did he land on feet, or how? He's little, then big.
Gene	He go out and he far away and he still same size—like airplanes—they go up and look really small but they still really big.
Jodi	Where is he?
Gene	Outside—don't you see the grass?
Jodi	Like a seven.
Teacher	It's the steps.
Jeff	What is black thing?
Gene	Carpet to wipe your feet on.
Jeff	I didn't hear you, Gene.
John	Why leaning? [steps]
Gene	Well, my steps are like that.
John	MY steps straight.
Gene	They Brenton's steps—he don't have no real steps—I just want to make like that.
Brenton	I have steps at my house!
Gene	'Cept up in your bedroom at top of your house.

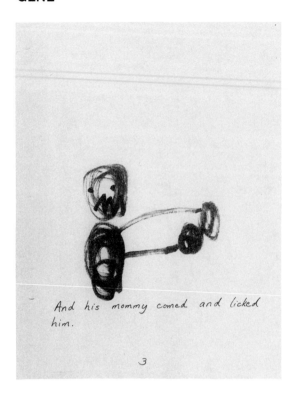

And his mommy comed and licked him.

3

Book II, First Draft, Page 3
Conference 2/23
Michelle Where is mom? Where Gene?
Gene Not in page. I'm down playing with little brother.
Michelle Where baby?
Gene No baby.
Teacher How come Brenton doesn't have a face?
Gene Didn't have time to draw.
Celeste Mom mad.
Gene Yeah, 'cause him made big hole in ceiling.

And his mommy comed and licked him.

Book II, First Draft, Page 3 revised
Conference 2/28
Teacher What did you do to make better?
Gene Changed words - added more words.
Teacher What else?
Gene No more—just words.
Celeste What about "I" in story?
Teacher We crossed it out because it didn't sound right.

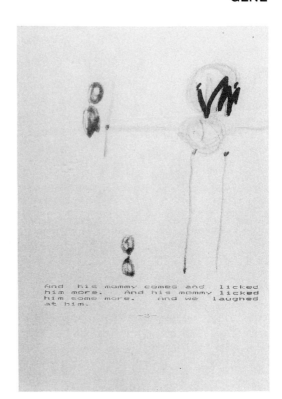

Book II, Final Copy, Page 3
Conference 3/22

Jeff	What's that?
Gene	His mom licking him.
Tyler	What's that?
Gene	Me laughing.
Michelle	Where arms?
Gene	Didn't draw them yet.
Brenton	Why don't she got no nose or mouth?
Gene	She does. Mad face—eyes.
Celeste	Where nose?
Gene	Right here.
Teacher	Can't see face?
Gene	He bawling and tears all over his face.
Teacher	Where's your face?
Gene	I laughing so hard, can't see my face.
Jeff	What are them lines?
Gene	All arms and fingers.

Book II, Final Copy, Page 3 revised
Conference 3/27

Teacher	What did you do to make better?
Gene	Color house, colored door, colored sun, and that's all.
Michelle	Where arms?
Gene	I don't want to make them.
Teacher	Will you need arms to hold things?
Gene	I'm laying on ground.
Michelle	You had to put arms different way.
Gene	I down on ground laughing. I lay flat. Well—I just want to make that!
Michelle	You need arms to be down. Where's your face—where you giggling?
Gene	Well, I on ground and you can't see face.
Michelle	Where's hair?
Gene	I want them to be bald.
Michelle	Where's slacks?
Gene	Boys don't wear slacks. These pants. These shirt.
Michelle	Where head, then?
Gene	Well—here pants, here shirt—here head. His mom not walking, she *licking* him!
Michelle	Where's mom's arms? She need legs. Where hair?
Gene	I don't want to make.
Brenton	Where tongue?
Teacher	Where's all parts that are missing—arms, hair, face, legs?
Gene	But, but—I draw it at recess.
Teacher	Why didn't you put them on—did it help your story?
Gene	I didn't want to. No [it didn't help story].
Damon	How come Brenton mom got mad face?
Teacher	What did story say?
Damon	What did he do that was bad?
Gene	I forgot.
Teacher	Wait a minute—back to page 2. If you hit him, and he hit the wall—how did he get outside?
Gene	He made hole in wall. Mom mad—made hole in wall.

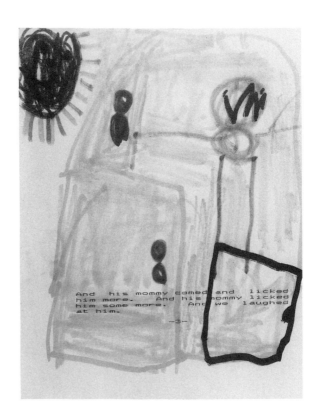

And his mommy licked him some more and next he was bawling ~~and us went roller skating.~~

4

Book II, First Draft, Page 4/5
Conference 2/23
Brenton   Next I'm gonna write a story about you.
Gene   I make 'nother one 'bout you.
Brenton   I gonna write *hundred* about you at home.

I jumped ~~down~~ out and he jumped on his mommy's head. And his mommy spanked him.

4

Book II, First Draft, Page 4/5 revised
Conference 2/28
[Gene has added a whole new page.]
Gene   I going make something up—and us laughing at him.
Jeremy   Who?
Gene   His brother and sister and me.
Teacher   What did you do? What did you do to your picture?
Gene   Made this [a whole new picture, with new text].
Michelle   Where's house?
Gene   They outside. Want everyone to see him get licked.
Brenton   Why don't he have rest of hat on?
Gene   It's his mom's hair.
Brenton   Don't got no teeth.
Gene   Mouth shut. And mommy laughing at you.
Brenton   Well, I made Tyler's mom happy in my story.

Book II, First Draft, Page 4/5, revised
Conference 2/28

Teacher	What did you do to make better?
Gene	Colored mom.
Jodi	Why you make face purple?
Gene	'Cause I wanted to.
Tyler	You can still see mad face.
Michelle	Where's Brenton?
Gene	Right there.
Michelle	Where you?
Gene	I ain't in this picture.
Michelle	Where your mom, your sister?
Gene	Not here.
Brenton	Why mom have round shoes on?
Gene	It *your* mom, and her tippy toes.
Michelle	Where Brenton's daddy?
Gene	He laying on sofa.
Brenton	No he don't—he work every day 'cept Saturday and Sunday.

And his mommy licked him some more and next he was bawling ~~and us went roller skating.~~

5

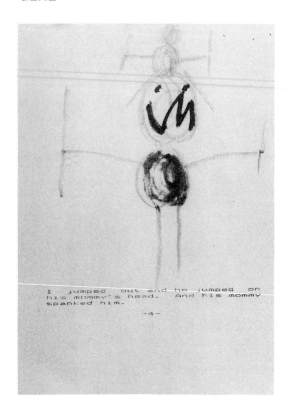

Book II, Final Copy, Page 4
Conference 3/22

Jeff	What is purple thing?
Gene	Mom tummy.
Brenton	Why purple tummy?
Gene	Purple shirt on.
Tyler	Why purple belly button?
Gene	Don't. Shirt over belly button. You see my belly button.
Brenton	Why blue hair?
Gene	She don't—that *you*, laying on her head.
Brenton	Where's her hair?
Gene	You sitting on it.
Jodi	No feet.
Gene	Uh-huh—long things.
John	Where legs?
Gene	These.
Jodi	You said *feet*!
Gene	They legs *and* feet.
Jodi	Where shoes?
Gene	Barefoot.
Celeste	Where toes?
Gene	They hiding.
Michelle	Where floor?
Gene	Words are floor.
Michelle	Where wall?
Gene	Don't see 'cause too far away.
Michelle	Can draw here [on edge of page].
Gene	I will draw over fingers. Can't.
Damon	What mad face for?
Gene	She mad he fall on her head.
Tyler	Where socks?
Gene	Socks?! She barefeeted.
Tyler	Why no socks? Can't go barefeeted outside.
Gene	She inside.

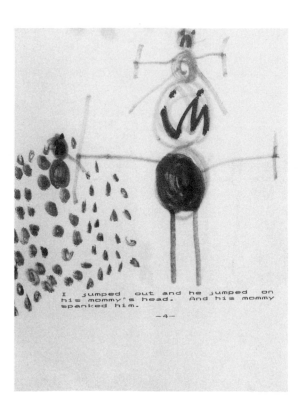

Book II, Final Copy, Page 4 revised
Conference 3/27

Teacher	What did you do to make better?
Gene	This when land on mom's head—this when getting licked.
Jodi	That should be you, laughing, and all your giggles coming out.
Gene	'Cept he sad.
Jodi	This could be you happy and this him sad.
Gene	I not in story.
Teacher	Listen—*I* jump out. [The teacher is warning children about behavior here, and is using the story text.]
Jeff	Why Brenton land on mom's head?
Gene	'Cause I jump out and he scared.

Book II, First Draft, Page 5/6
Conference 2/23
[No comments.]

Book II, First Draft, Page 5/6 revised
Conference 2/28

Teacher	What did you do to make better?
Gene	Drawed this and this.
Celeste	And roller skates?
Gene	No—just colored in balls.
Michelle	Where your dad?
Gene	He not there.
Michelle	Where's Brenton?
Gene	He behind me. He can't even skate, he holds on to side.
Brenton	Hey—you couldn't skate either! I see you. You stayed on side and couldn't even get started and went around with his mom!
Gene	Hey—this funny one—my daddy don't know how to skate.
Todd	My daddy can't skate.

Book II, Final Copy, Page 5
Conference 3/22
Celeste   Look at he tears!
Brenton   Where's tongue? Where's mom?
Gene   She left. She don't want to hear you bawling.

Book II, Final Copy, Page 5 revised
Conference 3/27
Teacher   What did you do to make better?
Gene   I color him stomach, made little dots his cries.
Jeff   What are them X?
Gene   That his hand.
Jeff   You made his arm and hand now!
Gene   That's his fingers.
Michelle   Where her hair and arms?
Gene   Right here.
Michelle   I can't see them.
Gene   Right there, one arm—not enough room for other arm.
Jodi   Is that Brenton's mom?
Gene   Yes.
Jodi   Does she eat too much?
Gene   No!
Jodi   Does your mom look like that—does she have blue skin?
Brenton   No, no!
Jodi   I can't see her belly button.
Gene   Her shirt over it.

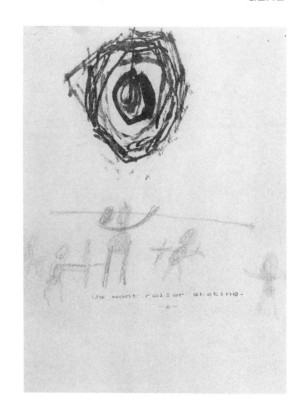

Book II, Final Copy, Page 6
Conference 3/22

Michelle What's this?
Gene Big golden thing hanging up. When lights off, goes around and makes dots on floor. Right, Brenton? Sorry—I should call you "Brenton Bear."
Jeff What's this?
Gene That's me and that Brenton holding on banister and I not hold on.
Brenton I see you fall and mom took you around!
Gene Well, so what. I can take myself around.
Todd I beat them little things [dots] go around. I Speedo.

Book II, Final Copy, Page 6 revised
Conference 3/27

Teacher What did you do to make better?
Gene I drawed that bigger (ball), draw hair, and more people skating. And right here roller skates.
Jodi Does he have blue hair? Who are they?
Gene No. That's me, his mom, him, my mom, and sister.
Brenton Where me?
Gene Right here—holding onto banister.

Book I, First Draft, Page 1
Conference 1/13
Jeff   Drew road to get to friend's house.

Conference 1/16 A.M.
John   Where snow?
Jeremy   Snow.

Book I, First Draft, Page 1 revised
Conference 1/16 P.M.
Teacher   What did you do to make the picture better?
Jeff   Bombs.
Tyler   From what?
Jeff   Rocks. Bombs are rocks. People have rocks.
Tyler   Who does?
Jeff   Me. Throw somewhere, pretend them bombs.

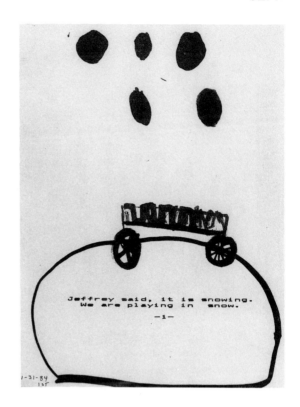

Book I, Final Copy, Page 1
Conference 2/1

Celeste	Where are you?
Jeff	In bus.
Gene	How he can be playing in bus with snow?
Jeff	Not playing in snow.
Michelle	But it say you playing.
Jeff	Bus came early.
Michelle	Where are you?
Jeff	Up front with Cameron.
Jeremy	How snow red, black?
Jeff	And orange. I made it that way.

Book I, Final Copy, Page 1 revised
Conference 2/2

Teacher	What did you do to make it better?
Jeff	Made more snow. And friends house. Our house. Chad's friend's house.
Gene	Where door?
Jeff	Here.
Gene	Where door knob?
Jeff	Chad's don't have one. Chad's friend don't have one. Them push button.
Tyler	Can't even reach no window or door.
Gene	Show us. No door.
Jeff	I make one soon.

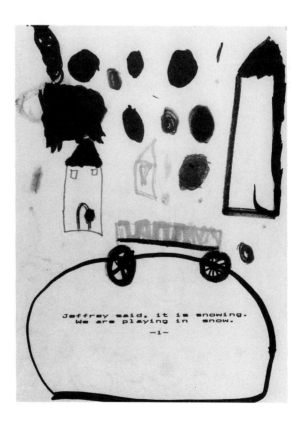

Book I, First Draft, Page 2
Conference 1/13

Jeff   Right here my bed. Christmas tree bed. There Derrick sleeping.
Celeste   What orange thing?
Jeff   Ladder.
Gene   What yellow thing go out?
Jeff   Chad bed.

Conference 1/16 A.M.

Jeff   I wrote "Gene."
Gene   'Cept ain't in story.
Jeff   I want to write it. Right here my Christmas bed [Christmas tree lying on its side]. Just wanted to make Christmas bed. Here Derrick's bed, Gene's bed.
Gene   I don't go to your house. Derrick sleep on your name.

Book I, First Draft, Page 2 revised
Conference 1/16 P.M.

Teacher   What did you do to make the picture better?
Jeff   Two blue dots—them are rocks coming in us bedroom. Really happened. Friend threw in—broke glass. My pop-pop got mad.

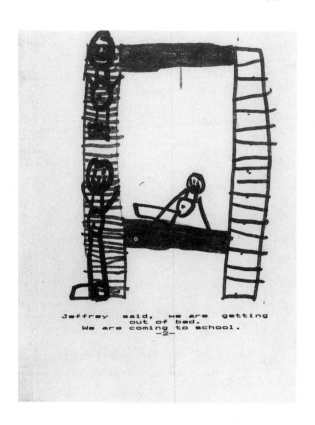

Book I, Final Copy, Page 2
Conference 2/1

Damon I never seen bed like that.
Jeff That us bunk beds.
Gene Why three persons?
Jeff Me, Chad [Jeff's twin brother], Derrick, 'cause mom sleeping in Derrick's bed.
Gene Who's Derrick?
Jeff Us brother. He's 8.

Book I, Final Copy, Page 2 revised
Conference 2/2

Teacher What did you do to make it better?
Brenton What's that?
Jeff Toys. Toy snow coming hitting Derrick.
John What's that?
Jeff Part of ladder.
Tyler Why only one leg [on Derrick]?
Jeff Is [illegible] other leg under cover.
Gene Why sleeping outside?
Jeff No. Us inside. Us in bed. Us bed ate it.
Brenton What's that?
Jeff Toys. Eyeballs.
Jeremy What's this?
Jeff Bed.
Tyler Why two beds?
Jeff 'Cause bunk beds.
Gene What's that?
Jeff Toy Christmas tree.
Gene Why blue?
Jeff I want to be that way and I not have 'nough time color.

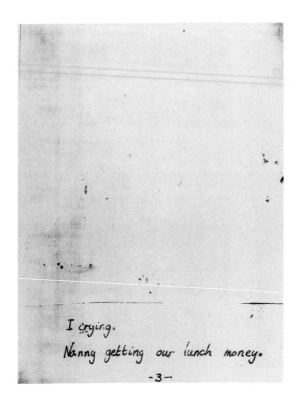

I crying.
Nanny getting our lunch money.
-3-

Book I, First Draft, Page 3
Conference 1/13
Jeff   No picture. Not have enough time.

Conference 1/16 A.M.
Celeste   He didn't have time do that [picture].

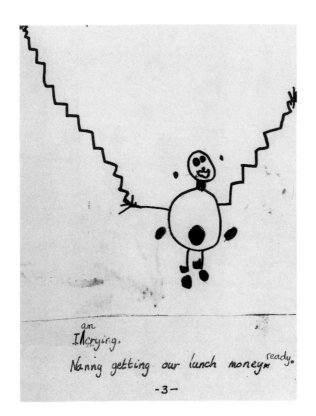

am
I crying.
Nanny getting our lunch money ready.
-3-

Book I, First Draft, Page 3 revised
Conference 1/16 P.M.
Teacher   What did you do to make the picture better?
Jeff   Money. Nanny's arms—look like steps.

Book I, Final Copy, Page 3
Conference 2/1
Celeste The bus is big.
Michelle Where's word "Nanny"?

Book I, Final Copy, Page 3 revised
Conference 2/2
Teacher What did you do to make it better?
Jeff Made hands. Made pennies.
Brenton What tiny dot?
Jeff Blinking light on bus.
John What that two things?
Jeff Feets. I not have shoes on yet.
Gene Why in sky?
Jeff Not.
Gene How you can be in house?
Jeff This my little hand. No. That is Damon.
Jeremy Little Damon.
Damon Where big Damon?
Jeff In bus.
Damon Look at that nose on bus!
Jeff That blinking light.
Tyler What is big dots?
Jeff Pennies.

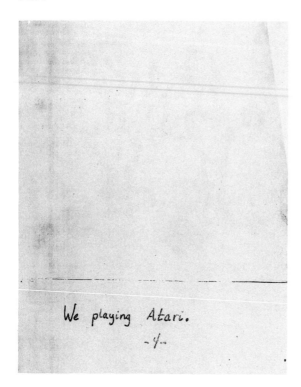

We playing Atari.
-4-

Book I, First Draft, Page 4
Conference 1/13
Celeste   Where Staci?
Gene   He didn't have time.

Conference 1/16 A.M.
[No comments]

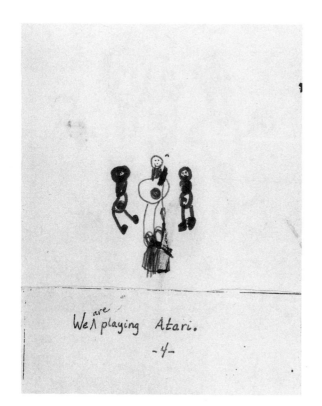

We are playing Atari.
-4-

Book I, First Draft, Page 4 revised
Conference 1/16 P.M.
Teacher   What did you do to make the picture better?
Jeff   Here Atari. Derrick play. Here me and he's Chad. My belly. Front, Gene, happy, mad, sad. Jeff, happy, mad, sad.

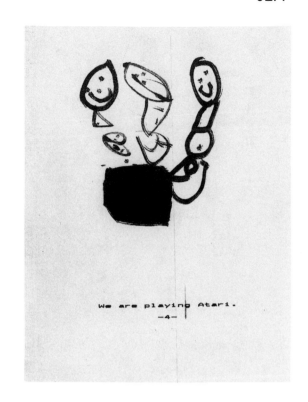

Book I, Final Copy, Page 4
Conference 2/1

Jodi　What's black thing?
Jeff　Atari box.

Book I, Final Copy, Page 4 revised
Conference 2/2

Teacher　What did you do to make it better?
Jeff　Maked dots. That how you play it. Count numbers what you want.
John　What that thing?
Jeff　Gun. Shoot.
Jeremy　Why do he have no feet?
Jeff　'Cause we sitting on us bottoms.
Jeremy　Why body ain't together?
Jeff　They are.
John　Why no arms?
Jeff　We laying down and playing.
Brenton　What's that?
Jeff　Handle of gun again—have two.

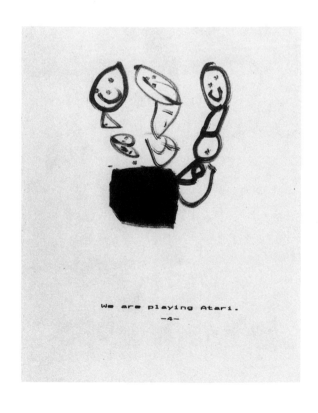

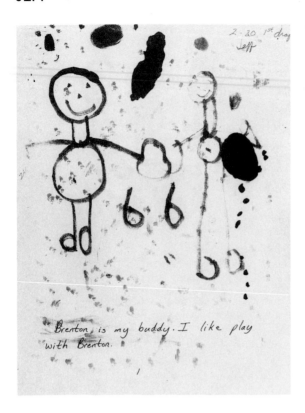

Book II, First Draft, Page 1
Conference 2/23

Brenton	What's red thing and that?
Jeff	Sun. Blood [on head].
Jeremy	Why [blood] on his head?
Jeff	'Cause he got blood-head.
Brenton	I don't have blood.
Jeff	I made it.
Gene	What's dot?
Jeff	On 'nother page.
Celeste	Where's hair?
Jeff	Not time have made it.
Brenton	What them? [a pair of sixes]
Jeff	Brenton is 6. I am 6.
Gene	What little dot?
Jeff	Belly button.
Gene	Why don't have shirt on?
Brenton	Why don't have shirt on?
Jeff	Didn't want.
Brenton	Why outside?
Jeff	Not.
John	Why sun out?
Jeff	Not sun—our toy.
John	Oh. He changed it.
Jeff	Yep.

Book II, First Draft, Page 1 revised
Conference 2/24

Teacher	What did you do to make better?
Jeff	Made two balls. Covered words. 'Cause I want to. Cover with brown.
Teacher	Why?
Jeff	To cover words.
Jodi	What red thing?
Jeff	Football.
Jodi	Not in your story.
Gene	No little footballs in story.
Jeff	I want to make.

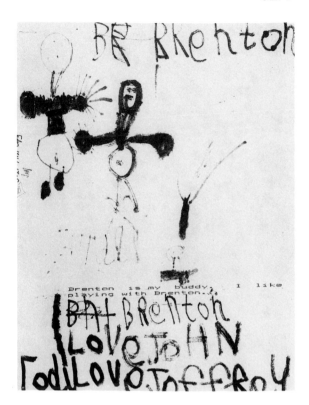

Book II, Final Copy, Page 1
Conference 3/23

Jodi	What's that thing?
Jeff	Roots growing out the grass, and here flowers.
Tyler	What's that little?
Jeff	You—Mr. Wenger [the teacher]. I want to make you into my story.
Gene	Who's that?
Jeff	Me and Brenton.
Damon	What is thing?
Jeff	Flowers.
Tyler	Jodi asked that.
Gene	What's that?
Jeff	Flowers flying off.
Gene	Flowers can't fly off.
Jeff	Uh-huh, at our house.
Todd	What word crossed out?
Jeff	Don't know.

Book II, Final Copy, Page 1 revised
Conference 3/27

Teacher	What did you do to make better?
Jeff	Make these roots—flowers ain't growing out yet.
Damon	How come they're bald-headed?
Jeff	I didn't have 'nough time to make.
Michelle	Yes you did!
Jeff	I forget.
Jodi	He [the teacher] said if you missed anything, do right now—didn't you listen?
Jeff	I make later.
Teacher	We already did things—you forgot.
Jeff	Oh.
Jodi	Why are they gloves or are they like this?
Jeff	Fingers.
Jodi	What are red things?
Jeff	I color in things.
Jodi	What is it?
Jeff	My shirt.
Jodi	You should make skin brown—don't have white. Shouldn't make red.

Book II, First Draft, Page 2
Conference 2/23

Jeremy	Why is big wheel and little wheel?
Jeff	'Cause is hot rod bus.
Todd	I thought that speedy one.
Gene	What dots?
Jeff	Snow.

Book II, First Draft, Page 2 revised
Conference 2/24

Teacher	What did you do to make better?
Jeff	Changed words.
Teach	What else?
Jeff	Made lines. Train coming and not enough time to finish.
Jeremy	What's this?
Jeff	My name.
Jeremy	Not have a "Y"
Jeff	I not want make "JEFFREY."
Jeremy	What yellow?
Jeff	Train tracks.
Jodi	What red?
Jeff	Snow.
Michelle	Snow not in story.
Jeremy	Who driving bus?
Jeff	Mrs. Robinson, I want make in story.
Tyler	Is that hot rod bus?
Jeff	No.
Michelle	You said yesterday hot rod.
Jeff	I just make on my story.
Jeremy	Bus not go on railroad tracks.
Jeff	We go on and back off.
Gene	'Cept don't go on tracks.
Todd	If want to get over you do.
Gene	'Cept bus don't go over.
Jeff	Uh huh. Remember road flooded and we went over?
Jodi	What's this say?
Jeff	Read story.
Jeremy	Then read story.
Jodi	"See" or "seeing."
Jeff	"Seeing."
Michelle	Doesn't sound right. "I like when I see the bus."
Jeff	No. That isn't better.
Michelle	It is, my mommy told me.
Jeff	I just want to say "I like seeing bus."
Todd	My mom tell me same thing. "I see a bus," my mom say. "I see a bus, I like to see bus."
Jeff	How does it sound to you?
Brenton	Yes. "I like seeing a bus"
Jeff	Put "a" (in).
Jeremy	Uh, oh—it going to sound different!
Todd	I don't like it that way.
Teacher	Why?
Jeff	I don't know.
John	What red spots?
Jeff	This is bomb, bomb, bomb, and snow.

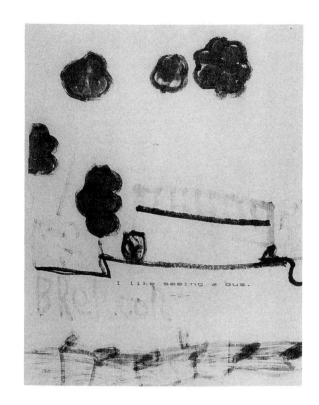

Book II, Final Copy, Page 2
Conference 3/23

Teach	What's thing on bottom?
Jeff	Some stuff belongs to bus seats.
John	What's that?
Jeff	Pink and green — some grass.
Michelle	What's that?
Jeff	Hill.
Jodi	What yellow thing?
Jeff	Bus!

Book II, Final Copy, Page 2 revised
Conference 3/27

Teacher	What did you do to make better?
Jeff	Write "Brenton."
Jeremy	That was there before — I saw it.
Jeff	I forgot.
Teach	What do?
Jeff	Make gate for me and Brenton. We are gate man.
Gene	What's that?
Jeff	Old sun.
Gene	Where new sun? Why purple trees?
Jeff	They're flowers.
Gene	Flowers not bigger than bus.
Jeff	I just make like that.
Jodi	Where people sitting in seats?
Jeff	Here.
Celeste	If they didn't have water — water flowers, them will get big. Flowers die if don't plant or water.
Damon	How come old sun is orange?
Jeff	I want make like that.
Damon	In desert, sun red and orange.
Jodi	What black thing?
Jeff	Hill (for buses).
Jodi	What's other thing?
Jeff	That hill too. Wheels.
Jodi	Only one wheel?
Jeff	No — here and here — two wheels.
Damon	Does battery [?] on wheels and be army bus tank.
Michelle	What are these?
Jeff	Dots of snow.

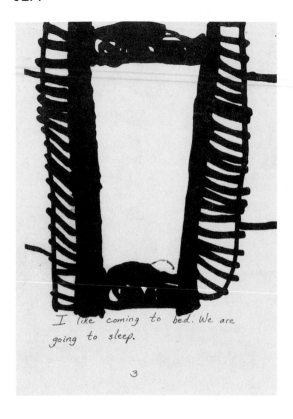

I like coming to bed. We are going to sleep.

3

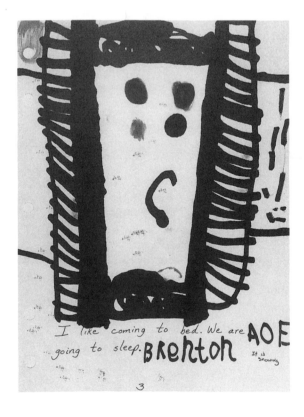

I like coming to bed. We are going to sleep. Brenton AOE It is snowing

3

Book II, First Draft, Page 3
Conference 2/23

Jeremy	What big ball for?
Jeff	Big snow coming down and try bite me.
Michelle	What streaks?
Jeff	Volcano come—blow bus up. I want made it that way.
Gene	What that on top?
Jeff	Bunk beds.
Gene	Where pillow?
Jeff	Here, little bump.
Gene	Where blanket?
Jeff	Here.
Michelle	What's this?
Jeff	Hang on bed so not bed fall down.
Michelle	We doesn't have that.
Jeff	We do.
Todd	Have four ladders on each side?
Jeff	Yes.
John	I have high bed.

Book II, First Draft, Page 3 revised
Conference 2/24

Teacher	What did you do to make better?
Jeff	Changed story—added "Brenton." I changed with no seeing.
Jodi	What four circles?
Jeff	Snow.
Jodi	It not snowing in house.
Jeff	Not on ceiling.
Jodi	How toys go to ceiling?
Jeff	Not on ceiling!
Jodi	This ground, this ceiling.
Jeff	Them in closet, toy snow. Is blanket on bed.
Jodi	'Cept where closet for toy snow.
Jeff	Not I have 'nough time to make.
	[Tried to put in story on own—"It is snowing."]
Jeff	We is playing in snow in us beds.
Jeremy	Who's under covers?
Jeff	Where?
Jeremy	On top.
Jeff	Me and Chad.
Tyler	Where Brenton?
Jeff	On bottom.
Jodi	Who this?
Jeff	Derrick.
Jodi	He has a long head?
Jeff	Yes.
Gene	Nuh-uh—has round head, everybody have round head.
Jeff	Not his head. Not enough time to make whole thing—IS his head.
Michelle	What's this? (black)
Jeff	I don't know.
Jodi	Then why you make it?
Jeff	I wanted to.
Todd	What's this?
Jeff	Head. Dot [is] his chin.
John	What green thing?
Jeff	Snow. Real snow.
Brenton	Snow not green.
Tyler	What black things?
Jeff	Just asked. Don't know.
Celeste	What's this?
Jeff	Brenton.
Celeste	He have no eyes. I don't see.
Jeff	He head under pillow. Not I have 'nough time make Brenton under pillow.

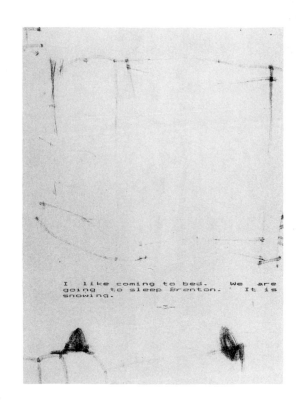

Book II, Final Copy, Page 3
Conference 3/23

Jeff   Where is "snow"? [the word]
Jodi   What's that?
Jeff   Tools.
Celeste Why tools?
Jeff   Break our bunk beds and put back together.
Jodi   What's "I" for?
Jeff   I want put there.
Jeff   [back to p. 2] I want to tell—these purple things flowers.

Book II, Final Copy, Page 3 revised
Conference 3/24

Teacher What did you do to make better?
Teacher Jeff added sentence and changed.
Jeff   Make tools to break bed and put back together.
Celeste They were there.
Teacher This is a new sheet [of paper] I just gave him.

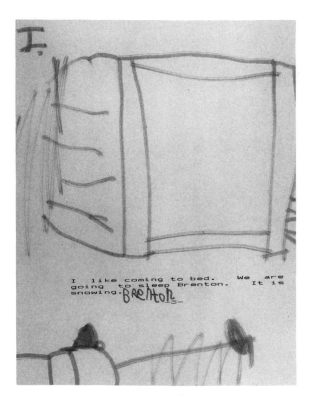

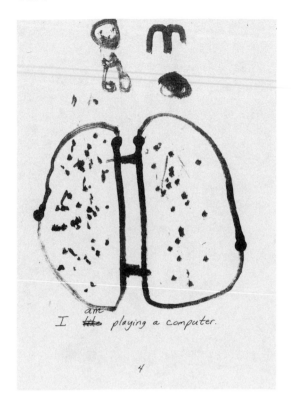

Book II, First Draft, Page 4
Conference 2/23

Celeste	What brown thing and green thing and dots?
Jeff	Part of computer. These buttons.
Celeste	What striped things?
Jeff	Hold on computer.
Brenton	What's that?
Jeff	Things hold on computer. This is button got out here— out of 'puter.
Damon	What's this?
Jeff	A bird.
Brenton	What's this?
Jeff	My hands.
Brenton	You have long hands.
Jeff	They're playing computer.
Michelle	Why hands not touch? You have to touch to play.
Jeff	I not playing yet.

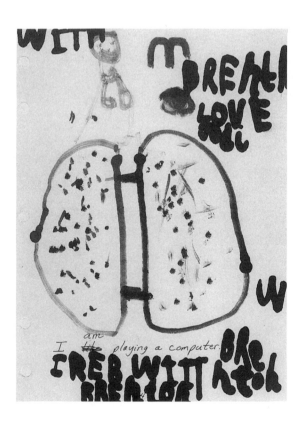

Book II, First Draft, Page 4 revised
Conference 2/24

Teacher	What did you do to make better?
Jeff	[added words "with Brenton"]
Gene	Where Brenton?
Jeff	Right here.
Gene	Where you?
Jeff	Not 'nough time to make.
Teacher	Why not enough time?
Jeff	Bell rang.
Teacher	No.
Gene	What round purple thing?
Jeff	Button.
Jeremy	What are these?
Jeff	Buttons to compute.
Michelle	What's this?
Jeff	Buttons. Out of computer.
Jodi	I'm not in your story.
Jeff	I know. I want to make it that way.
Jodi	Why make my name?
Jeff	I want to.
Tyler	What [are the] two lines?
Jeff	I forget.
Jodi	What two dots?
Jeff	Buttons.

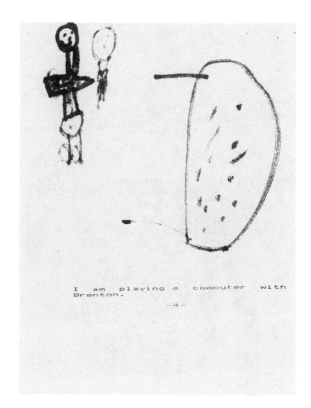

Book II, Final Copy, Page 4
Conference 3/23

John   Me see "Brenton"! See Brenton's name.
Jodi   What's that?
Jeff   Brenton.
Jodi   Who other one?
Jeff   Me.
Celeste   No Brentons coming out of computer no more. No—Buttons!
              [She accidentally said "Brentons" instead of "buttons."]
Jeff   I put back in.

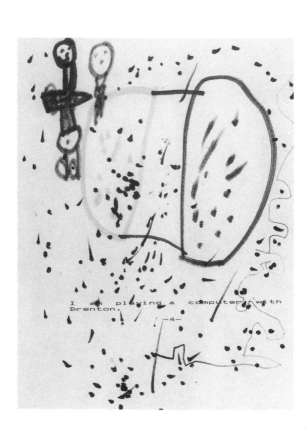

Book II, Final Copy, Page 4 revised
Conference 3/24

Teacher   What did you do to make better?
Jeff   Right here, Brenton here, tell computer how to play it.
Celeste   All dots coming out of computer—all buttons, I mean.
Jeff   Uh-Huh—I want to make that way.
Celeste   You were gonna make all buttons in—now popped out.
Michelle What black stripe?
Celeste   I know—to hold computer together.
Jodi   What's yellow?
Jeff   Computer.
Jodi   Buttons all over computer?
Jeff   Yes.
Celeste   What is black thing?
Jeff   This me, this Brenton.
Jodi   You said this you and this Brenton—that's what you said before.
Jeff   Oh no, this Brenton, this me—I make mistake last time.

Book I, First Draft, Page 1
Conference 1/12

Jodi   I put roller skates on. I happy, then I mad 'cause we not go.
Tyler   Why not go?
Gene   Her daddy's leg hurt.
Jeff   His *foot*.

Conference 1/16 A.M.
[Student] Jodi's not here.
Teacher   Read it anyway.

Book I, First Draft, Page 1, revised
Conference 1/18
[no comments]

Book I, Final Copy, Page 1
Conference 2/1
Jeff   Right there's "we." [pointed out word]
Todd   I think we went roller skating.

Book I, Final Copy, Page 1 revised
Conference 2/2
Teacher   What did you do to make better?
Jodi   Make this—wrote "Manning"—cursive.

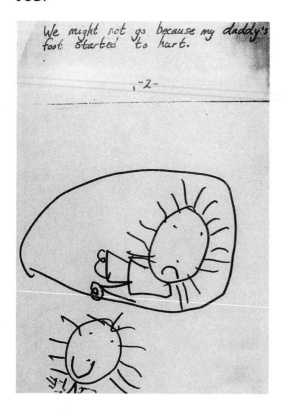

We might not go because my daddy's foot started to hart.

-2-

Book I, First Draft, Page 2
Conference 1/12

Celeste	Daddy in bed?
Jodi	Daddy on couch.
Celeste	Him laying on it.
Tyler	What is this thing around him?
Jodi	That's couch.
Jeremy	What's around head?
Jodi	Hair.

Conference 1/16 A.M.
[Jodi was absent, but her story was discussed.]

John	Me know "dad." [the word]
Tyler	What's this little thing?
Celeste	Maybe foot.
Tyler	He already have two foots.
Gene	Maybe hand?

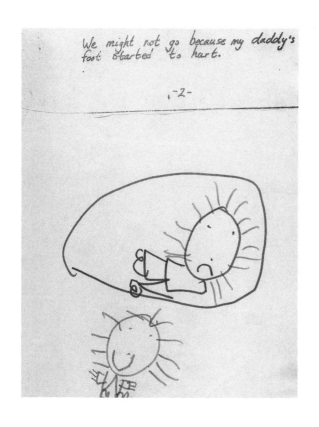

We might not go because my daddy's foot started to hart.

-2-

Book I, First Draft, Page 2 revised
Conference 1/18

Tyler	What is that, Jodi?
Jodi	Dad's foot.
Tyler	He's got three feet.
Jodi	They're his toes.

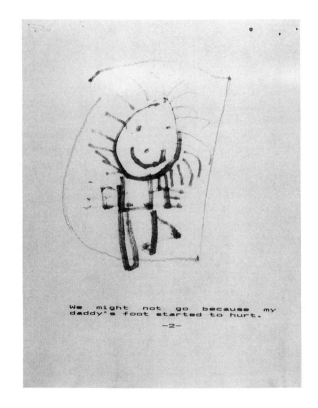

Book I, Final Copy, Page 2
Conference 2/1
Todd   Where?
Jodi   This one, that [illegible].
Todd   I mean—where are feet?
Jodi   [points]
Todd   Then where hands?
Jodi   Short ones!

Book I, Final Copy, Page 2 revised
Conference 2/2
Teacher   What did you do to make better?
Jodi   Colored this in [clothes] and put "foot."
John   What these?
Jodi   His hands.

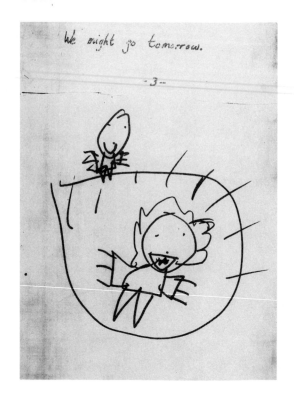

Book I, First Draft, Page 3
Conference 1/12
Jodi   I'm jumping on bed saying "Yeah! Yeah!"
John   Who other?
Jodi   Me, too.
John   Two yous?
Jodi   I'm pretending.

Conference 1/16 A.M.
[Jodi was absent, but her story was discussed.]
Todd   Her said they both her.
Gene   That's her mother.
Todd   No it's not.

[Note: During the Friday conference, Jodi said both figures were pictures of herself—one "Jodi" was what she would *want* to do—jump on the bed; the other "Jodi" was a picture of what she *really* did.]

Book I, First Draft, Page 3 revised
Conference 1/18
Celeste   Who's them?
Jodi   Both me.
Jeff   One is a fake one.
Jodi   I don't know why two.
Celeste   You forgot to put hair on one.

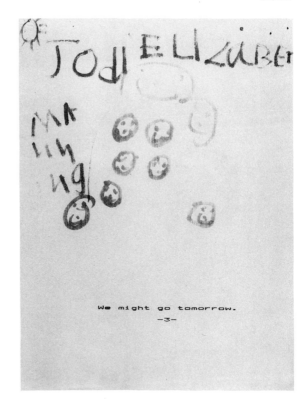

Book I, Final Copy, Page 3
Conference 2/1
Jeremy No bodies.
Tyler Nobody driving—not even a steering wheel.
Jeremy Head up top. Happy roof with face on top?
Jodi I didn't make bodies.
Jeremy I make bodies on mine.

Book I, Final Copy, Page 3 revised
Conference 2/2
Teacher What did you do to make better?
Jodi I putted hands here. The hair. A sun.

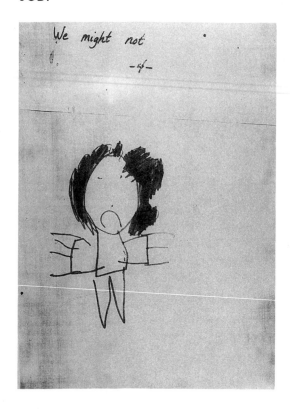

Book I, First Draft, Page 4
Conference 1/12
[no comments]

Conference 1/16 A.M.
[no comments]

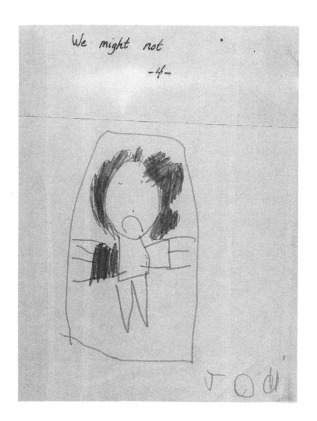

Book I, First Draft, Page 4 revised
Conference 1/18

Tyler	You could put the car on there.
John	What's that?
Jodi	Me.
Tyler	'Cause how far can you go without a car?
Jodi	I didn't go.
Tyler	How can them live in a house?
Jodi	I'm gonna make a house.
Celeste	And a car.
Jodi	Yes.
Celeste	Big or little car?
Jodi	Little.
Tyler	Car can be far away.
Jeff	Car can be on other page, far away.

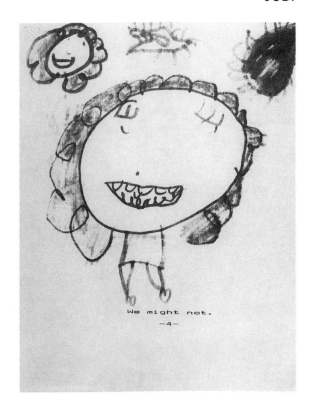

Book I, Final Copy, Page 4
Conference 2/1

John   Where you?
Celeste Oh, look at you! [eyes rolled up]
Jodi   Eyes rolled up.
John   One eye.
Brenton What's that?
Jodi   Sister.
Tyler   What are green things?
Jeremy   What are green things?
Jodi   Sun.
Tyler   There's not two suns, and anyway, not green.
Jodi   I make that way.
Todd   Just one sun!

Book I, Final Copy, Page 4 revised
Conference 2/2

Teacher What did you do to make better?
Jodi   Nothing.

Book II, First Draft, Page 1
Conference 2/23

Jeff   Like Michelle's story.

Jodi   'Cept they didn't come home.

Celeste   Her name on here.

Jeff   There "Jodi." [in writing]

Book II, First Draft, Page 1 revised
Conference 2/28

Teacher   What did you do to make better?

Jodi   I make diapers, make diaper bag and I wrote these. This an "A." I don't know why, just wrote.

Tyler   Hey, no—she didn't add diapers—they there before.

Jodi   Not these—I add these orange ones.

Tyler   They look grey.

Book II, Final Copy, Page 1
Conference 3/23

Gene	What's this, and little dots?
Jodi	Grass outside.
Gene	'Cept grass ain't round?
Jodi	I just make it. That's the door and people come inside.
John	Where are you?
Jodi	This me and my sister.
Michelle	What are these?
Jodi	Diapers.
John	Where mom?
Jodi	Here.
John	Where dad?
Jodi	Not home.
John	Where brother?
Jodi	Not home.
Michelle	Where Amy?
Jodi	Here. This my aunt. And cousin.
Jeff	What's that dot?
Jodi	Doorknob.
Tyler	What's that dots?
Jodi	Grass.
Michelle	Where dog?
Jodi	The dog on next page.
Gene	What's this?
Jodi	Diapers.

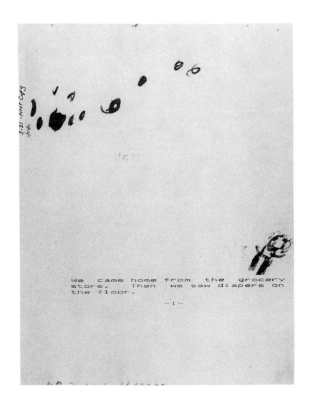

Book II, Final Copy, Page 1 revised
Conference 3/27

Teacher	What did you do to make better?
Jodi	Here's diapers. I maked diaper bag, and here's dog getting them out.
John	What that?
Jodi	Diapers.
Gene	What's that?
Jodi	Door.
Gene	Door not in story.
Jodi	Well, we're coming home and we need a door to get in.
Gene	Well, didn't write words about door.
Jodi	Don't have to—it's my story.

Book II, First Draft, Page 2
Conference 2/23

Gene I got doggy—don't bite.
Damon Hey what's this word, "R-N-T"?
Jodi That's "AMY." [Jodi has not mastered the diagonal line yet, and the diagonals in "AMY" are rendered as mostly horizontal lines.]
Damon Dog name?
Jodi NO! Dog Skippy.
Jeff What's this?
Jodi Other page.

Book II, First Draft, Page 2 revised
Conference 2/28

Teacher What did you do to make better?
Jodi Colored in mommy them I wrote "MY MOM YELLED AT DOG."
Celeste How you write "AMY" and "STEVEN"?
Jodi We have a plate hanging on wall and I used to copy it. I need to copy middle name like I used to write.
Tyler There's no plates on the wall.
Jodi It not in my story. It how I copy my name.
Tyler I thought was on the school walls.
John What's that?
Jodi My puppy. This his tongue.
Celeste Look how I didn't know how to write my name—just went like that [gestures in air]. When I at church—didn't even know name.

Book II, Final Copy, Page 2
Conference 3/23

Jeff	What's that gray thing?
Jodi	The paper my mom hitting dog with. She does that. I do too. Even sister and brother.
Jeremy	My mom does spank my dog with paper sometimes.
John	What word?
Jodi	"BACK FEET." "FRONT FEET."
John	Where puppy?
Jodi	Here.

Book II, Final Copy, Page 2 revised
Conference 3/27

Teacher	What did you do to make better?
Jodi	I make cousin Angie and my sister and me.
Michelle	What's this say?
Jodi	"Back foot, front foot."
John	What's that?
Teach	What did Jodi just say?
John	Jodi sister, she mom [cousin].

Then we ~~the~~ got the broom.
Then we sweep them.

— 3 —

Book II, First Draft, Page 3
Conference 2/23

Michelle	Where's broom?
Jodi	Here.
Jeff	What's this?
Jodi	Sky.
Celeste	What's that?
Jodi	Sky too.
Gene	Is diapers outside?
Jodi	No.
Gene	Then how you see sun?
Jodi	I just put there.
Michelle	Where's house?
Jodi	In here.
Jeff	What are these?
Jodi	Diapers.
Jeff	Yuck!
Jodi	They were clean.

Then we ~~the~~ got the broom.
Then we sweep them.

— 3 —

Book II, First Draft, Page 3 revised
Conference 2/28

Teacher	What did you do to make better?
Jodi	Colored this in and make sky. Then put red around my mom's hair.
Celeste	This was there.
Jodi	No wasn't. I maded this sky.
Celeste	It was there.
Jeremy	It was there.
Jodi	Then I make more diapers. These sticks of broom.
Michelle	What's this dot?
Jodi	That's a diaper.
Jeff	I said make it bigger.
Jeremy	I said little wee one.

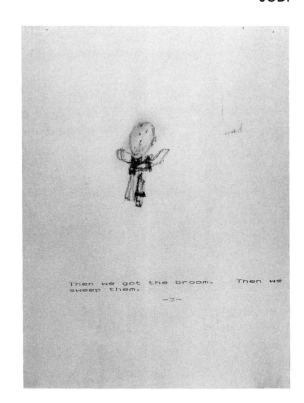

Book II, Final Copy, Page 3
Conference 3/23

Celeste	What these are?
Tyler	SWEPT diapers?
Jodi	Yes.
Tyler	I don't sweep. I just put on my baby. My dog chew up and still put them on.
Jodi	'Cept put them on, they smell like dog.
Tyler	Wash them.
Jodi	Can't.
Michelle	Where's broom?
Jodi	Right here.
Michelle	You're not holding it.
Jodi	I'm going to get it.
Michelle	If diapers everywhere they wet. And dog tongue wet.
Jodi	We swept on to dust pan. My aunt helped.
Michelle	Where aunt?
Jodi	I forgot to make.

Book II, Final Copy, Page 3 revised
Conference 3/27

Teacher	What did you do to make better?
Jodi	Put these in [more diapers] and make my aunt and mom.
Jeff	What are yellow things?
Jodi	I told you—it's a broom.
Gene	Where's the broom? What do you sweep with?
Jodi	Here.

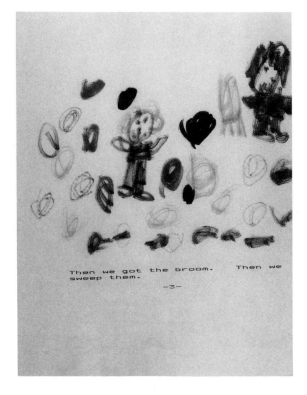

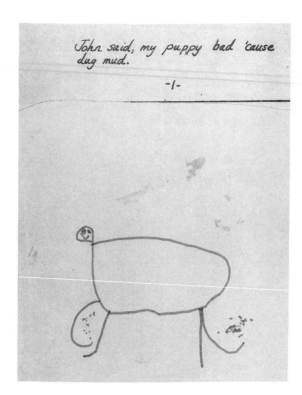

John said, my puppy bad 'cause dug mud.

-1-

Book I, First Draft, Page 1
Conference 1/12
Jeremy Where's "dug?" [again asked] Where's "DUG?" Thought name Doug.

Conference 1/16 A.M.
Celeste "DIGGED" mud.
Damon "DUG" mud.
Celeste Don't see the word.
Damon Here! My daddy's name "D-o-u-g."
Gene Why bofe of 'em have mad faces?
John Dog mad at me.
Gene I know why bofe got mad faces—dog mad at him and him mad at dog.
Tyler Is your house far far away?
Celeste You can't see edges?
John Yes.
Gene Is it soggy-foggy?
John Yes.
Teacher What happens when its foggy?
Tyler Not allowed to go outside.

John said, my puppy bad 'cause dug mud.

-1-

Book I, First Draft, Page 1 revised
Conference 1/16 P.M.
Teacher What did you do to make the picture better?
John Nothing.

Book I, Final Copy, Page 1
Conference 2/1

John   There my puppy. There me. There's grass. There a door. There floor. There you go in.

Jeff   Where dog?

Tyler   Didn't you see him point?

Book I, Final Copy, Page 1 revised
Conference 2/2

Teacher   What did you do to make better?

John   Make sun. Make window. Made door.

Tyler   Two doors.

John   Yes. Bathroom door, outside door. Colored my puppy. Puppy bite doorbell.

Brenton   What's that?

John   Doorbell. You push. New door bell.

Brenton   How do you do it?

John   Knocker. Pull up and down.

Damon   What's that?

Teacher   We already asked.

Book I, First Draft, Page 2
Conference 1/12

Jodi	How did he make his face?
John	Who?
Jodi	How dog face when mad?
Jeremy	Where's you?
John	Where's my hand?
Celeste	John mad. 'Cause mouth up-and-down.
John	Not see my house—far, far away.
Michelle	These your hands—three.
John	No, [this one is] my FOOT hand.

Book I, First Draft, Page 2 revised
Conference 1/16 P.M.

Teacher	What did you do to make the picture better?
John	Colored house. Colored hand [thumb purple].

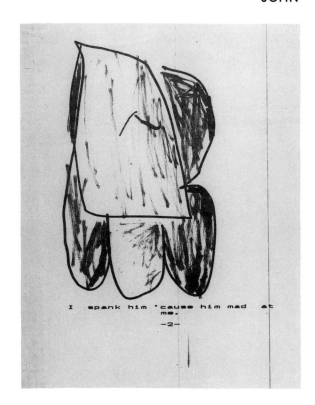

Book I, Final Copy, Page 2
Conference 2/1
John   There my hand and me not make body yet. There door. There
floor. Grass. That my house. There window.

Book I, Final Copy, Page 2 revised
Conference 2/2
Teacher   What did you do to make better?
John   There my puppy. And mad. There grass. Make bathroom,
downstairs bathroom. Front door.

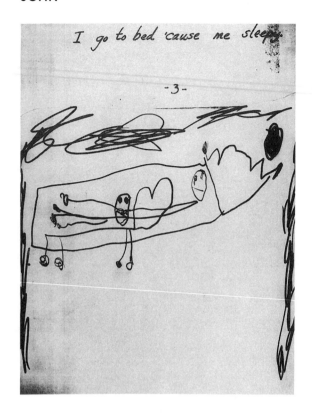

Book I, First Draft, Page 3
Conference 1/12
Jodi   Where word "sleepy"?
John   Me and mommy bed.

Conference 1/16 A.M.
Gene   What's green stuff?
John   My walls.
Gene   Brown? Maybe it pillow.

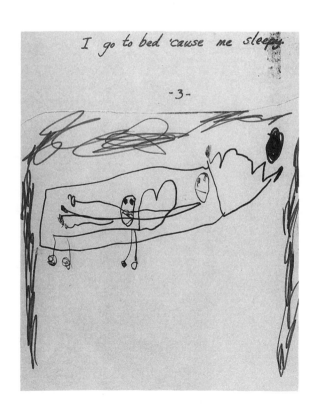

Book I, First Draft, Page 3 revised
Conference 1/16 P.M.
Teacher   What did you do to make the picture better?
John   Nothing.

Book I, Final Copy, Page 3
Conference 2/1

John   There my window. No door. There my window.
Teacher What in window?
John   Picture. Todd.
Jeff   Next when we done, when we done . . . not about story.
Gene   What orange?
John   Todd hair.
Gene   Todd hair not orange.

Book I, Final Copy, Page 3 revised
Conference 2/2

Teacher What did you do to make better?
John   There my ladder. Me go bed. There Todd, me. My bed [drew]
             and there grass. My bed far far away.
Jeremy   Todd not in story.
John   I just maked it.

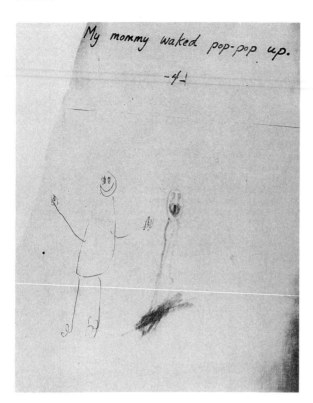

Book I, First Draft, Page 4
Conference 1/12
[no comments]

Conference 1/16 A.M.
Tyler   How can mommy be gray and pop-pop blue?
Teacher   She's blue too.
Tyler   One dark, one light.

Book I, First Draft, Page 4 revised
Conference 1/16 P.M.
Teacher   What did you do to make the picture better?
John   Nothing. Wrote "Brenton," "Gene," "John" on back.

Book I, First Draft, Back of Page 4

Book I, Final Copy, Page 4
Conference 2/1
John   There Mommy. Say "Uppy-up!" There Gene.
Gene   I not purple.

Book I, Final Copy, Page 4 revised
Conference 2/2
Teacher   What did you do to make better?
John   That pink — pop-pop nightie. Mom nightie too. Made mom say
             "Up." There Brenton's picture. Windows. [The brackets at the
             four corners of the drawing were identified as "windows."]
Tyler   Hey — I thought that Todd.
John   I change it.
Brenton   What's that?
John   My door.
Brenton   Little door.
John   My door far far away.
Damon   What's "L" ? A hook?
John   All windows. Glass in it.

My puppy bad, cause he woke me up.

Book II, First Draft, Page 1
Conference 2/23

Jodi	He's already woke up.
Todd	Nuh-uh. Dog wake him up.
Gene	Where is John's hands?
John	In there, and other no me get write my hand [sic].
Brenton	What's that?
John	My puppy.
Jeff	What is this?
John	My mom.
Jeremy	Your puppy looks like a fire.
John	Not a fire.
Gene	Where Mom's body?
John	No me make—no room.
Jeff	[I have a] Good idea—these be mom body. [the "h o h" letters]
John	No.
Jeff	Maybe mom body under covers.
John	Yes.

My puppy bad, cause he woke me up.

Book II, First Draft, Page 1 revised
Conference 2/24

Teacher	What did you do to make better?
John	Make them—snow. [large red dots]
Brenton	He made a face.
John	Yes—there beard.
Jodi	Who that?
John	Peter Rabbit.
Gene	Snow ain't red.
John	No, white.
Jodi	Peter Rabbit not in story.
John	Rabbit outside.
Jodi	Then she outside.
John	She look out window.
Jodi	Where is puppy waking you up?
John	There.
Celeste	It look like fire.

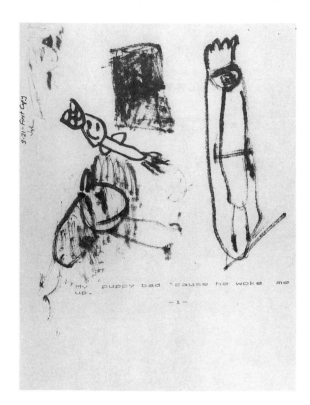

Book II, Final Copy, Page 1
Conference 3/22

John There Brenton.
Michelle He's not in story!
John I think make it.
Michelle What's that?
John Bed.
Michelle But you're supposed to be in bed if puppy woke you up.
John I in bed. Right here. My pillow.
Jeremy What's that?
John My mom. Laughing.
Jeremy What's brown thing on doggie?
John That bird, two birds. My birds break out of cage.
Jodi What around puppy head?
John Hair.
Jodi Black thing?
John Picture of Brenton.

Book II, Final Copy, Page 1 revised
Conference 3/27

Teacher What did you do to make better?
John Colored in birds, made face.
Jodi Of who?
John Mommy.
Jodi What does it say?
Jodi Is that him—did he wake you up first?
John Puppy woke me up and I say "I have—"
Teacher Did that happen in story?
John No.
Jodi What's this?
John Bed—me in.
Jodi Is that your 'jamas you're wearing?
John Yes.
Michelle What's this say?
John "Todd love Michelle. Jodi love Todd."
Celeste What is face?
John That is Brenton.

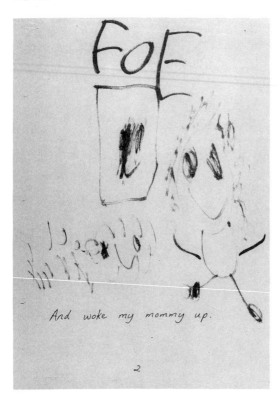

And woke my mommy up.

Book II, First Draft, Page 2
Conference 2/23

John	There mommy.
Brenton	What say? [the letters F-O-E]
John	"Jeff."
Jeff	Not my name.
John	Didn't make "Jeffrey."
Jodi	What "F-O-E"?
John	"Eat."
Michelle	"Eat" is "E-A-T."
Jeff	What's this?
John	Me face.

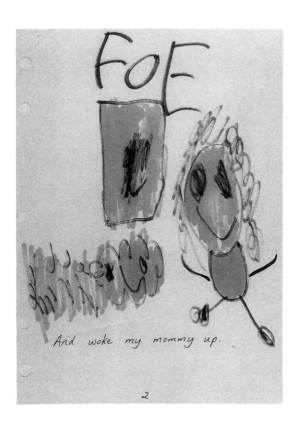

And woke my mommy up.

Book II, First Draft, Page 2 revised
Conference 2/24

Teacher	What did you do to make better?
John	Colored my puppy. Color my mom.
Jodi	This Mommy?
John	Yes.
John	I no can make feet. Me make one foot.
Brenton	I know who it is! Peter Skunk!

Book II, Final Copy, Page 2
Conference 3/22
John   There my puppy running.
Michelle What's this say?
John   "Tyler love Todd. Brenton love Jodi. Michelle love Todd."

Book II, Final Copy, Page 2 revised
Conference 3/27
Teacher   What did you do to make better?
John   Colored my mommy. This "Michelle." "Todd love Tyler."
Jodi   Where's Mommy?
John   There in bed.
Michelle What's this say?
John   "Todd love Tyler. Brenton love Michelle. Jodi love Todd. Todd
              love Michelle."
Teacher   Was that in story?
John   No.

And woke up my Pop-Pop.

3

Book II, First Draft, Page 3
Conference 2/23
John   These windows. These clothes.
Jeff   What is this?
John   Puppy.
Jeff   In pop-pop bedroom?
John   Yes.
Jeff   My dog sleep outside.
John   Hey, big one and little sleep inside. Little one woke me up. Dogs, two boys.

And woke up my Pop-Pop.

3

Book II, First Draft, Page 3 revised
Conference 2/24
Teacher What did you do to make better?
John   Color puppy.
Jodi   Did do this?
John   First time.
Jodi   That feet?
John   Them arms.
Jodi   Pop-pop have curly hair?
John   No, straight. This grass. Bottom grass. Attic.
John   This door. I no make yet face.
Gene   Them look like bones.
John   They feet. They bones.
Gene   No—they dippytoes.
Brenton What this?
John   Pop-pop mirror.

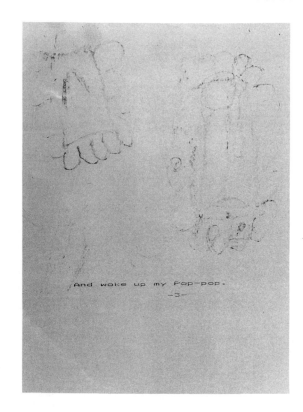

Book II, Final Copy, Page 3
Conference 3/22
John   There my pop-pop.
Jodi   What did he do, just jump on bed?
John   Yes.
Celeste   Who this on picture?
John   It's you.

Book II, Final Copy, Page 3 revised
Conference 3/27
Teacher   What did you do to make better?
John   Colored in.
Jodi   Is that your pop-pop?
John   Yes.
Jodi   Why do you have a picture of me hanging in his room when he
doesn't even know me?
Michelle   What's that?
John   My puppy.

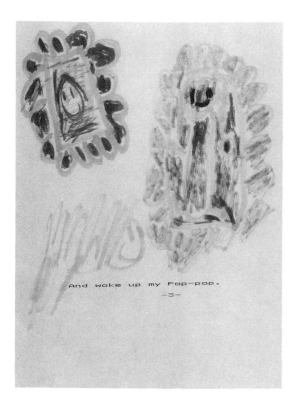

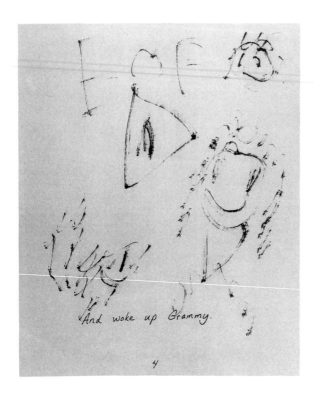

Book II, First Draft, Page 4
Conference 2/23
John   There Granny.
Jodi   They live with you?
John   Yes.
Jeremy   What word? [the letters E-O-F]
John   "Wash."

Book II, First Draft, Page 4 revised
Conference 2/24
Teacher What did you do to make better?
Gene   What that?
John   Peter Rabbit.
Gene   What you looking at?
John   My puppy jumping down steps.
Jodi   Who this?
John   Me.
Jodi   No body?
John   No room.
Jodi   Can make it a little.
John   Maybe.

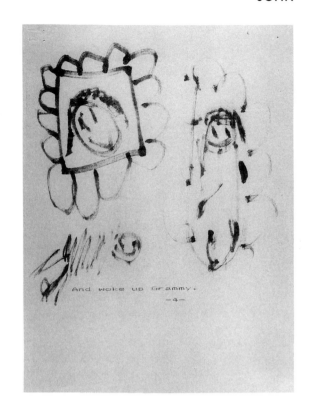

Book II, Final Copy, Page 4
Conference 3/22

Celeste	Who this?
John	Jodi kiss Celeste.
Tyler	What's this one?
John	My puppy again.
Jodi	What thing flying through air?
John	Puppy.
Jodi	Other thing?
John	Grammie. Happy. Puppy jumped on her. My puppy fly— do this.
Jeff	What that picture?
John	Jodi.

Book II, Final Copy, Page 4 revised
Conference 3/27

Teacher	What did you do to make better?
John	Draw that in—not color in yet.
Jodi	Who's that on wall?
John	Celeste.
Jodi	Who's that?
John	My puppy.
Michelle	Where is wall? Where is floor?
John	No me draw yet.
Jodi	Or don't you want to draw it?
John	Me want draw—no time draw yet.

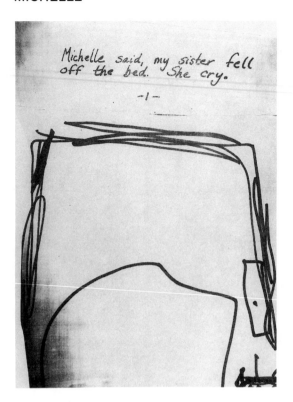

Michelle said, my sister fell off the bed. She cry.

— 1 —

Book I, First Draft, Page 1
Conference 1/13
John   Where bed?
Tyler   That's a big bed.
Gene   Red thing on edge of bed?
Michelle   Jammies hanging on bed. Tree I see on my window.
Celeste   What's that?
Michelle   Baby sister.

Conference 1/16 A.M.
Michelle   She was being "pinky."

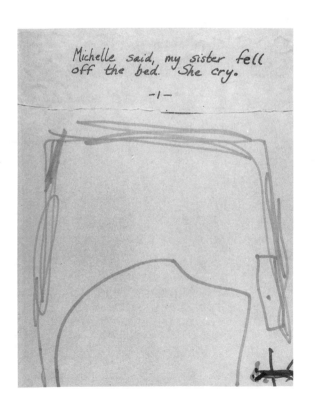

Michelle said, my sister fell off the bed. She cry.

— 1 —

Book I, First Draft, Page 1 revised
Conference 1/16 P.M.
Teacher   What did you do to make the picture better?
Michelle   I forgot to make pillows.

Book I, Final Copy, Page 1
Conference 2/1
Celeste There's a playpen.
Michelle No it's a crib. We don't have a playpen. That's why Marilyn broke it.
Gene What's that?
Michelle Light.
Todd What's that?
Michelle Marcella. That's her jammies that doesn't fit her.
Gene Looks like little man.
Michelle Huh-uh that's a wheel on crib. She's crying.
Brenton What's that?
Michelle Strawberry Shortcake pillow.

Book I, Final Copy, Page 1 revised
Conference 2/2
Teacher What did you do to make better?
Michelle Marcella's changing [table]. And made crib.

Book I, First Draft, Page 2
Conference 1/13
John   Where mom? Where you?
Teacher   [That's the] Shirt you wear to school.

Conference 1/16 A.M.
Jeremy   Same shirt. Same shirt again.
Michelle   She being green.

Book I, First Draft, Page 2 revised
Conference 1/16 P.M.
Teacher   What did you do to make the picture better?
Michelle   The house—drew it.

Book I, Final Copy, Page 2
Conference 2/1
Gene   What's green thing?
Michelle My couch.
Gene   Slippers.
Michelle No — sneakers.

Book I, Final Copy, Page 2 revised
Conference 2/2
Teacher   What did you do to make better?
Michelle Nothing.

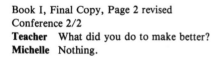

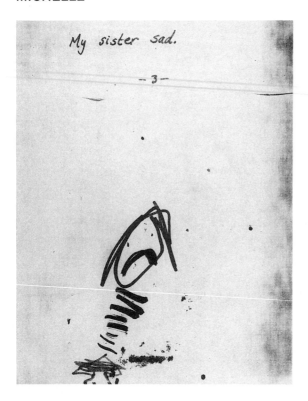

Book I, First Draft, Page 3
Conference 1/13
[Drew shirts she and Marilyn wear to school.]

Conference 1/16 A.M.
Michel [pointed out shirt differences—lines horizontal and have white stripe. Other shirt slanted like one she had on today]

Book I, First Draft, Page 3 revised
Conference 1/16 P.M.
Teacher　What did you do to make the picture better?
Michelle　My ponytails, headband, window, chimney, and snow.

Book I, Final Copy, Page 3
Conference 2/1
Michelle She wearing short sleeves. She wasn't supposed to wear red short sleeves.

Book I, Final Copy, Page 3 revised
Conference 2/2
Teacher What did you do to make better?
Michelle Made snow. The floor.
Damon What are things up there?
Michelle Snow.
Damon Never seen like that.
Michelle Just made it.
Celeste What green things?
Michelle Sofa—colored it.
John What red in hair?
Michelle Just made it.
Brenton What's that?
Michelle That's her pillow. When she grow up she go in that bed.
Tyler That your pillow yesterday.

Book I, First Draft, Page 4
Conference 1/13
John   Where you mom?
Celeste   Where sister?

Conference 1/16 A.M.
[no comments]

Book I, First Draft, Page 4 revised
Conference 1/16 P.M.
Teacher   What did you do to make the picture better?
Michelle   Make snow and window and door and green things on mom's
    shirt.

Book I, Final Copy, Page 4
Conference 2/1
Gene   What's that?
Michelle Crib.
Gene   Why brown, was pink.
Michelle No it's brown—that Marcella's jammies.

Book I, Final Copy, Page 4 revised
Conference 2/2
Teacher   What did you do to make better?
Michelle Gave Marcella black hair—when she grow up gonna be blonde.

MICHELLE

Book II, First Draft, Page 1
Conference 2/23

John	Should be "*with* diapers."
Michelle	I just wanted to say that.
Brenton	What's that?
Michelle	Diapers. Diaper box.
John	What's that yellow thing?
Michelle	Diapers and bed.
John	What that?
Michelle	Diaper box. Called Pampers.
Jodi	Diapers is on bed?
Michelle	Uh huh.
Jeff	What long black line?
Michelle	My hand, to get diapers out.
Jodi	Other hand go like that?
Michelle	Yes.
Jodi	'Cept that one shorter?
Michelle	I playing with hand tuck in shirt.
Jodi	One grow longer?
Michelle	No, just tuck in shirt.
Celeste	How baby don't have no feet?
Michelle	Just want have no feet.
Gene	Where fingers?
Michelle	Didn't draw.

Book II, First Draft, Page 1 revised
Conference 2/24

Teacher	What did you do to make better?
Michelle	Get arms longer. More diapers. Wrote "S-U-N-day."
Brenton	What's block?
Michelle	My bedroom.
John	What that purple?
Michelle	That a diaper.
Gene	You mean you got purple diapers?
Michelle	No I wanted purple.
Gene	Why you not color brown? That more better. It look like diapers.
John	Why you make diapers?
Michelle	I little—only 1 [year old]—and throw them down.
John	What that lines?
Michelle	I don't know. I was little and didn't know what them are.
Jodi	What's this?
Michelle	Diapers. I broke the diapers.
Jodi	That looks like something you ride on. This a book?
Michelle	No—my arms.
Gene	What little dots?
Michelle	Diapers I make in a circle.
Gene	'Cept them pop open.
Michelle	No they won't—they sticky and have tape on.
Celeste	I didn't make my bed and my blanket was like this.
Jeremy	What's this?
Michelle	I told you two times! That's ceiling.
Celeste	You said was your bedroom.
Michelle	Ceiling, wall, wall, floor [she points to each part].

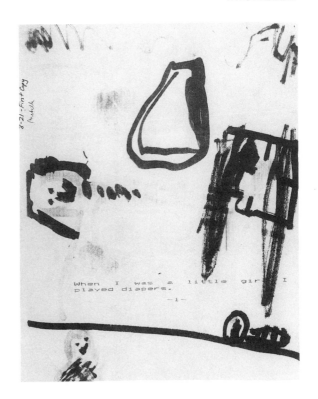

Book II, Final Copy, Page 1
Conference 3/23

John	Played diapers! Bad, bad, bad.
Michelle	I 1 year old.
Jeremy	Who's this?
Michelle	Me and sister Marilyn.
Celeste	Her was little baby?
Michelle	No, she came first and she was 2 years old then. November 24 her birthday, November 25 my birthday.
Teacher	Have same birthday.
Michelle	Yes, but I want Marilyn to be 2 there.
Jeff	What's that?
Michelle	Light.
Tyler	What purple stuff?
Michelle	My ceiling.
Jeremy	What's that?
Michelle	My curtains—long time ago—old curtains.
Celeste	What's that?
Michelle	Part curtain broke.
Teacher	Where's drapes?
Michelle	Under curtain. I didn't make them.

Book II, Final Copy, Page 1 revised
Conference 4/2

Teacher	What did you do to make better?
Michelle	Make big light in room.
Brenton	Did you really play diapers?
Michelle	Yes long time ago I did.

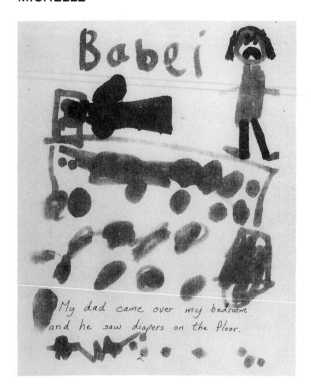

Book II, First Draft, Page 2
Conference 2/23
Gene   Where dad?
Michelle Here.
Jeremy   He mad.
Jeff   No he sad.
Gene   Where pillow?
Michelle Here.
Gene   Where bed?
Michelle Here.
Brenton   What's that?
Michelle Diapers. Did like this, to rip them.
Todd   Why no wheel on this side?
Michelle Sister Marilyn broke it.

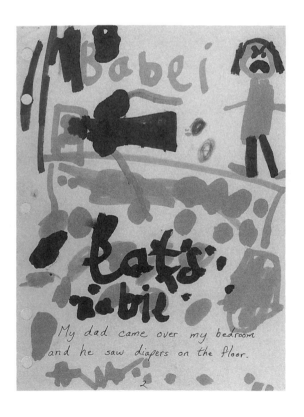

Book II, First Draft, Page 2 revised
Conference 2/24
Teacher   What did you do to make better?
Michelle Spelled "Barbie."
John   What that?
Michelle I mess my "B" up.
Brenton   What's that?
Michelle Diapers and that's me.
Jodi   What's this?
Michelle My bed.
Jodi   What's it say?
Michelle I told you already I mess my "B" up. I don't know. Didn't know
              what blue was. Didn't know what was 'cause I little.

Book II, Final Copy, Page 2
Conference 3/23

Michelle	I was hiding in bathroom too.
Celeste	What's that say?
Michelle	"I love Gene."
Jodi	Ooh—I hear her say I love him!
Jodi	What's brown thing?
Michelle	Daddy.
Jodi	Is he a "I"?
Jodi	Like "I." Looks like "J" now.
Celeste	Like "4."
Michelle	Is a "Y."

Book II, Final Copy, Page 2 revised
Conference 4/2

Teacher	What did you do to make better?
Michelle	I wrote "Love," made heart, made bedroom light.
Tyler	Bedroom night light?
Michelle	Yes, but I don't got anymore.
Tyler	I used to have little pink night light but don't work no more.
Jeremy	What's this?
Michelle	I smash my bed.
Damon	Beds don't smash, them have mattresses on.
Brenton	Where's your mom?
Michelle	She at work—she don't work no more—just daddy work in Lebanon.

Book II, First Draft, Page 3
Conference 2/23

Jeff   Nah—nah.
Michelle   Yes! I went under bed.
Gene   Why diapers under bed with you?
Michelle   Because diapers had to go under there. I put them there to let daddy not see.
Gene   'Cept daddy can see falling down.
Michelle   He looking down. I baby. [Made balloon with words in it, "Go back to bed."]
Jeff   Maybe Michelle dad thinking.
Michelle   No, I was there—Daddy thought I under pillow. You don't know where my sister Marilyn.
Teach   Where is she?
Celeste   In hospital sick.

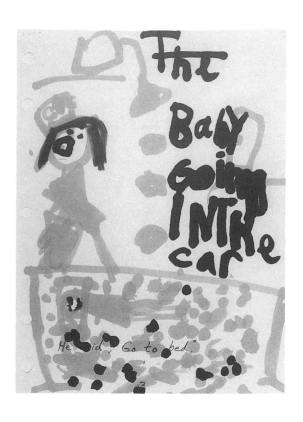

Book II, First Draft, Page 3 revised
Conference 2/24

Teacher   What did you do to make better?
Michelle   Made more diapers.
Jodi   Who's this?
Michelle   My dad.
Jodi   What this say?
Michelle   "Barbie goes in a car." That's crossed cause doesn't sound right.
Jodi   Sounds right.
Michelle   I didn't know that.
Brenton   What's this?
Michelle   That's me.
Tyler   What red things?
Michelle   I told you—dirty diapers. [Jumping up and down] I told you!
Jeff   What's this?
Michelle   My diaper thing and diapers coming down.
Todd   What's this?
Michelle   Me and my blue eyes.

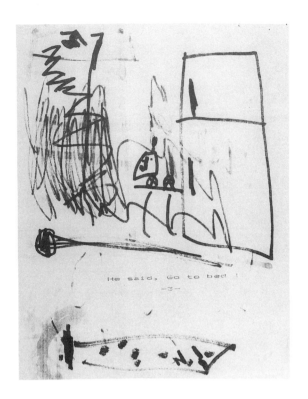

Book II, Final Copy, Page 3
Conference 3/23

Michelle I didn't go bed. I run under bed.

Jodi Is that "Amy" in cursive?

Michelle No. That's refrigerator in our room. I making mashed potatoes and I FIRED everything [burnt?]. That's crack where I did that.

Jeremy Why you have messy hair?

Michelle I went to bed and put pillow under head.

Jodi What's that?

Michelle That's fire.

Teacher Who's missing?

Michelle Daddy. He put himself in the refrigerator.

Celeste I see something here.

Michelle That's a sink and refrigerator.

Damon He could get fire extinguisher and push button down and fire go out.

Book II, Final Copy, Page 3 revised
Conference 4/2

Teacher What did you do to make better?

Michelle Draw my sister under bed. She didn't comb her hair right.

Brenton I thought that was you.

Michelle That *was* me, but I went to bathroom to hide.

Brenton Where's bathroom?

Michelle He shut door.

Brenton Where's bed?

Michelle Here's door—far far away

Brenton Why door far away?

Michelle Big room.

Tyler Why a huge bed?

Michelle I just got a new bed—it's bigger.

MICHELLE

He spanked me.

Book II, First Draft, Page 4
Conference 2/23
Jodi   Was real story?
Michelle Yes.
Jodi   Really spank?
Michelle Yes.
Gene   You must be bad girl.
Michelle No—I just 1 year old, I don't understand.
Todd   I UNDERSTAND when I a baby.
Jodi   My cousin only 1 year, she don't understand.

He spanked me.

Book II, First Draft, Page 4 revised
Conference 2/24
Teacher   What did you do to make better?
Michelle Make my lights. 'Cause that's my living room.
Jodi   You make this.
Michelle Made yesterday.
Jeremy   When my mom spank me I don't cry.
Jeff   What's red?
Michelle My ceiling.
Jodi   What box?
Michelle My suitcase to get ready to come to my house.
Jodi   Not in your story.
Michelle My mom put it there. I stay at my grandma.
Jodi   You said my house.
Michelle I made a mistake, so excu-u-se me!

Book II, Final Copy, Page 4
Conference 3/23

Jodi Who brown thing?
Michelle My mommy, she spank me. Daddy spank me.
Teach Where's dad?
Michelle Cousins in my living room.
Jodi What's brown thing?
Michelle His hand—long—he's 37 years old.
Jeremy Why spanking you?
Teacher What story say?
Jeremy Playing diapers.
Celeste What's that?
Michelle My tears.
Tyler What's that?
Michelle My bed.
Jeff What's that?
Michelle My dad long hair.
Tyler What's that on other page?
Michelle Daddy's long hair.
Gene When you go in army you have to get a buzz. They give you haircut and all hair come off.
Michelle I know—he was starting go in army.

Book II, Final Copy, Page 4 revised
Conference 4/2

Teacher What did you do to make better?
Michelle Made diapers.
Damon Can I see what's back?
Brenton Diapers ain't green.
Michelle I want to make it green.
Brenton Why?
Michelle I make diapers green—I colored, I have crayons at my house.
Teacher Real story?
Michelle No, I just make that way.
Brenton You should make white diapers.
Michelle I didn't color long ago.
Gene She can't make white—[because] paper white.
Damon She could use black and not color in.
Michelle That my mom hand to spank me.
Brenton You said Daddy spank you.
Michelle Mom just came home and Dad looking for Marilyn.
Celeste What's this?
Michelle That's the diaper I squish really hard.
Brenton If door is teeny can't get through it.
Michelle My bathroom, the whole way [hallway?], hall, living room.
Celeste It look like small in living room and when get close looks big.

225

Todd said, I love you.

-1-

Book I, First Draft, Page 1
Conference 1/13
Gene   Oh—you love kisses. 'Cause he love kisses.
John   Purple hearts.
Celeste   If put heart, you love.
Todd   Love mom and dad.
Gene   That's maybe they love you. Gene said all mom and dad DON'T love kids.
Michelle Don't know if mom and dad don't love.
Damon   At our house they sure do.
Jeff   Yes—some mom and dad DON'T love kids.
Tyler   What about if you're bad. Don't love you if bad but love if good.
Brenton   Think some mom and dad don't love boys and girls—all daddies DO love, moms DON'T love.
Celeste   All LOVE.

Conference 1/16 A.M.
Tyler   He loves kisses.
Todd   No.
Gene   You love kisses and that's why you draw hearts.
Todd   NO!
Celeste   No—mom and daddy.
Gene   One for Mom, one for dad—and black one for you. See—you love kisses.
Todd   No I don't—I just put for mom and dad.

Todd said, I love you.

-1-

Book I, First Draft, Page 1 revised
Conference 1/16 P.M.
Teacher   What did you do to make the picture better?
Todd   Beds. Ladders. Spare room.

[*Note*: Most of Todd's revisions to Book 1, First Draft, are not shown; he used the blank facing pages of his book.]

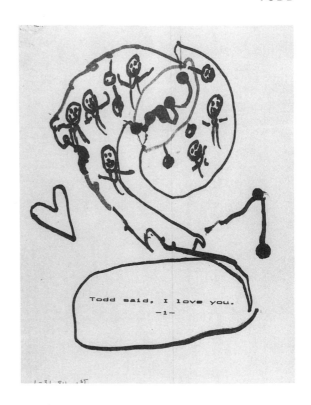

Book I, Final Copy, Page 1
Conference 2/1

Jeff   I know when Todd loves kisses? 'Cause Todd all time kiss Jodi.
Todd   Only one time.
Brenton   What's that?
Todd   A baseball park.
Michelle   What's these?
Todd   Lights.
John   What's that?
Todd   A road.
Celeste   What's pink stuff?
Todd   That's outside of it.
Celeste   Green and orange stuff?
Todd   That's the house.

Book I, Final Copy, Page 1 revised
Conference 2/2

Teacher   What did you do to make better?
Todd   Make houses and pipes.
Jodi   That's not about the story.
Todd   That home.

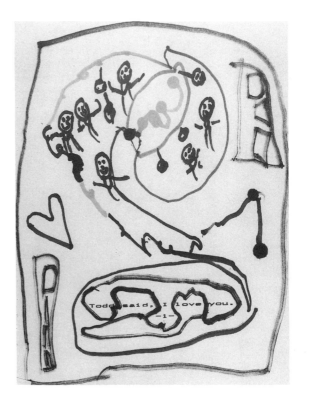

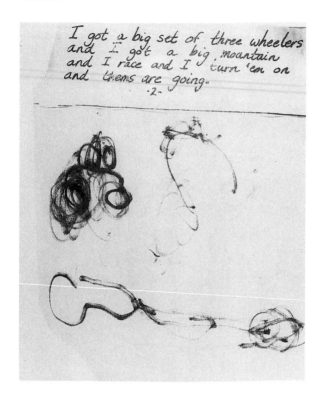

I got a big set of three wheelers
and I got a big mountain
and I race and I turn 'em on
and thems are going.
-2-

Book I, First Draft, Page 2
Conference 1/13

John Where kids?
Todd No kids.
John What's racing?
Jeff I know—stompers. Stompers can be cars or trucks.
          Conference 1/16 A.M.
Jeff He talk about one go up, one go under, one push 'nother one.
Gene Where cars?
Gene What's that?
Todd Bridge.
Gene Big hill?
Todd Here!

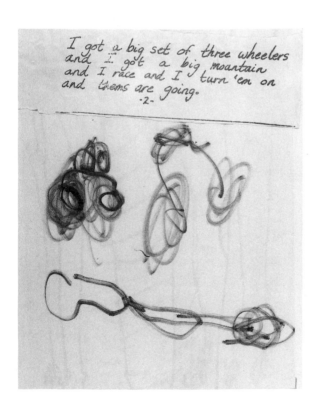

I got a big set of three wheelers
and I got a big mountain
and I race and I turn 'em on
and thems are going.
-2-

Book I, First Draft, Page 2 revised
Conference 1/16 P.M.

Teacher What did you do to make the picture better?
Todd Me, Daddy and Mom having a fight. Not saying nothing, just fighting. Tickling and wrestling.
Teacher Laughing?
Todd No.
Teacher Mom feels?
Todd Funny.
Teacher Dad feels?
Todd Funny.
Teacher You feel?
Todd Don't watch. Playing upstairs on mom and dad's bed. Jumping on them's bed.

Book I, Final Copy, Page 2
Conference 2/1

Todd	Steps and bathrooms and brick.
Brenton	What's that?
Todd	Sky and black are moon and sky covering moon and one go here and sun go down.
Gene	What's that?
Todd	My toy. Need to be big 'cause *is* big.
Celeste	What's that?
Todd	Doorknobs for bathrooms.
John	What's that?
Todd	The floor.
Gene	Why make that so little?
Todd	'Cause no room for 'em.

Book I, Final Copy, Page 2 revised
Conference 2/2

Teacher	What did you do to make better?
Todd	Moon coming out right here, and the pipes and this sun.
Michelle	You tell us yesterday.
Todd	I know—this different, it coming up.
Jodi	You didn't make hair on people.
Todd	I know, I not do it.
Damon	Maybe went to hairdresser and got all hair cut off.
Todd	No. Them have hair.

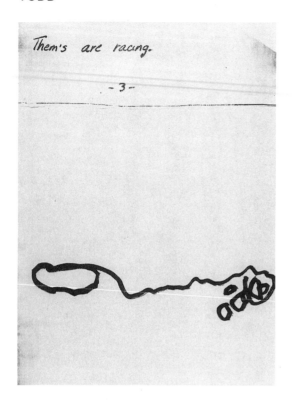

Book I, First Draft, Page 3
Conference 1/13
Gene   Right there's motorcycle.
Todd   This one going up, one under.

Conference 1/16 A.M.
John   Where car?
Gene   Look like motor cycle.
Todd   Don't have none.
Gene   Well, looks like.

Book I, First Draft, Page 3 revised
Conference 1/16 P.M.
Todd   Daddy have big legs goin' down here. Mom have big legs, go down, then I have big legs.
Teacher   What's good about big legs?
Todd   Get on bed.
Teacher   Added?
Todd   House.

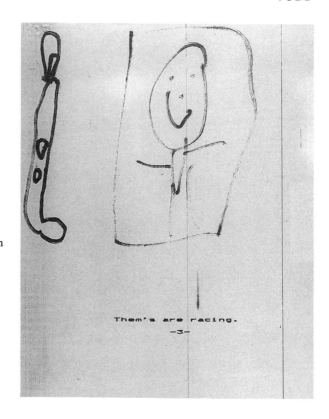

Book I, Final Copy, Page 3
Conference 2/1

Gene   What's this big thing?
Todd   Them's racing.
Celeste What's that?
Todd   Floor. Them's racing and I lay on floor and fix 'em and put 'em back on racing.

Book I, Final Copy, Page 3 revised
Conference 2/2

Teacher   What did you do to make better?
Todd   Colors. Floor blue lines. This red is box.
Brenton   That ain't in story.
Todd   I got this for Christmas and this Christmas box [race track came in].
Damon   But why didn't he say tracks in Christmas box?
Todd   'Cause I take it out and Dad putted it together.
Michelle What's blue?
Todd   Floor.

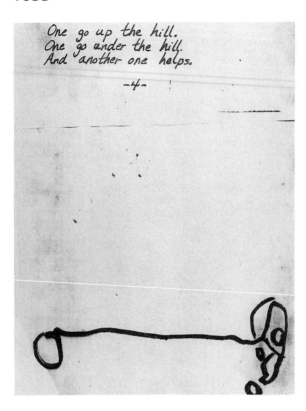

Book I, First Draft, Page 4
Conference 1/13
John   Where helps?
Todd   This one.
John   Where come out?
Damon   Guess what my dad's gettin' me?

Conference 1/16 A.M.
Tyler   Where one under?
Todd   These two same, this one different.

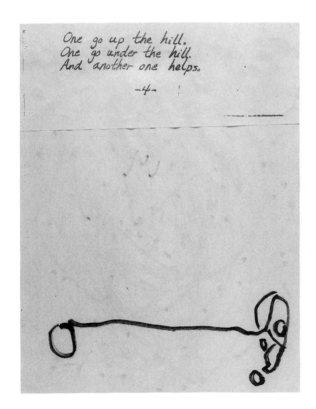

Book I, First Draft, Page 4 revised
Conference 1/16 P.M.
Teacher What did you do to make the picture better?
Todd   Drew tall bed with just mom on. Dad not climbing up yet.
Teacher Where are you?
Todd   Downstairs.

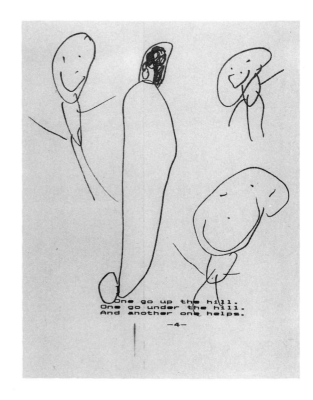

Book I, Final Copy, Page 4
Conference 2/1

Todd   Right here circles — one going in, that one underneath that go
            up. Then go down, down, down.
Damon   What's that?
Todd   Racers.

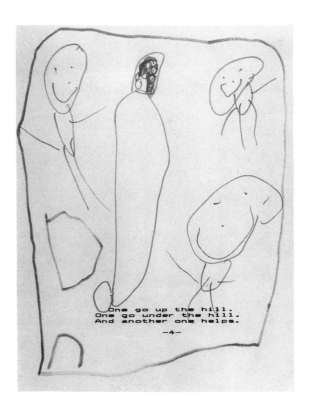

Book I, Final Copy, Page 4 revised
Conference 2/2

Teacher What did you do to make better?
Todd   Make a mouse hole. I mean it's a door and window.
Damon   That's a mouse window and door.
Todd   No — I just have one in bathroom downstairs.
Jodi   What does story say? He didn't write hair on there.
Todd   Uh-huh — pointy things is hair.

Book II, First Draft, Page 1
Conference 2/23

Celeste	He have cave girl—like cave man.
Jeff	Like cave girl and cave sister.
Todd	Her not with us—her in our house.
Jeff	What is these?
Todd	Feet.
Jeff	Little dinosaur feet.
Todd	Looked at book to draw.

Book II, First Draft, Page 1 revised
Conference 2/27

Teacher	What did you do to make better?
Todd	Made rainbow [with tape].
Jodi	How?
Todd	With tape. Put roll like that.
Jeremy	Where's tape?
Todd	What tape? Don't know.
Teach	What else?
Todd	Made words. Names dinosaurs. Found words in book.
Gene	What's that circle?
Todd	Thems are our caves.
Gene	How you get in?
Todd	Here are our door.
Gene	It's little!
Todd	Far, far away.
Gene	Caves ain't purple.
Todd	Wallpaper.
Gene	Where you get paper? No stores at where dinosaurs at.
Todd	Yes. Dinosaur store.
Gene	No. Dinosaurs eat off of trees.
Todd	I know—thems have different ones. Him a store one.
Teacher	What paper made of?
Todd	Skin.
Gene	These have black skin.
Tyler	Black.
Michelle	Green.
Jeff	Brown.
Todd	White skin. Them put stuff—paint in it.
Gene	No paint at dinosaur.
Todd	We have pet and we ride on him when go store. When us have snow us go to Mt. Joy 'cause them don't let dinosaurs in Mt. Joy.
Michelle	No wonder you don't have dinosaurs at Mt. Joy. I didn't see none at Mt. Joy. Todd got them away.

Book II, Final Copy, Page 1
Conference 3/22
Jodi   Is that a cave man?
Todd   No that us pets—Peppie.
Jodi   What's that stuff?
Todd   Crocodinosaur. Mousey Mousey [in picture—*Mousey Mousey* is
             a toy]. That my dad with sunglasses. I'm here. Here mom.
Jodi   That a monkey?
Todd   No, Peppie.
Jodi   Where cave?
Todd   Here. Crocodinosaur, two-headed dinosaur.
Gene   What if two-headed want to go two different ways?

Book II, Final Copy, Page 1 revised
Conference 4/2
Teacher What did you do to make better?
Todd   Make furry, hairy [gave a texture to the paper by rubbing the
             marker repeatedly over the same spot]—this is Mousey Mousey
             friend.
Teacher Who's Mousey Mousey?
Todd   Car.
Tyler   I have one—it's a toy.
Todd   Make 'nother animal.
Brenton What's this?
Todd   Two-headed. Body.
Michelle But that was too sticky.
Brenton But that don't make your story better.
Todd   I knew it—I just did it.
Brenton Why did you do it?
Todd   I do it first but then I don't do anymore.
Brenton Did he copy off Damon?
Todd   No—Damon copy off me.
Tyler   Hey I thought these heads.
Todd   Two heads. Him turn around.
Tyler   Whose face?
Todd   That is face. Them's animals—them have two faces.
Jeremy   They were there before.
Todd   This part wasn't. That's my dad's beard.
Celeste Todd said this was dad other day.
Todd   Him moves on faces—that beard moves—it alive.
Tyler   What's this?
Todd   Nothing—it's his house.
Tyler   Don't look like a house.
Todd   We live underground.
Tyler   One devil live underground.
Damon   And he have lots of kids underground with him.
Tyler   Only one devil in whole world.
Damon   Well, kid devil.
Celeste He have a wife,
Todd   I read in Bible, and only one.
Damon   Well, my Grandmother say he have lots of kids.
Tyler   She not right.
Damon   Well I have big Bible . . .
Celeste I went to church and I looked at book about devils—them
             didn't have any NO kids and NO husbands—just one BOY devil
             and I'm a GIRL.
Michelle Who's this?
Todd   A helper.
Michelle Well what's his name?
Todd   I don't care what's his name.

Book II, First Draft, Page 2
Conference 2/23

Jeff	Yuck. I never eat dinosaur.
John	Real story?
Todd	[Nods head yes]
John	Who did it with you?
Todd	Daddy. Mom cooking.
John	She cook dinosaur? She cut?
Todd	No.
Jodi	You're 'posed to cut if too big for pot.
Michelle	Have to cut head out, get teeth out.
Todd	Us just hit it with hand and he fall down.
Celeste	You have tooth soup?
Todd	No—take out when cook.
Gene	You get whole lot of money from tooth fairy.
Michelle	What's this?
Todd	All kinds of dinosaurs. 'Cept people. That mom, dad, and me. Make bird up here.
Tyler	Only you and mom and dad. That's all? No brother and sister?
Todd	All my friends. Birds is my friend and fat ones we eat. Others my friends.
Damon	What they?
Todd	Little dinosaurs peoples.

Book II, First Draft, Page 2 revised
Conference 2/27

Teacher	What did you do to make better?
Todd	Make more dinosaurs, more bird dinosaurs, dragons.

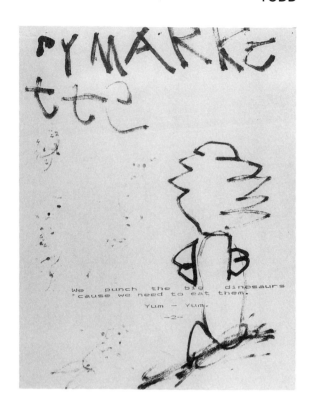

Book II, Final Copy, Page 2
Conference 3/22

Jodi   What does "Yum-yum" mean?
Todd   We like dinosaur.
Teacher Who's this?
Todd   Mom, dad, Todd punching dinosaur.
Jodi   This a real story, Todd?
Todd   Yes. Real. We just ride on them.
Jodi   You didn't answer my question.
Todd   Just mom and dad not real—rest is.
Teacher Really?
Todd   No, not true, just ride dinosaurs little bit. My robot one. My robot one have little friend and never see him. I go out late at night and see him. 'Cept when my dad work late, then he might see him. I never do when Dad works. I have secret tunnel under bed, I go out and look at dinosaur. Go whole way down under couch. Can't do alone, I call one friends and them help me.

Book II, Final Copy, Page 2 revised
Conference 4/2

Teacher What did you do to make better?
Todd   Draw more dinosaurs—I mean more people.
Gene   What's that?
Todd   That's us.
Damon   Todd, do you have a tunnel under your bed for real?
Todd   Yeah.
Damon   Do you go to Hawaii where dinosaurs are? It's hot there and lava keep them warm.
Tyler   There's no dinosaurs in whole wide world.
Damon   I know—volcanoes kill them off.
Gene   What's this?
Tyler   Bird.
Gene   'Cept bird ain't in your story.
Todd   Dinosaur bird.
Gene   Ain't no dinosaur birds.
Todd   I make that way.
Celeste What's that say?
Todd   Nothing [a word he has copied from the magic marker].

Book II, First Draft, Page 3
Conference 2/23

Todd   Here is dinosaur.
Jeff   'Cept you kill that one?
Todd   No, our friend.
John   Did you [the teacher] tell to put "yum-yum"?
Teacher No—I write on board.

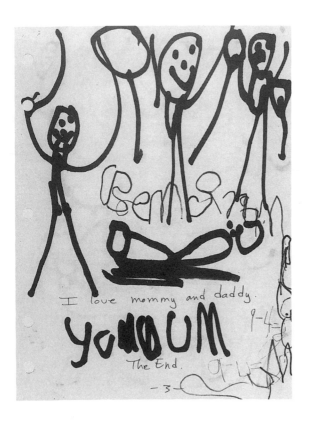

Book II, First Draft, Page 3 revised
Conference 2/27

Teacher What did you do to make better?
Todd   Made 'nother name dinosaur. I don't know—that's cursive. [Ben Franklin, copied from the cigar box in which the magic markers are kept.] This is him pet—Ben Franklin.
Jeff   What this say?
Todd   "Yum-yum."

Book II, Final Copy, Page 3
[This is another version of Page 3, which was produced after the conference for First Draft, Page 3. There is no conference associated with it, but the added words are incorporated into the text of the Final Copy.]

[The Xerox copy is not available for this page.]
Book II, First Draft, Page 3
Conference 3/22

Todd	[Everyone clapping; hands over ears] I don't like it.
Jeremy	What's that?
Todd	"L."
Jodi	Who are the people?
Todd	Me. Dad. Mom.
Jodi	You should be this one.
Todd	No 'cause I bigger than mom. When I be bigger. Everybody have nail in their foot.

Book II, Final Copy, Page 3 revised
Conference 4/2

Teacher	What did you do to make better?
Todd	Made big dinosaur that we eating. Here's big body and here's neck—him alive—here's face—him happy.
Teacher	What's in your hands?
Todd	We holding hands.

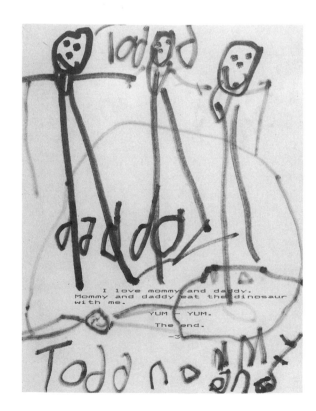

Book I, First Draft, Page 1
Conference 1/12
Jeremy Where's snow?
Jodi What's thing in sky?
Tyler Snow too.

Conference 1/16 A.M.
Jeremy I like it when snows.

Book I, First Draft, Page 1 revised
Conference 1/16 P.M.
Teacher What did you do to make the picture better?
Tyler Make me.

Book I, Final Copy, Page 1
Conference 2/1

John Where snow?

Tyler Don't you see!

Celeste Green?! It supposed to be white.

Tyler But then you wouldn't see any circles.

Todd and

Celeste If blue paper could use white.

Tyler Besides we don't got white markers.

Jodi You could leave white.

Tyler Oh. Was gonna make Christmas tree but upside down. I don't know what words say when you would start at other end. [i.e., if turned paper upside down]

[Jeff is staring off into space.]

Teacher What thinking about?

Jeff John's story.

Teacher Really.

Jeff Going outside.

Book I, Final Copy, Page 1 revised
Conference 2/2

Teacher What did you do to make better?

Tyler Snowing.

Teacher Where? What else?

Tyler Colored in. Made a window.

Jeremy Christmas tree not yellow.

Tyler Not a tree.

Book I, First Draft, Page 2
Conference 1/12
Michelle Has name on.
Celeste No snow coming down.
Teacher Do you need snow?
Tyler Yes.

Conference 1/16 A.M.
Jeremy Orange snowman.
Tyler No! That's me, the gray one is snowman.
Damon Guess what I had supper last night?
Teacher Not talking about now.

Book I, First Draft, Page 2 revised
Conference 1/16 P.M.
Teacher What did you do to make the picture better?
Tyler No—forgot to make snow.

Book I, Final Copy, Page 2
Conference 2/1

Gene Where snowman?
Tyler Don't you know—bigger than me. I made Rudolph.
Gene But little?
Tyler Hey don't you know—he's real far away.
Gene What's that?
Tyler Don't you know—it's my house.
Jeremy Far away.
Tyler Nuh-uh—next to me.
Brenton Why smoke bigger than house?
Tyler 'Cause cooking a lot of stuff.

Book I, Final Copy, Page 2 revised
Conference 2/2

Teacher What did you do to make better?
Tyler Make snowman.
Teacher Was Tyler yesterday.
Tyler Changed mind, colored in and made me. Made Rudolph.
Damon Why everyone like Rudolph?

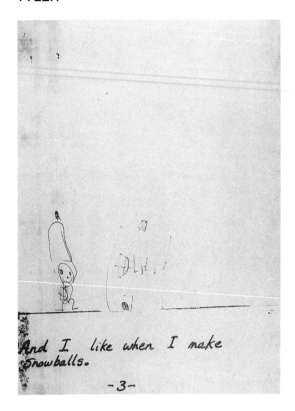

And I like when I make snowballs.

-3-

Book I, First Draft, Page 3
Conference 1/12
Michelle Where snowballs?

Conference 1/16 A.M.
Jeremy Snowballs! Where snowballs?
Tyler I only draw one on my hat.
Jeremy [rolled eyes] I throw snowballs at my mom. She don't say anything. I throw at brother. She throw at me. She didn't say anything. She just throw snowballs.
Michelle I throw at my sister.
Gene You didn't do mine.
Teacher Oh yes.
John Me throw big balls at puppy. Me throw balls and puppy bite pop-pop.

And I like when I make snowballs.

-3-

Book I, First Draft, Page 3 revised
Conference 1/16 P.M.
Teacher What did you do to make the picture better?
Tyler Made snowballs. Michelle [stripe slanted on shirt.] Sun is wearing sunglasses. A star.

Book I, Final Copy, Page 3
Conference 2/1

Tyler   It's snowing and I throwed it. I throwed this one and it's ripping apart.

Celeste I see one circle.

Brenton Why is snow green and red?

Tyler   I drawed it like that. I decided.

Jeff   I think this eye so little.

John   What's that?

Tyler   My hat.

Michelle What is this?

Tyler   Part of snowball ripping.

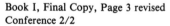

Book I, Final Copy, Page 3 revised
Conference 2/2

Tyler   I throwed all green ones.

Teacher Added?

Tyler   Snowballs.

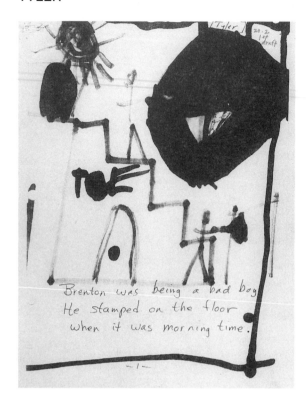

Brenton was being a bad boy
He stamped on the floor
when it was morning time.

—1—

Book II, First Draft, Page 1
Conference 2/23

Jeff   What that?
Tyler   Mom getting food out.
Gene   What that?
Tyler   Mom bedroom.
Jeff   Under steps?
Tyler   Yes.
Jeremy   Where's Tyler?
Tyler   Mom and him [Brenton] stamping down steps.
Brenton   Why green people?
Tyler   'Cause wanted to.
Jeff   People are white.
Celeste   I brown.
Michelle   John brown.
Todd   I have stairs and down on bottom have a work room.
John   What that?
Tyler   Table.
Gene   What 'bout robbers finding skunk in, and skunk starts to stink?
Tyler   Hey—door locked.
Gene   What 'bout door knob?
Tyler   Not a real door. Real door somewhere else.
Damon   Where's the gun to kill robber?
Tyler   No robber.
Brenton   Why make door there?
Tyler   I wanted to.

Brenton was being a bad boy
He stamped on the floor
when it was morning time.

—1—

Book II, First Draft, Page 1 revised
Conference 2/27

Teacher   What did you do to make your story better?
Tyler   Make this snow.
Jodi   What's this?
Tyler   Big light. On ceiling. I made it big. Have to be on ceiling.
Celeste   What's that?
Tyler   My bedroom. NO. that's Brenton's bedroom. [added] Red stuff.
Teacher   You added the doorknob.
Celeste   What blue thing?
Tyler   Pan, to cook the scrambled eggies.
Celeste   You didn't have blue thing.
Tyler   YES I DID!
Jodi   What red around [the edge of the drawing]?
Tyler   My house. Everybody have a square house.
Jodi   I have a triangle.
Tyler   I just have a square house, that's all.

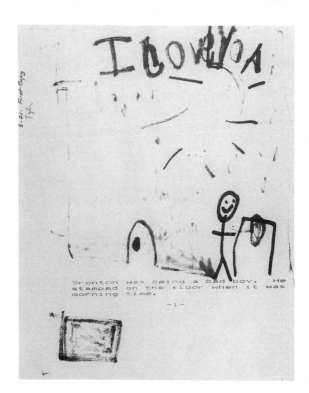

Book II, Final Copy, Page 1
Conference 3/22

Gene	What does that say?
Tyler	Brenton, saying "I love you" to mommy.
Gene	'Cept that YOU mom.
Tyler	No—HIS mom.
Jodi	Outside or in?
Tyler	Don't you know—inside.
Gene	Then why people outside? See—here is house.
Tyler	No.
Brenton	Why sun in house?
Tyler	It's not.
Jeremy	What's that?
Tyler	That's Brenton—fell down, hit his head on box of toys.
Gene	Did mom come up and spank him! 'Cause he stamp his feet— then he fell down hit head on toy box.
Jeff	What's that?
Tyler	Making scrabled [sic] eggies.
Jodi	What's this thing?
Tyler	Brenton's room.
Jodi	'Cept not in your story.
Tyler	'Cept I just drawed it.

Book II, Final Copy, Page 1 revised
Conference 3/26

Teacher	What did you do to make your story better?
Tyler	These fell down and mom give spanking and step down steps and he tripped down here.
Michelle	Why ain't got no clothes on?
Tyler	Just here's his head and he have pants and shirt on.
Teacher	Hair.
Tyler	Brenton bald. Mom bald too.
Jodi	What's that?
Tyler	This her and pan and making scrambled eggies.
Brenton	What's that?
Tyler	That's the trap.
Brenton	That's not in your story!
Tyler	I just want to make it.
Brenton	You copied off of me.
Tyler	It's not a mouse trap, just a trap.
Jodi	It's a trap for boys like you.
Damon	What kind of trap?
Tyler	Just a trap.

Book II, First Draft, Page 2
Conference 2/23

Jeff	Why Brenton sitting backward?
Tyler	Because he a bad boy.
Brenton	Why red sun?
Tyler	Wanted to.
Teacher	Where Brenton?
Tyler	Here.
Teacher	Where syrup?
Tyler	Didn't have time to make.

Book II, First Draft, Page 2 revised
Conference 2/27

Teacher	What did you do to make your story better?
Tyler	Snow and sun.
Michelle	It's like in *Pierre* [the storybook].
Tyler	But he didn't say to pour syrup on head. It say pour syrup on HAIR.
Michelle	But just like it. Like he sit backwards in chair in *Pierre*.
Tyler	I don't care.
Jodi	What's this?
Tyler	Snow. You don't even know anything. I drew he's new. [Brenton]
Jodi	Snow's in the house.
Tyler	No ain't, outside. In front window.
Jodi	Where's window?
Tyler	I didn't have 'nough time and not 'nough room else I write on stuff.
Jeremy	You can write down here.
Tyler	I don't care [goes to page 3] anyways I did black stuff.

Book II, Final Copy, Page 2
Conference 3/22

Jeremy How can Brenton yell at mom same time his making eggs?

Tyler He's not yelling at mom. He's stamping down stairs and she's making eggies.

Jeremy He is! [Look at words]

Tyler They can do at same time.

Gene I see house — see little dot.

John What's that? [purple]

Tyler Outside door.

Book II, Final Copy, Page 2 revised
Conference 3/26

Teacher What did you do to make your story better?

Tyler Colored in syrup.

Brenton Where's chimney, roof?

Tyler Right here.

Brenton Roof supposed to be triangle!

Tyler Some can be square.

Jodi What's that thing?

Tyler Bottle with syrup in.

Jodi Then what's purple thing with X?

Tyler Chair.

Jodi Then what's lines and green things?

Tyler Grass.

Jeff What is long X, little one?

Tyler Part of chimney.

Damon Why X on chimney? Is it made out of steel?

Tyler Made out of steel.

Book II, First Draft, Page 3
Conference 2/23

John	Why a girl there?
Jeremy	A pony tail?
Tyler	It's word she saying out of her mouth. Showed on TV on Bugs Bunny.
Brenton	Not talking.
John	Says in story?
Tyler	But not when mom talking.
Brenton	What's that?
Tyler	Sky.
Damon	What pointy things?
Tyler	Clouds.

Book II, First Draft, Page 3 revised
Conference 2/27

Teacher	What did you do to make your story better?
Tyler	This [(lines) drew X on house]. That's not house. It's so little we ain't in there.
Jeremy	I see something new.
Tyler	Nuh-uh. That was there.
[Four others said wasn't there.]	
Tyler	Yes it was.
Jodi	Is that your Mommy?
Tyler	No, it's Brenton's.
Jeremy	Why did he color this in?
Tyler	No I did it. It like that before.
Michelle	No.
Jeremy	No.

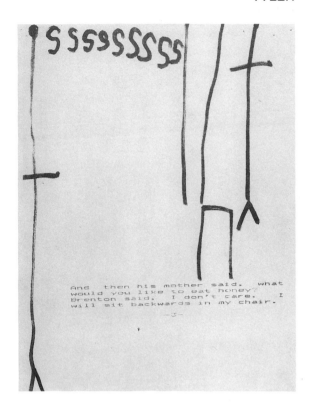

Book II, Final Copy, Page 3
Conference 3/22

Teacher What did you do to make your story better?
Tyler Syrup in here, and he's pouring on head.
John Where Brenton?
Tyler Here.
Brenton Why I outside?
Tyler 'Cause you have a picnic.
Brenton Where's mom?
Tyler With me.
Gene Where's syrup?
Tyler Don't you know—from in the house.
Gene What things going down?
Tyler Grass.
Jodi I don't like "SYRUP ON HEAD," it's wrong. You should pour on hair.
Tyler I think it's right.
Todd I think it's OK.
Jodi Raise your hand if you want hair.
Tyler That's Brenton sitting on big chair. Gots little head. Mom gots big head.
Jodi What on "SSS"?
Tyler Words talking.

Book II, Final Copy, Page 3 revised
Conference 3/26

Teacher What did you do to make your story better?
Tyler Made Jodi's little house.
Jodi But I'm not in story.
Tyler I just want to make it.
Teacher What does that have to do with the story?
Tyler I just want to make it.
Jodi What lines?
Tyler Back of chair.
Gene What's that?
Tyler Sun—two suns. I want to make two suns.
Jeff Why is smoke blue?
Tyler 'Cause I make it blue.
Jeff Mine black.
Jodi Mine white.
Celeste Mine white.
Damon Gray.
Jodi Who's big man?
Tyler That's my Mommy—no—his mom.
Gene What's them?
Tyler She's saying, "What would you like?"

Book II, First Draft, Page 4
Conference 2/23
No comments.

Book II, First Draft, Page 4 revised
Conference 2/27

Teacher	What did you do to make your story better?
Tyler	Colored ME and put mommy and daddy hiding.
Jeff	What these?
Tyler	That's Gene's army truck.
Gene	That ain't in your story.
Tyler	I don't care.
Michelle	He always say "I don't care."
Tyler	But I don't care.
Gene	If you don't care maybe YOU TURN INTO Pierre.
Jeremy	What's this?
Tyler	Gene's army tank, I already told you.

Book II, Final Copy, Page 4
Conference 3/22

John	Where Brenton?
Tyler	Right here, and Mom spanking him.
Tyler	That's father and spanking him with his yardstick.
Jodi	What's all this?
Tyler	The father → mother spanked in story.

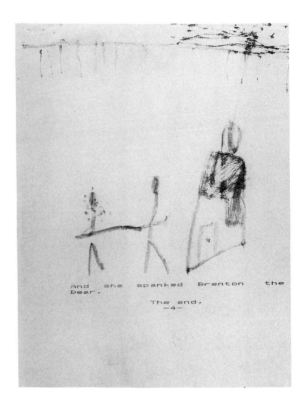

Book II, Final Copy, Page 4 revised
Conference 4/2

Teacher	What did you do to make your story better?
Tyler	Sun. It raining on Brenton. Rain coming from cloud. Raining and mom give him spanking.
Jodi	What's brown thing?
Tyler	Birdie.
Jodi	Blue thing?
Tyler	New sun. Old sun—old will fall in there.
Brenton	You copied off of me!
Tyler	I didn't copy suns in there.
Brenton	So—you still said old sun falling down.
Teacher	How you feel when someone copies your idea?
Brenton	I don't know—I feel mad.
Tyler	Well I didn't copy suns in here.
Teacher	But you made boxes and you made hand.
Brenton	And you made a trap!
Tyler	I just wanted to do it.
Brenton	So—you copied. Oh, shame, shame!
Michelle	What's that?
Tyler	Grass.
Michelle	Grass not red.
Tyler	But I want to make all colors.
Gene	Brenton has green sky and blue sky.
Tyler	He didn't do all this—I wanted to make it blue and green.
Brenton	Hey, you copied off of me.
Tyler	I just wanted to make it.
Brenton	You copied!
Teacher	What do you think about copying ideas?
Michelle	I don't care—wouldn't copy off of someone else—they will get mad at me.
Teacher	If they wouldn't [illegible] [know?] ?
Michelle	I don't care.
Teacher	Would you copy ideas?
Celeste	Sometimes I don't want, sometimes do.
Teacher	Jeremy?
Jeremy	No—don't want to—get mad.
Teacher	If won't get mad?
Jeremy	Might be sad.
Teacher	Damon?
Damon	Might get mad. No—if I copy off Brenton I won't be able to sit next to him.
Teacher	Jeff?
Jeff	No—I don't want Brenton get mad. 'Cause Brenton my buddy.
Teacher	Brenton?
Brenton	No. I don't know. Wouldn't do.
Jodi	Sometimes I would, sometimes no—Celeste used to copy off me.
Gene	No—Except only if I want to. 'Cause maybe I do maybe don't.
Celeste	We drawed something like Christmas tree where are them? You put tape on them and said mom and dad can write on them. I think we take them home. Look how I make my name on that picture—I didn't know how to write name then.

Appendix B:
Book Covers

Brenton—Book I, First Draft, Front Cover

Brenton—Book I, Final Copy, Front Cover

Celeste — Book I, Final Copy, Front Cover

Damon — Book I, Final Copy, Back Cover

Gene—Book I, First Draft, Front Cover

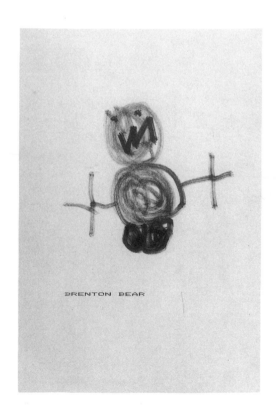

Gene—Book II, Final Copy, Front Cover

Jeff—Book I, Final Copy, Front Cover

Jeff—Book I, First Draft, Back Cover

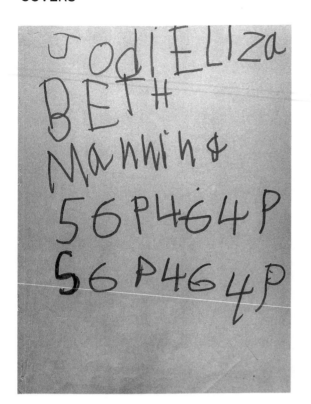

Jodi—Book I, First Draft, Front Cover

Jodi—Book I, Final Copy, Front Cover

Jodi — Book I, Final Copy, Back Cover

Michelle—Book I, First Draft, Front Cover

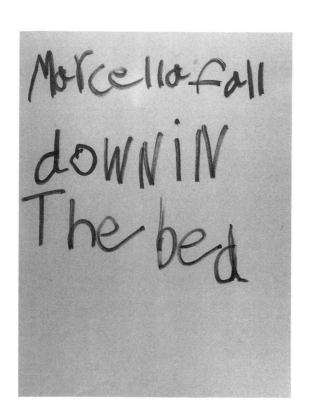

Michelle—Book I, Final Copy, Front Cover

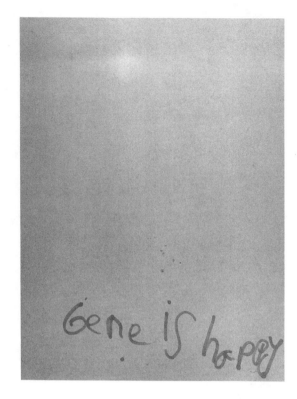

Michelle — Book I, First Draft, Back Cover

Michelle — Book I, Final Copy, Back Cover

Todd—Book I, First Draft, Front Cover

John—Book I, Final Copy, Front Cover

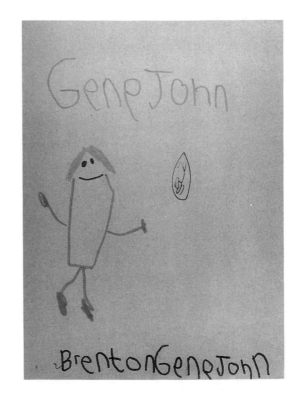

John—Book I, First Draft, Back Cover

John—Book I, Final Copy, Back Cover

Tyler — Book I, First Draft, Front Cover

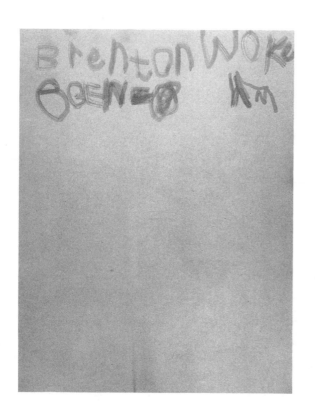

Tyler — Book I, First Draft, Back Cover

Tyler—Book II, Final Copy, Front cover
Tyler has added a cover page with the words "Brenton was a bad boy,"
which he displays at the beginning of the last conference.

Brenton You copied off my hand! You wanted to make fat hand like
mine!

Tyler No—it's not as fat as yours.

Brenton Well, you just wanted to copy.

Tyler So—I just wanted to make it. See—it's not as fat. I wanted to
make a hand. He's holding a mouse and he making a sandwich
out of mouse and he got scared and he bawled when he took
bite out of it. That's a number I just want to make, 105—
remember we put on library books. [the number of the class-
room]

Tyler—Book II, Final Copy, Back Cover

References

Adams, M. J. (1990). *Beginning to read: Thinking and learning about print*. Cambridge, MA: MIT Press

Applebee, A. N. (1978). *The child's concept of story*. Chicago: The University of Chicago Press.

Aukerman, R. C. (1984). *Approaches to beginning reading* (2nd ed.). New York: Wiley.

Avery, C. S. (1988). Laura's legacy. *Language Arts*, *65*, 110–111.

Avery, C. S. (1989). A teacher's first text. *Language Arts*, *66*, 729–732.

Barrs, M. (1988). Drawing a story: Transitions between writing and drawing. In M. Lightfoot & N. Martin (Eds.), *The word for teaching is learning: Language and learning today* (pp. 51–69). London: Heinemann.

Bissex, G. (1980). *GYNS AT WORK: A child learns to write and read*. Cambridge, MA: Harvard University Press.

Brigance, A. (1978). *Brigance Diagnostic Inventory of Early Development*. Woburn, MA: Curriculum Associates.

Bruner, J. V. (1985). Vygotsky: A historical and conceptual perspective. In J. V. Wertsch (Ed.), *Culture, communication, and cognition: Vygotskian perspectives* (pp. 21–34). Cambridge, England: Cambridge University Press.

Bruner, J. V. (1986). *Actual minds, possible worlds*. Cambridge, MA: Harvard University Press.

Calkins, L. M. (1986). *The art of teaching writing*. Portsmouth, NH: Heinemann.

Clay, M. M. (1975). *What did I write?* Auckland, New Zealand: Heinemann Educational.

Cook-Gumperz, J., & Gumperz, J. J. (1981). From oral to written culture: The transition to literacy. In M. Farr-Whiteman (Ed.), *Writing: The nature, development and teaching of written communication: Vol. 1. Variation in writing: Functional and linguistic-cultural differences* (pp. 89–109). Hillsdale, NJ: Lawrence Erlbaum Associates.

Dyson, A. H. (1988). Unintentional helping in the primary grades: Writing in the children's world. In B. A. Raforth & D. L. Rubin (Eds.), *The Social construction of written communication* (pp. 175–194). Norwood, NJ: Ablex.

Egan, K. (1987). Literacy and the oral foundations of education. *Harvard Educational Review*, *57*, 445–472.

Emig, J. (1981). Non-magical thinking: Presenting writing developmentally in schools. In C. H. Fredericksen & J. F. Dominic (Eds.), *Writing: The nature, development and teaching of written communication: Vol. 2. Variation in writing: Functional and linguistic-cultural differences* (pp. 21–30). Hillsdale, NJ: Lawrence Erlbaum Associates.

Ferreiro, E., & Teberosky, A. (1982). *Literacy before schooling*. Portsmouth, NH: Heinemann.

Frawley, W. (1987). *Text and epistemology*. Norwood, NJ: Ablex.

Frawley, W., & Lantolf, J. P. (1984). Speaking and self-order: A critique of orthodox L2 research. *Studies in Second Language Acquisition*, *6*, 143–159.

Frawley, W., & Lantolf, J. P. (1985). Second language discourse: A Vygotskyan perspective. *Applied Linguistics*, *6*, 19–44.

Galda, L., & Pellegrini, A.D. (1988). Children's use of narrative language in peer interaction. In B. A. Raforth & D. L. Rubin (Eds.), *The social construction of written communication*, (pp. 175–194). Norwood, NJ: Ablex.

Gardner, H. (1980). *Artful scribbles: The significance of children's drawings*. New York: Basic Books.

Gee, J. P. (1985). The narrativization of experience in the oral style. *Journal of Education*, *1*, 9–35.

Gibson, J., & Yonas, P. (1968). A new theory of scribbling and drawing in children. In H. Levin, E. J. Gibson, & J. J. Gibson (Eds.), *The analysis of reading skill* (final report). Washington, DC: U. S. Department of Health, Education, and Welfare, Office of Education.

Goodman, Y. (1989). Kidwatching: An alternative to testing. In G. Manning & M. Manning, (Eds.) *Whole language: Beliefs and practices, K–8* (pp. 115–123). Washington, DC: NEA Professional Library.

Goody, J. (1977). *The domestication of the savage mind*. New York: Cambridge University Press.

Graves, D. (1983). *Writing: Teachers and children at work*. Exeter, NH: Heinemann.

Green, G. M., & Morgan, J. L. (1981). Writing ability as a function of the appreciation of differences between oral and written communication. In C. H. Fredericksen & J. F. Dominic (Eds.), *Writing: The nature, development and teaching of written communication: Vol. 2. Variation in writing: Functional and linguistic-cultural differences* (pp. 177–188). Hillsdale, NJ: Lawrence Erlbaum Associates.

Grinnell, P. C., & Burris, N. A. (1983). Drawing and writing: The emerging graphic communication process. *Topics in Learning and Learning Disabilities*, *3*, 21–32.

Gundlach, R. A. (1981). On the nature and development of children's writing. In C. H. Fredericksen & J. F. Dominic (Eds.), *Writing:*

The nature, development and teaching of written communication: Vol. 2. Writing: Process, development, and communication (pp. 133–152). Hillsdale, NJ: Lawrence Erlbaum Associates.

Harste, J. C., Woodward, V. A., & Burke, C. L. (1984). *Language stories and literacy lessons*. Portsmouth, NH: Heinemann.

Havelock, E. A. (1986). *The muse learns to write: Reflections on orality and literacy from antiquity to the present*. New Haven: Yale University Press.

Heath, S. B. (1983). *Ways with words: Language, life and work in communities and classrooms*. Cambridge, MA: Cambridge University Press.

Hicks, D. (1990a). Narrative skills and genre knowledge: Ways of telling in the primary grades. *Applied Psycholinguistics, 11*, 83–104.

Hicks, D. (1990b). Narrative skills and literacy learning. *Penn WPEL, 6*, 23–51.

Hubbard, R. S. (1989). *Authors of pictures, draughtsmen of words*. Portsmouth, NH: Heinemann.

Jastak, S., & Wilkinson, G. S. (1984). *Wide Range Achievement Test (Revised)*. Wilmington, DE: Jastek.

Johnson, D. W., & Johnson, R. T. (1986). *Learning together and alone: Cooperation, competition, and individualization* (2nd ed.). Englewood Cliffs, NJ: Prentice Hall.

Kellogg, R. (1970). *Analyzing children's art*. Palo Alto, CA: Mayfield.

Kozulin, A. (1985). Vygotsky in context. In L. Vygotsky, *Thought and Language* (pp. xi–lvi). (Trans. by A. Kozulin. Original work published in 1934). Cambridge, MA: MIT Press.

Kozulin, A. (1986). The concept of activity in Soviet psychology: Vygotsky, his disciples and critics. *American Psychologist, 41*, 264–274.

Lave, J. (1988a). *Cognition in practice: Mind, mathematics and culture in everyday life*. Cambridge, MA: Cambridge University Press.

Lave, J. (1988b). *The culture of acquisition and the practice of understanding* (Report No. 88-0007). Palo Alto, CA: Institute for Research on Learning.

Leontiev, A. N. (1978). *Activity, consciousness, and personality*. Englewood Cliffs, NJ: Prentice-Hall.

Liebermann, P. (1984). *The biology and evolution of language*. Cambridge, MA: Harvard University Press.

Luria, A. R. (1982). *Language and cognition*. New York: Wiley.

Manning, M. M., Manning, G. L., Long, R., & Wolfson, B. J. (1987). *Reading and writing in the primary grades*. Washington, DC: NEA Association.

Moll, L. C. (Ed.). (1990). *Vygotsky and education: Instructional implications and applications of sociohistorical psychology*. Cambridge, MA: Cambridge University Press.

Newkirk, T., & Atwell, N. (Eds.). (1988). *Understanding writing: Ways of observing, learning and teaching*. Portsmouth, NH: Heinemann.

Ninio, A., & Bruner, J. S. (1978). The achievements and antecedents of labelling. *Journal of Child Language, 5*, 5–15.

Olson, D. R. (1977). From utterance to text: The bias of language in speech and writing. *Harvard Educational Review, 47*, 257–281.

Ong, W. J. (1982). *Orality and literacy*. New York: Methuen.

Read, C. (1975). *Children's categorization of speech sounds in English*. Urbana, IL: National Council of Teachers of English.

Rivers, W. J. (1988). *Problems in composition: A Vygotskian perspective*. Unpublished doctoral dissertation, University of Delaware, Newark.

Sendak, M. (1962). *Pierre*. Scranton, PA: Harper & Row.

Scollon, R. & Scollon, S. (1981). The literate two-year-old: The fictionalization of self. in *Narrative, literacy and face in interethnic communication*. Norwood NJ: Ablex.

Slavin, R. E. (1990). *Cooperative learning*. Needham Heights, MA: Allyn & Bacon.

Smolkin, L. B., Conlon, A., & Yaden, D. B. (1988). Print salient illustrations in children's picture books: The emergence of written language awareness. *Thirty-seventh Yearbook of the National Reading Conference*. Rochester, NY: NRC.

Snow, C. E. (1983). Literacy and language: Relationships during the preschool years. *Harvard Educational Review, 53*, 165–189.

Snow, C. E., & Ninio, A. (1986). The contracts of literacy: What children learn from learning to read. In W. H. Teale & E. Sulzby, (Eds.), *Emergent literacy*, Norwood, NJ: Ablex.

Spalding, R. B. (1986). *The writing road to reading: The Spalding method of teaching speech, writing and reading*. New York: William Morrow.

Sulzby, E. (1982). Oral and written language mode adaptations in stories by kindergarten children. *Journal of Reading Behavior, 16*, 51–59.

Sulzby, E. (1986). Writing and reading: Signs of oral and written language organization in the young child. In W. H. Teale & E. Sulzby (Eds.), *Emergent literacy: Writing and reading* (pp. 50–89). Norwood, NJ: Ablex.

Taylor, D., & Dorsey-Gaines, C. (1988). *Growing up literate: Learning from inner-city families*. Portsmouth, NH: Heinemann.

Teale, W. H. (1986). Home background and young children's literacy development. In W. H. Teale & E. Sulzby (Eds.), *Emergent literacy: Writing and reading*. Norwood, NJ: Ablex.

Tharp, R. G., & Gallimore, R. (1988). *Rousing minds to life*. Cambridge: Cambridge University Press.

Vocate, D. R. (1987). *The theory of A. R. Luria: Functions of spoken language in the development of higher mental processes*. Hillsdale, NJ: Lawrence Erlbaum Associates.

Vygotsky, L. S. (1962). *Thought & Language* (E. Hanfmann & G. Vakar, Eds. & Trans.). Cambridge, MA: MIT Press. (Original work published 1934)

Vygotsky, L. S. (1978). *Mind in society: The development of higher psychological processes* (M. Cole, V. John-Steiner, S. Scribner, & E. Souberman, Eds.). Cambridge, MA: Harvard University Press.

Weir, R. (1962). *Language in the crib*. The Hague: Mouton.

Wenger, R. N. (1985). *Reading, writing, and literacy: The application of a whole language approach to the education of learning disabled students*. Paper presented at the 38th Education Conference, Millersville University, Millersville, PA.

Wertsch, J. V. (1981). *The concept of activity in Soviet psychology*. Armonk, NY: Sharp.

Wertsch, J. V. (1984). The zone of proximal development: Some conceptual issues. In B. Rogoff & J. V. Wertsch (Eds.), *Children's learning in the "zone of proximal development"* (pp. 3–21). San Francisco, CA: Jossey-Bass.

Wertsch, J. V. (Ed.). (1985). *Culture, communication, and cognition: Vygotskian perspectives*. Cambridge: Cambridge University Press.

Wood, D. J., Bruner, J. S., & Ross, G. (1976). The role of tutoring in problem solving. *Journal of Child Psychology and Psychiatry, 17*, 89–100.

Zebroski, J. T. (1982). Soviet psycholinguistics: Implications for teaching of writing. In W. Frawley (Ed.), *Linguistics and literacy* (pp. 51–63). New York: Plenum.

Index

INDEX

INDEX